on track ...
Fairport
Convention

every album, every song

Kevan Furbank

SONIC**BOND**

sonicbondpublishing.com

Sonicbond Publishing Limited
www.sonicbondpublishing.co.uk
Email: info@sonicbondpublishing.co.uk

First Published in the United Kingdom 2020
First Published in the United States 2020

British Library Cataloguing in Publication Data:
A Catalogue record for this book is available from the British Library

Copyright Kevan Furbank 2020

ISBN 978-1-78952-051-4

Typeset in ITC Garamond & ITC Avant Garde
Printed and bound in England

Graphic design and typesetting: Full Moon Media

on track ...

Fairport Convention

Contents

Acknowledgements

Writing a book always has a knock-on effect on friends and family so I would like to apologise for ignoring them for four months. Thanks to my wife Elizabeth and daughters Sarah and Emily for their support, encouragement and quite reckless blind faith in my literary abilities. In particular, I'd like to give three cheers and a tiger to Sarah for helping me with the penultimate chapter of this book so I could hit the deadline.

I would also like to thank Stephen Lambe of Sonicbond Publishing for offering me the opportunity to write this book and his cheerful encouragement. And, finally, thanks to Fairport Convention for more than 50 years of great music. May your bus roll on…

Come all ye rolling minstrels...

If there was any justice in the world, Fairport Convention would be as revered in the UK as, say, The Grateful Dead are in the US. They took British roots music and dragged it kicking and screaming into the 20th century – and, in the process, created a whole new genre: British folk-rock.

Their career spans an astonishing 53 years at the time of writing, putting them in the same rarified atmosphere of apparently immortal musicians such as The Rolling Stones and Paul McCartney. They have released 29 studio albums and their fourth, *Liege And Lief*, has been voted by BBC Radio 2 as the Most Influential Folk Album Of All Time and is in Mojo magazine's list of the 100 Records That Changed The World.

The many musicians who have passed through the band – and anyone who has seen Pete Frame's family tree for Fairport will know that it is as twisty and entangled as an ancient forest of gnarled oaks – include a who's-who of folk-rock legends. There is Richard Thompson OBE (no less), regarded as one of Britain's finest songwriters and one of the world's greatest guitarists. There is the brief, beautiful flame that was Sandy Denny, a singer and songwriter of rare beauty who was cut down in her prime.

You'll also find the demon fiddler Dave Swarbrick, Jethro Tull bassist Dave Pegg, Elton John, XTC and Paul McCartney drummer Dave Mattacks. And, standing astride the genre like a genial colossus, there's Ashley Hutchings – founder of Fairport, Steeleye Span and The Albion Band, and described by Bob Dylan as 'the single most important figure in English folk-rock'.

In 2019 the current incarnation – singer/guitarist Simon Nicol, bassist Dave Pegg, fiddler Ric Sanders, multi-instrumentalist Chris Leslie and drummer Gerry Conway – was still touring across the UK and Ireland and celebrating 40 years of the Cropredy Festival. Not bad for a band with a combined age of 338!

The story of Fairport Convention starts with bass player Ashley Stephen 'Tyger' Hutchings, born in 1945, who formed bands out of people he knew at the North Bank Youth Club in Muswell Hill. One of those was Simon John Breckenridge Nicol, five years younger, whose father was a doctor with a surgery at the family home, Fairport. By 1966 Ashley and Simon were playing together in the Ethnic Shuffle Orchestra.

Richard Thompson, from nearby Totteridge and a year older than Simon, was next to join and, with Ethnic Shuffle Orchestra drummer Shawn Frater, the new group rehearsed above Dr Nicol's surgery at Fairport – and it was another friend of Simon who dubbed them Fairport Convention. Frater only lasted one gig, replaced by Martin Francis Lamble (same age as Richard).

The band found a vocalist in 18-year-old librarian Judy Aileen Dyble and also pulled in Scunthorpe-born Ian Matthews MacDonald, born June 1946, from defunct pop trio Pyramid. Fairport became part of London's 'underground' music scene, sharing the bill at venues such as Middle Earth and the Electric Garden with the likes of Soft Machine and Procol Harum. They were spotted by American record producer Joe Boyd, who was immediately impressed, especially by the guitar skills of the then 17-year-old Richard Thompson. They signed a contract with Boyd's Witchseason management company and the producer got them a recording deal with Track Records. Fairport Convention were ready to unleash their music upon the world.

More than 50 years later, the band may not have the same energy as it did back in 1967 – as well as only one of the original members – but there's still a simple, almost naive joy in the music-making that has survived half a century of trials and tribulations. As Simon Nicol said in a 2016 interview: 'I want the next CD we make to be outstanding in its own right, without reference to the arc of music preceding it over the last 50 years. I don't want to be part of a tribute band to Fairport Convention, nor to have our music put under glass in an exhibition case.'

Just how successful Fairport have been in reinventing themselves in the studio can only be assessed by looking at their albums in some detail, examining the motivations, inspirations and artistic decisions behind them – and that is what this book attempts to do. It is not a detailed history of the band, but it is, of course, impossible to separate what went on behind the scenes with what ended up in the record shops.

Finally, it attempts to shine a gentle light on what must be one of the most overlooked British bands of the 20th century – I'm a Fairport fan and I want everyone else to love them just as much as I do, warts and all.

Fairport Convention (1968)

Personnel:
Judy Dyble: lead vocals, electric and acoustic autoharps, recorder, piano
Ian MacDonald: lead vocals, jaw harp
Richard Thompson: vocals, lead electric and acoustic guitars, mandolin
Simon Nicol: vocals, electric 12 and 6 string and acoustic guitars
Ashley Hutchings: bass guitar, jug, double bass
Martin Lamble: percussion, violin
Claire Lowther: cello
John Wood: engineer
Produced at Sound Techniques, London, by Joe Boyd and Tod Lloyd for
Witchseason Productions
Record label: Polydor
Release dates: June 1968 (UK), 1970 (US)
Highest chart positions: Uncharted
Running time: 37:46 (original release)
Current edition: 2003 reissue on Polydor/Universal with bonus tracks

Some bands come straight out of the traps with their sound fully-formed, their debut albums acting as templates for most of what follows. Others need a little time to find their feet, to hone their style and sound. Fairport Convention fall into the latter category. Indeed, their self-titled debut in 1968 carries few hints of their future musical direction. Instead, it's a mixture of American singer/songwriter covers and quirky psychedelia. Even the original compositions owe something to the West Coast sound.

But before the album came a single – a cover of an obscure 1936 swinging ballad by Huey Prince and Lou Singer called 'If I Had A Ribbon Bow'. Whose idea was this? Perhaps it came from the record collection of Ashley's dance-band father – or even from Richard's eclectic tastes. Certainly, he seemed very upset when the single sank without trace following its 23 February 1968 release. He said: 'I was so mortified [it] wasn't a hit. I mean, I had invested so much in believing in this song, and in believing that it was going to be a successful record, that when it wasn't I thought "never again".'

Before the single was released, they were in Sound Techniques studio in London recording their debut album. Like a lot of bands at the time, Fairport tried to find songs that weren't too well known so they could stand out from the crowd – and they weren't prolific and accomplished enough as songwriters to record an entire album of originals. Thanks to Joe Boyd's contacts in the industry they heard 'I Don't Know Where I Stand' and 'Chelsea Morning' from a demo tape left behind by Joni Mitchell. They pulled tracks from obscure albums and singles, from parts of their live repertoire, and the well-listened Boyd no doubt dropped a few hints into young ears eager to learn.

The result is, understandably, an uneven album that has been criticised for its flat production and for Judy Dyble's distant, somewhat hesitant vocal delivery. But there are many delights to be found, not least the moments when Richard unleashes his distinctive lead guitar and in the interesting arrangements, chord sequences and delivery of some of the original material.

Polydor's promotion was low-key, with one advertising blurb describing the album as 'one put together by unusual personalities for that insignificant minority of seekers to whom real music, oddly enough, seems to matter'. The record cover hardly helps. Shot in semi-gloom, it shows two and a half band members' faces sitting around a table, possibly having a séance lit by an art deco 1930s lamp – you had to open the gatefold to see everyone else. As a result, an insignificant minority of seekers bought it.

'Time Will Show The Wiser' (Emitt Rhodes)
This busy, fast-paced rocker is the perfect opening number, showcasing Richard's confident guitar riffing and licks, with strong ensemble vocals and a catchy, singalong one-line chorus. If Fairport were playing this when Joe Boyd first saw them, then no wonder he thought they showed promise. The song comes from The Merry-Go-Round, the 1967 debut album by a band with the same name featuring US multi-instrumentalist Rhodes. In comparison, the original is a sparse, lightweight affair – Fairport give it the cojones it demands, with a catchy opening guitar riff, strong vocals from Ian and Judy and pounding drums from Martin. Richard clearly liked it so much he used it to open his 1976 career retrospective *(guitar, vocal)*.

'I Don't Know Where I Stand' (Joni Mitchell)
The first of two Joni songs here, this eventually appeared on her second album, *Clouds*, the following year. Joni's version of this wistful ballad about emotional insecurity – one of her favourite subjects – is gently finger-picked on a solo guitar to allow her gorgeous voice to soar. Fairport throw guitar, drums and bass on it, while Judy's vocal is pleasant but unremarkable. All wistfulness is crushed under a somewhat heavy-handed arrangement, although Richard's solo manages to be clever and entertaining. But this is a track where less would definitely have been more.

'If (Stomp)' (Ian MacDonald, Richard Thompson)
The first self-penned song on the album, it's less a stomp and more a good ol' Chet Atkins-style country-pickin' number, mostly written by Richard but with some help on the lyrics from Ian. Not that the lyrics are anything special – 'If I were rich enough, if I could pitch enough, if you were bitch enough'. But the song is a pleasant ditty and, as always, one can enjoy Richard's accomplished electric guitar picking, as well as a delightful country-style instrumental. An earlier version supplied the B side for the 'If I Had A Ribbon Bow' single.

'Decameron' (Paul Ghosh, Andrew Horvitch, Richard Thompson)
Written with two school friends, this wistful ballad in 6/8 reveals the first
stirrings of Richard's rather cynical, world-weary lyrical approach. 'Every
time the sun shines, to me it's a rainy day' sings Ian in one of his best vocal
performances on the album, supported with gentle harmonies from Judy.
Structurally it feels like two songs welded together – the rhythmic verses in A
major alternate with a slower, sparser section in D major that gently fades away
before lurching back into the verse again. There doesn't appear to be any sort
of chorus nor any explanation of the title in the lyrics. Decameron is Greek
for '10 days' and is best known as the title of a collection of novellas by 14th-
century writer Giovanni Boccaccio.

'Jack Of Diamonds' (Bob Dylan, Ben Carruthers)
Talk about obscure! This one was a strange amalgam of the lyrics to a Texas
gambling song from the back of Bob Dylan's third album, set to music by US
actor Ben Carruthers, who appeared in *The Dirty Dozen* movie in 1967. He
released it as a single and, according to Fairport biographer Patrick Humphries,
it was used in a BBC *Play For Today* that also starred Carruthers. Ashley thinks
the single was given to Richard by Hugh Cornwell, later of The Stranglers. Of
all the songs on the album, this one deserves the 'British Jefferson Airplane'
tag – sinister electric guitar notes drenched in reverb launch into an aggressive,
bluesy thrash alternating between B flat minor and E flat before a surprise
melodic major key middle eight. It's marred by Judy Dyble's terribly out of
tune recorder solo (!) and the fact that Ian's voice is a bit too nice for it. But,
along with the opening track above, it showed what this band could do when
firing on all cylinders.

'Portfolio' (Judy Dyble, Ashley Hutchings)
A silly little throwaway instrumental played on a badly-tuned piano, with Martin
squeaking along on violin. At 2:05 it is 2:05 too long.

'Chelsea Morning' (Joni Mitchell)
The second Joni song from the same album and a much more successful
attempt – the style and subject matter suit a rock band approach. Fast,
inventive percussion from Martin and Richard's rising guitar phrases give it
a sense of pace and urgency, especially with racing car sound effects over
chopping flamenco-style chords at the end. One quibble: In the slower middle
eights, Ian sounds like he's singing from the next-door studio. Strange.

'Sun Shade' (Paul Ghosh, Andrew Horvitch, Richard Thompson)
A lovely little ballad with jazzy chord progressions (C to G minor then D flat
major seventh. Try it, it sounds lovely), gentle, wistful singing from Ian and
faultless and tasteful electric guitar playing from Richard. And 'Chuckles'

Thompson supplies suitably uplifting lyrics: 'Dying's not easy today'. A small but perfectly formed little song.

'The Lobster' (George Painter, Ashley Hutchings, Richard Thompson)

This is where things get a little weird. Some apparently aimless, high-pitched guitar twiddling leads into plodding bass and minor key autoharp sweeps before the entire band thrashes away, with Martin going all-out on the tom-toms. As things calm down, Ian sings a poem by George Painter about a ferocious crustacean, and then the band go quiet for a bit before everyone has another thrash. At times, Richard's fast electric guitar picking sounds similar to Robert Fripp's work with Giles, Giles & Fripp. It's the sort of thing a band plays after saying 'Hope you like our new direction.' Thankfully, it leads into…

'It's Alright Ma, It's Only Witchcraft' (Ashley Hutchings, Richard Thompson)

The title of this song is clearly inspired by Bob Dylan, particularly 'It's Alright Ma, I'm Only Bleeding'. A walking bass shuffles into view, Ian sings a jaunty understated verse, Martin's drums swing beautifully beneath him and then everything bursts into life into a rocking chorus, punctuated by Richard's unique lead guitar. It's a simple almost-blues, but the sheer energy and musical chutzpah make this a highpoint of the album, especially when the band break into the chorus of 'This is the season, stormy weather's on the way'.

'One Sure Thing' (Harvey Brooks, Jim Glover)

From one of the best tracks on the album to, sadly, one of the worst. 'One Sure Thing' came from Jim & Jean's 1966 album *Changes* and was a fairly dreary minor key moan in its original incarnation. Fairport speed it up a bit but they can't save it from sounding plodding, bland and listless. Thank whatever musical god you believe in then for Richard's angular, discordant lead guitar section that briefly drags the song into a completely different territory.

'M1 Breakdown' (Ashley Hutchings, Simon Nicol)

The sound of a van – probably a Transit – leads into a banjo-like thrash while Ian twangs a jaw harp. Apparently, it cut his mouth so badly he listened to the playback while dripping blood. After a minute or so, the van and the song break down. A throwaway piece of studio fun, to be sure, but quite spookily prophetic considering what was going to happen to them 18 months later.

2003 Bonus Tracks
'Suzanne' (Leonard Cohen)

Tinkling percussion introduces a spirited version of Cohen's debut single – some may say it's so busy, with pounding drums, Simon's staccato electric guitar strum and Richard providing strong licks throughout, that its wistful nature is pretty much lost. It certainly overstays its welcome by about the four-minute mark – but there's still nearly two minutes more to go! It illustrates a Fairport trait that was both a strength and a weakness: they didn't just cover songs but made them their own through imaginative, sometimes counter-intuitive arrangements that worked better with some songs than others.

'If I Had A Ribbon Bow' (Hughie Prince, Lou Singer)
A major ingredient of British psychedelia in the 1960s was a return to Edwardian fashion and song styles, as evidenced by The Beatles' *Sgt Pepper* album and Paul McCartney's 'Honey Pie' on the *White Album*. So it's quite reasonable to believe Fairport Convention really did think this could be a hit. First recorded in 1936 by jazz singer Maxine Sullivan as a quirky novelty song, Fairport's version pretty much follows the original note for note. Richard plays classy jazz guitar and percussionist Tristan Fry provides vibes while Martin delivers a click-clacking rhythm, occasionally using brushes to swing on the drum kit. Judy's vocal is a little colourless – listen to the original and you'll hear the difference. It's a pleasant, quirky, totally un-Fairport-like number that should never have been released as a single and predictably bombed.

'Morning Glory' (Larry Beckett, Tim Buckley)
A live TV recording with all the sound imperfections that implies – tinny, distant guitar accompaniment, Judy's slightly out of tune recorder and a vocal performance from Ian that's flat and dreary. Highlights are Martin's busy drums and, of course, a dramatic Richard guitar solo. The original song first appeared on Tim Buckley's second album, *Goodbye And Hello*, in 1967.

'Reno, Nevada' (Richard Farina)
Another live TV recording but considerably better quality than 'Morning Glory'. Vocals are a little hesitant, but instrumentally it is approached with much more confidence, with a lengthy Richard guitar break taking up most of its 7:43 length and showing why Joe Boyd was so impressed with him live (despite one or two dodgy notes!). Farina was a US protest singer and author who died aged just 29 in a motorcycle crash a year before this was recorded.

What We Did on Our Holidays (1969)

Personnel:
Alexandra Elene MacLean Denny: vocals, guitars, piano, harpsichord
Ashley Hutchings: bass, backing vocals
Martin Lamble: drums, percussion, violin, tabla & footsteps
Ian Matthews (nee MacDonald): vocals, congas
Simon Nicol: guitars, electric autoharp, electric dulcimer, backing vocals
Richard Thompson: guitars, piano accordion, sitar, vocals
Brice Lacey: robots on 'Mr Lacey'
Claire Lowther: cello on 'Book Song'
Kingsley Abbott: coins on 'The Lord Is In This Place...', backing vocals on 'Meet On The Ledge'
Paul Ghosh, Andrew Horvitch and Marc Ellington: backing vocals on 'Meet On The Ledge'
Peter Ross: harmonica on 'Throwaway Street Puzzle'
Recorded at Sound Techniques, Olympic Studios and Morgan Studios, all in London, by Joe Boyd
John Wood: engineer
Record label: Island (UK), A&M (US)
Release dates: January 1969 (released as 'Fairport Convention' in US)
Highest chart positions: Uncharted
Running time: 38:07 (reissue 47:53)
Current edition: 2003 Island Remasters

Let us pretend, you and I, that this was actually Fairport Convention's debut album. A lot of compilations do just that. Why? Because this is head and shoulders above its predecessor, an album of such confidence and quality that several of the tracks have become classics in the band's repertoire – and one, in particular, is Fairport's end-of-show anthem. Another, more prosaic, reason may be that Joe Boyd moved all his acts to Island Records before the album's release, and most compilations tend to take their material from one record label. The choice of material, the performances and the original compositions are all superb, with scarcely any filler. Two things, in particular, stand out – the voice of Sandy Denny and the songwriting of Richard Thompson.

Before the recording came the first of Fairport's many, many splits. Judy Dyble was asked to leave – Ashley says it was because the band was getting stronger, louder and heavier and her light voice was getting lost. On her website, Judy depicts her ousting as being quite brutal, saying she was 'unceremoniously dumped' The band thought they could carry on as an all-male five-piece, but fans kept asking where the girl singer was. After all, Jefferson Airplane had one... So Fairport held auditions, and that was when they met Sandy Denny, According to Simon, she 'stood out like a clean glass in a sinkful of dirty dishes'.

Alexandra Elene Maclean Denny, born in London in 1947, was already a well-seasoned performer when she met the Fairports. She had played the folk clubs, appeared on the BBC, recorded two released albums with Scottish folk singer Alex Campbell and British folk and blues artist Johnny Silvo and been, briefly, a member of The Strawbs. Her early composition 'Who Knows Where The Time Goes?' had been covered by Judy Collins, so Sandy was already well-known as a singer and songwriter.

Her influence on Fairport was immediate. One of her compositions opens the album, she encouraged them to include two traditional songs – one of which, 'She Moves Through The Fair', is basically what Sandy did in the clubs with electric backing – and her expressive, versatile and emotive voice gives the band a confident swagger.

The album also sees Richard Thompson's debut as a solo songwriter. Growing in confidence and skill, he was rapidly creating a distinctive voice for himself – dark, cynical and world-weary, set against catchy, sometimes jaunty melodies. In all, he contributes to five of the original album's twelve tracks and gives the band a sense of weight and gravitas.

Even the cover was an improvement on the debut – a blackboard covered in a chalk picture by the Fairports in the dressing room of a university, the title taken from a typical start-of-term essay teachers give to their students.

Once again, the album failed to chart, but time has shown the wiser as it is now viewed as one of the two or three essential Fairport releases.

'Fotheringay' (Sandy Denny)

A sombre one to open with but, gosh, what a lovely song and what a heartrending subject matter – the imprisonment of Mary, Queen of Scots in Fotheringhay Castle, Northamptonshire, before her execution for attempting to overthrow Queen Elizabeth I. Sandy demoed the tune to different words back in 1966 – it was called 'Boxful Of Treasures' – but changed the lyrics after a visit to the 12th century castle in Northamptonshire (while misspelling the name). Structured like a folk song, it has just four verses in A minor, moving very nicely to A major for a slightly baroque-sounding instrumental after the third verse. Sandy and Richard finger-pick acoustic guitars together while Simon adds autoharp, Ashley bass and Martin bells, giving the song just the right amount of backing to create a performance that is heartfelt and touching. The song meant so much to Sandy that she used the title for the name of the band she formed after her first departure from Fairport.

'Mr Lacey' (Ashley Hutchings)

Ashley's only solo composition on the album pays tribute to 'Professor' Bruce Lacey, an eccentric British performer who made odd mechanical devices, appeared in Richard Lester films including The Beatles' *Help!* and constructed the props for Michael Bentine's TV series *It's A Square World*. The song is a straightforward twelve-bar blues rocker with Richard playing some searing guitar licks while Lacey's robots provide buzzing noises in the instrumental break. Some 35 years later Lacey appeared live on stage with the Fairports.

'Book Song' (Ian Matthews, Richard Thompson)

Matthews (who had changed his name from Ian MacDonald to avoid confusion with Ian McDonald of King Crimson) had the lyrics, written about his future wife, and Richard supplied the waltz-time melody, with Simon adding some low-key sitar. It's a gentle, wistful little number, beautifully sung by Ian and Sandy together in close harmony, with a tasteful Richard guitar solo. Martin is suitably restrained on drums, confining himself mostly to rimshots.

'The Lord Is In This Place, How Dreadful Is This Place' (Richard Thompson, Ashley Hutchings)

Inspired by a gospel blues song performed by Blind Willie Johnson called 'Dark Was The Night, Cold Was The Ground', this was a bit of an experiment combining Richard's slide guitar abilities with the cavernous, echoing recording atmosphere provided by a nearby church. Sandy hums a suitably bluesy tune, with gentle harmony humming behind her. So it wouldn't be taken too seriously, Kingsley Abbott, a friend of the band, drops some coins in Richard's cup, and Martin's footsteps can be heard walking away.

'No Man's Land' (Richard Thompson)

Richard's first solo composition epitomises his unique combination of grim, gallows-humour lyrics matched to a jaunty tune. It sounds like a leather-trouser-slapping, beer-spilling knees-up, with Thompson providing rumbustious accordion and the band overdubbing handclaps. The music sounds almost triumphant, with massed vocals on the verses. But the lyrics! Read this: 'It's no use to be free/ If lies are all the truth they see/ They'll screw up what you do/ When you're through'. Believe it or not, this was later covered by The New Seekers!

'I'll Keep It With Mine' (Bob Dylan)

Fairport were still turning to US songwriters for the bulk of their material, particularly for their live set, and this is one written by Dylan in 1964 but first recorded by Judy Collins (all Dylan's released versions are out-takes). It bears some similarities to Sandy's 'Who Knows Where The Time Goes' with its ascending chord structure, and her performance on this song is rich, emotional and powerful. It opens with a gentle electric guitar strum before subdued bass and drums come in, gaining in volume and power for the chorus. It was released as a single with 'Fotheringay' as the B-side but failed to trouble chart compilers.

'Eastern Rain' (Joni Mitchell)

Another West Coast song, this time from the pen of the mighty Joni and one that never appeared on any of her studio albums, although it was part of her live repertoire during the late 1960s. Fairport treat it with great respect, fading in on Simon's autoharp, giving it some drums rolling like thunder and a sharp, angular guitar solo. Sandy shows how to cover a Joni song – compare her nuanced, lyrical rendition with Judy's vocals on the debut album's Mitchell numbers.

'Nottamun Town' (Trad)
Trad was to become a prolific writer of songs for the Fairports, but this was the first time they explored British folk music. Surprisingly, it didn't come from Sandy but was known to the band through the version Shirley Collins recorded with Davy Graham for their 1964 album *Folk Roots, New Routes*. A bit of a 'riddle' song with nonsense lyrics, Nottamun may be a corruption of Nottingham. It contains an acoustic guitar solo by Richard that draws heavily on the 'drone' sound of traditional instruments such as Scottish bagpipes – his father was Scottish and had a large collection of traditional folk records – but also owes something to the scales of Indian music. Coupled with Martin's bongos, the track also has an exotic Eastern feel to it. It's performed by the massed Fairport vocal department of Sandy, Ian, Richard, Simon and Ashley, with simple drone-like harmonies. The result is an unusual blend of folk styles and influences.

'Tale in Hard Time' (Richard Thompson)
Another of Richard's gloomy/jaunty songs, an upbeat, rhythmic number with slit-your-wrists lyrics including 'Take the song from my heart/ Let me learn to despise'. Yet Thompson isn't doing it for effect – that's how he writes – and the song works because it is so damn catchy, with a guitar solo that never goes where you expect it to. It opens with two finger-picked guitars in harmony before Ian comes in with the vocal. There's a repetitive three-note motif played high up on a piano or harpsichord that lasts through most of the song, disappearing during the instrumental but returning for the final verse. It's a superbly put-together track with excellent musicianship and great attention to detail.

'She Moves Through The Fair' (Trad anon)
This was part of Sandy's repertoire when she did the folk club circuit at the start of her career. An Irish song from Co Donegal, it tells of a couple who are due to be wed, but she dies – possibly at the hands of her disapproving family – and returns to him as a ghost. The song is basically performed solo with acoustic guitar accompaniment, Simon on autoharp, Richard providing tasteful lead guitar and gentle rolling drums from Martin. Once again, Sandy's singing is superb, investing the song with a sense of mystery and passion, and the entire arrangement hints at what Fairport would later achieve with traditional material.

'Meet On The Ledge' (Richard Thompson)

With 29 albums to draw from, it is almost impossible to predict what Fairport Convention will play in any particular gig. But one thing is certain – they will end with this, a song that has become an anthem for the band, a reaffirmation of life but also a tribute to those who are no longer with us. I've seen grown men cry at this and it still brings a lump to my throat, no matter how many times I have heard it. The title came from a tree Richard and his friends used to climb as children – it had a large, hanging limb they dubbed 'The Ledge'. Some of the braver ones would climb to the very top of the tree, while others would only get as far as The Ledge. The lyrics suggest loss and the futility of ambition – but they also provide hope in the suggestion that 'The Ledge' is some kind of afterlife, a place where we will all meet, with intimations of reincarnation in the line 'it all comes round again'. Subsequent events made the song seem spookily prescient, and with key band members such as Sandy, Martin, Dave Swarbrick and Trevor Lucas now dead it inevitably rekindles old feelings and memories for both the band and the audience. There are many versions of 'Meet On The Ledge' – in this, the original, Ian sings the first verse, Sandy the second and then everyone joins in for a moving singalong chorus that can be repeated as many times as you like because, you see, it all comes round again. Issued as a single in November 1968, it went the same way as 'If I Had A Ribbon Bow'.

'End Of A Holiday' (Simon Nicol)

Simon songs are few and far between. This is a short solo acoustic guitar instrumental that started life with lyrics by Ian. Simon says it was put on the album as 'a sop' but it is a gentle, winding-down to the record, especially after the emotion of the preceding track.

Bonus Tracks

'Throwaway Street Puzzle' (Ashley Hutchings, Richard Thompson)

A bluesy 'Mr Lacey' clone played with great energy, originally released as the flipside of 'Meet On The Ledge'. Chopping, muted guitar chords open proceedings, Sandy and Ian sing some 'come in and see the show' blues lyrics while guest Pete Ross provides harmonica and Mr Thompson gives us a powerful lead guitar break. Its first album appearance was on Richard's *(guitar, vocal)* solo compilation.

'You're Gonna Need My Help' (McKinley Morganfield)

A swampy 12-bar blues number recorded at the BBC for *Symonds On Saturday* and first broadcast on 9 February 1969. Fairport do a gutsy, confident version that does the song justice. McKinley Morganfield was the real name of Muddy Waters, the American blues singer regarded as the father of modern Chicago blues. He first released it as the flipside of his 1950 single 'Sad Letter Blues'.

'Some Sweet Day' (Felice & Boudleaux Bryant)

This spirited country stomp was part of Fairport's repertoire for some time and first recorded in 1967 with Judy Dyble on vocals. A second version was laid down in 1968 for John Peel's *Top Gear* radio show, and this third attempt was made during the sessions for this album as a possible third single. The Bryants were an American husband and wife team who wrote and performed country songs – 'Some Sweet Day' was first recorded and released by The Everly Brothers in 1960 although the Bryants later did their own version. Fairport's recording pretty much follows the Everlys' – it's a gentle, upbeat, swinging little number with pleasant harmonies. Ian takes most of the vocal duties while Richard plays his electric guitar with a bit of country slide.

Unhalfbricking (1969)

Personnel:
Sandy Denny: vocals, harpsichord
Martin Lamble: drums, stacked chairs
Simon Nicol: electric and acoustic guitars, electric dulcimer, backing vocals
Ashley Hutchings: bass, backing vocals
Richard Thompson: electric and acoustic guitars, electric dulcimer, piano accordion, organ, backing vocals
Additional personnel:
Dave Swarbrick: fiddle on 'Si Tu Dois Partir', 'A Sailor's Life' and 'Cajun Woman', mandolin on 'Million Dollar Bash'
Trevor Lucas: triangle on 'Si Tu Dois Partir'
Marc Ellington: vocals on 'Million Dollar Bash'
Ian Matthews: backing vocals on 'Percy's Song'
Dave Mattacks: drums on 'Ballad Of Easy Rider'
Recorded at Sound Techniques, London.
Produced by Joe Boyd, Simon Nicol & Fairport
John Wood: engineer
Record label: Island
Release dates: 3 July 1969
Highest chart positions: 12 (UK)
Running time: 39:24 (reissue 47:50)
Current edition: 2003 Universal Island with bonus tracks

Unhalfbricking is seen as a transition album as Fairport Convention's inspiration moved from the West Coast of America to the highways and byways of rural Britain and Ireland. Its centrepiece, a bold eleven-minute re-imagining of the tragic ballad 'A Sailor's Life', created a loose template for what was to follow on *Liege And Lief*. It also gave Fairport their one and only hit single – a French-language version of Bob Dylan's 'If You Gotta Go, Go Now' – and an appearance on Top Of The Pops. Sandy's classic song 'Who Knows Where The Time Goes?' makes its first appearance here as a Fairport number and, out of just eight tracks on the album, there are no fewer than three Dylan songs.

It also saw the departure of Ian Matthews, who went on to form his own group, Matthews' Southern Comfort. Ian was not happy with the new traditional direction in which the band appeared to be going and had apparently made that view crystal clear to the rest of the group. After singing on just one track on the new album, he discovered the band had booked a traditional session – probably 'A Sailor's Life' – without informing him. He said:

Joe Boyd wanted to move on to phase 3 quickly, and sentiments had no place in his plan. I was asked to leave and was dumped on the same day. Presuming that he meant soon, I got in the van to go to the show, Ashley turned to me and said, "Where do you think you're going." Sandy, bless her, turned to him and said, "You heartless bastard." I got out and away they sped.

Fairport's revolving door policy saw the departure of one member but the arrival of someone who would play a pivotal part in their development as a folk-rock band and end up becoming 'de facto' leader until 1979. Fiddler Dave Swarbrick, born in New Malden, south-west London in 1941, was even more of a grizzled folk veteran than Sandy. He had joined the hugely-respected and influential Ian Campbell Folk Group in 1960 before working as a duo with another giant of traditional music, Martin Carthy. He even had a solo album to his name that no budding folk fiddler could afford to ignore.

Joe Boyd called him in as a session musician to play on Richard's 'Cajun Woman'. Dave knew 'A Sailor's Life' because it was part of the Carthy-Swarbrick repertoire, and he also ended up playing fiddle on 'Si Tu Dois Partir' and mandolin on 'Million Dollar Bash'. Soon he would become a full-time member, telling his old partner Carthy: 'I just played with this guy Richard [Thompson] and I want to play with him for the rest of my life.' Two other non-Fairporters appear on the album. Marc Ellington was a Scottish folk singer and multi-instrumentalist (actually born in Boston, USA) and Aussie Trevor Lucas was Sandy's boyfriend at the time and bass player in the folk band Eclection.

Unhalfbricking is seen by some as unfairly overlooked, sandwiched between two great albums. In my view it has a slightly incomplete and unfocused feel, due to its over-use of Dylan covers, its baffling title (taken from a game of Ghost in which players add letters to fragments of words) and enigmatic cover, showing Sandy's parents standing at the entrance to their garden, the band sitting in the background having tea.

There's also an atmosphere of loss surrounding the album because, between the recording of the tracks and the album's release, Fairport suffered a terrible tragedy that robbed them of one of their members, forcing Joe Boyd to put together a tracklist while the band was recuperating.

On the back cover of the album is a picture of Fairport enjoying a meal. Ashley later said: 'The shirt and the leather waistcoat I'm wearing are what I had on when the crash happened. I can clearly remember them being bloodstained. You don't forget things like that.'

'Genesis Hall' (Richard Thompson)
The album opens with an absolute classic from Richard, a composition that uses folk structures and styles to create a modern-day protest song. The title came from a squat in Drury Lane, London, that had been raided and cleared out by the police, creating a moral ambiguity for Richard, whose father was a Scotland Yard detective. But his sympathies clearly lie with the squatters who were evicted, and the lyrical vitriol grows as it goes along, ending with 'It was all I could do to keep myself/ From taking revenge on your blood'. The rousing chorus is simple and direct: 'Oh, oh, helpless and slow/ And you don't have

anywhere to go'. The sting of the song is blunted a little by having it sung by Sandy – Richard was still unsure about his voice at this stage – and by the slightly swinging waltz rhythm. Richard's electric guitar is warmer and more subdued than usual, and there's an electric dulcimer following the melody line. It's a powerful song but perhaps one that is a little too dark to be the album opener.

'Si Tu Dois Partir' (Bob Dylan)

According to Fairport biographer Patrick Humphries, this slightly-dodgy French version of Dylan's 'If You Gotta Go, Go Now' came about as a spontaneous and somewhat impetuous decision in the dressing room of Middle Earth. Let's do it Cajun-style, said the band, and the call went up through the PA system for a Frenchman in the house to provide a translation. Apparently, three people turned up and the song was eventually written by committee. For the recording, Richard plays the accordion, Trevor the triangle, Dave Swarbrick on fiddle and Martin a pile of plastic chairs, which fell over towards the end, to create a Cajun-style washboard sound. It reached No 21 in the UK singles chart and gave Fairport their one and only *Top of the Pops* appearance. Sandy later disowned it as 'a load of rubbish' because it misled people into thinking they were a French group. The original song was written around 1965 but first appeared as a Manfred Mann single.

'Autopsy' (Sandy Denny)

Richard supposedly suggested the unusual time signature of 5/4 – think of the rhythm in Jethro Tull's 'Living In The Past', although 'Autopsy' shifts into 4/4 for the middle eight. A song about a girl who is always crying, it may have been partly autobiographical as Sandy was an emotional person able to burst into tears at the slightest provocation. It's a minor key lament with a bit of a jazzy swing to it – 5/4 does that to a song. The transition to the 4/4 section is a bit abrupt and plodding, and it's a relief when it goes back into the original rhythm. Sandy sings it as only she can, stretching single words out across multiple bars in an exquisite legato, but some of the meaning is lost in all the vocal gymnastics.

'A Sailor's Life' (Trad)

This is the moment that marks the beginning of British folk-rock. The most important song on the album that set the course for Fairport's future direction came about, once again, as a spur-of-the-moment dressing-room decision. Sandy had started playing it just before a gig, the band joined in and the arrangement, including its long electric instrumental ending, was pretty much formed then. It went down so well on stage it was pencilled in for the next album.

In the studio, they did one (or possibly two) run-throughs and then recorded the song in a single, 11-minute take. Sandy had a cold at the time, which probably adds to the dense, claustrophobic atmosphere. Martin's drums and cymbals roll like the ocean swell, Dave Swarbrick's rhythmic violin screams like a seagull and Richard provides relatively subdued lead while Simon and Ashley chug along relentlessly. When they listened to it afterwards, everyone knew Fairport had just recorded something special.

Credit must be given to Joe Boyd, who was pushing the band into a more traditional direction and had booked 'Swarb' to play violin because he knew he would give the recording some real folk authenticity, as well as deliver the goods in one or two takes. Swarb knew the song well as he had recorded it with Martin Carthy in 1966.

The 18th-century ballad about a girl going to sea to find her 'Sweet William' – only to discover that he's been taken by the briny – was part of Sandy's folk club repertoire and she probably didn't consider it anything special. But it excited Ashley and sparked off his interest in traditional music as he rummaged through the archives at Cecil Sharp House, looking for additional verses and stumbling across other songs he thought would be great for the band. So without Sandy's impromptu dressing-room performance Fairport may have remained the 'British Jefferson Airplane' and there would have been no *Liege And Lief* – and no Steeleye Span and Albion Band. But it also started a process that would lead to Ian quitting and Sandy's and Ashley's departure from the band after just one more album.

'Cajun Woman' (Richard Thompson)
After 'A Sailor's Life' everything else on the album was inevitably going to sound like an anti-climax. 'Cajun Woman' is a bit of a throwaway number from Richard, a Cajun pastiche recorded early on in the sessions with Swarb on fiddle. Having said that, it cracks along powerfully thanks to Martin's solid drumming and, on close inspection, contains some lyrics to make your blood run cold – 'Well, it's welcome to the graveyard/ And welcome to the throne/ Welcome to the orphanage/ Where your family sit and moan'.

'Who Knows Where The Time Goes?' (Sandy Denny)
Sorry, did I say the rest of the album was an anti-climax? Well, apart from this, Sandy's most famous composition and one that links her to Fairport for evermore. Many have sung it in the last 50 years – there are about 90 known released studio recordings – but, on each occasion, they are channelling Sandy. They have no choice – the song simply doesn't work unless you try to sing it exactly as she did. Musically it does share some similarities with Bob Dylan's 'I'll Keep It With Mine' – both have an ascending chord pattern with ringing open strings (although Dylan's is in G major and Sandy's in E) and both have the same gentle plodding rhythm. But Sandy's is an even more poignant, slow-paced and reflective affair with lyrics that touch on the passing of life but also that some things are timeless.

Sandy originally taped it as a demo in 1967 before re-recording it later that year when she was briefly a member of The Strawbs, although that version wasn't released until 1973. Judy Collins heard the demo in 1968 and made it the title track of her eighth album – Fairport recorded it only because Richard asked Sandy to play the song Judy had covered.

Fairport's version was the last track recorded for *Unhalfbricking* and the final one to feature Martin Lamble on drums. It was completed in one take – Ashley admits he messed up the bass part at one point, but the rest of the performance was perfect. It opens with acoustic and electric guitars, bass and restrained drumming before Sandy's solo voice enters with the first line 'Across the evening sky' – she had originally sung 'Across the purple sky', but Richard suggested changing it. Her vocal is exquisite – powerful and melodically adventurous yet with that fragile edge to it that makes her sound so vulnerable and yearning. Richard's provides very tasteful electric guitar phrases, and the band support her sensitively all the way through – and I can't spot Ashley's fluff.

The song has become even more poignant as the time goes, performed by a variety of female singers at the Cropredy festival in tribute to the sadly-departed Sandy, as well as by Simon on Fairport's 21st album of the same name, and has been used on the soundtracks of TV shows and movies. In 2007 it was voted Favourite Folk Track Of All Time by BBC Radio 2 listeners.

'Percy's Song' (Bob Dylan)

The first song Fairport recorded for the album and the only one with Ian Matthews on vocals. He supports Sandy, who sings an impassioned narrative about a driver in a fatal car crash who is sentenced to 99 years in prison for manslaughter, which appears to him to be a little on the steep side. The lyrics were written by Dylan in 1963 – based, he claimed, on the story of a friend – while the tune is traditional. Fairport take the original 4/4 song and perform it in waltz time, with the rousing repeat of 'turn, turn again'. It opens with acapella harmony vocals, before an acoustic guitar joins in, followed by bass, drums and electric dulcimer. The track builds into a powerful singalong before fading out on guitar, dulcimer and organ. It's a fine version but, compared to what has gone before on this album, you can't help feeling they have left songs like this behind.

'Million Dollar Bash' (Bob Dylan)

Recorded in one take, the third Dylan cover on the album features practically everyone taking a verse, including Ashley attempting an American accent, while Dave Swarbrick plays mandolin. Fairport learned the song from the 1967 bootleg of Dylan's *The Basement Tapes* – it's said to be about all the strange people in Dylan's songs so far coming together into one big party. In 1992 Ashley rewrote the lyrics to tell Fairport's story for the 25th-anniversary concert at Cropredy.

2003 Bonus Tracks
'Dear Landlord' (Bob Dylan)

The FOURTH Dylan cover recorded during the sessions but wisely left off because, quite frankly, you can have too much Dylan. Fairport perform it pretty much as Dylan did on his 1968 album *John Wesley Harding*, although it's not a patch on Joan Baez's cover. Notable for being one of the last songs Fairport recorded with Martin on drums.

'The Ballad Of Easy Rider' (Roger McGuinn)

Dylan also had a hand in writing this, penned by The Byrds singer for the cult 1969 movie Easy Rider, but refused a credit. Fairport's version should really be a bonus track on *Liege And Lief* (it turns up on the now-deleted 2007 deluxe edition) as it was recorded during those sessions with new drummer Dave Mattacks. A waltz-time ballad with similarities to Sandy's own 'Who Knows Where The Time Goes?', it used to be the band's live encore song. It's the last remnant of the West Coast sound that provided the bulk of Fairport's material and clearly does not fit with anything else on *Liege And Lief*, which may explain why it appears here instead.

Liege And Lief (1969)

Personnel:
Sandy Denny: vocals
Ashley Hutchings: bass, backing vocals
Dave Mattacks: drums
Simon Nicol: guitars, backing vocals
Richard Thompson: guitars, backing vocals
Dave Swarbrick: violin, viola
Recorded at Sound Techniques, London, 16 Oct-2 Nov 1969.
Produced by Joe Boyd, Witchseason Productions Ltd
John Wood: engineer
Record label: Island (UK), A&M (US)
Release date: December 1969
Highest chart position: 17 (UK)
Running time: 40:33 (2002 reissue 50:55)
Current edition: 2002 reissue

In the early hours of 12 May 1969, having wrapped up work on the tracks that would become *Unhalfbricking*, Fairport Convention were returning from a concert at Mothers in Birmingham. Sandy was travelling separately with her boyfriend, Trevor Lucas, while the rest of the band and Richard's girlfriend, fashion designer and magazine columnist Jeannie Franklyn, were in a transit van driven by roadie Harvey Bramham. At Mill Hill, North London, the vehicle veered off the M1, cartwheeling across the road. Bodies and musical equipment were flung out at all angles. Simon Nicol told a BBC documentary:

> Our driver had got a bad stomach and he'd been complaining about being tired and unwell all day. I did wake up in the van as it was somersaulting down the M1 and I was concussed and knocked out. When I came to I was the only person, or thing, left inside the vehicle. The doors had all burst open, the windows were out, everybody and all the kit was thrown out the back door. Somehow or other I'd remained inside. Everybody was on the ground either dead or out for the count or moaning.

Two people were killed in the crash – Fairport's 19-year-old drummer Martin Lamble and Richard's girlfriend Jeannie. Ashley suffered a broken nose, broken cheekbone, broken pelvis, a lot of head injuries and an ankle injury. His eyes were so bruised and swollen he thought he had gone blind. Richard had a broken shoulder, while Simon suffered a concussion and superficial injuries from flying glass. Bramham was later jailed for causing death by dangerous driving, even though the band didn't blame him at all.

The crash knocked the stuffing out of them, and they seriously considered whether they should continue. Simon said: "In the aftermath, we thought a lot about what to do, whether to call it a day. It had been fun while it lasted, but it took a definite effort of will to continue. It had given us a lot, but now it had taken away a lot: was it worth it if it was going to cost people their lives?"

Two things probably helped to keep them going. One was the fact that their single 'Si Tu Dois Partir' had reached No 21 in the UK charts and they were invited to perform on *Top Of The Pops*. The other was the excitement they had felt at the new folk-rock direction they were now pursuing after the success of 'A Sailor's Life'. They made the decision to carry on and immediately invited Dave Swarbrick, who had guested on *Unhalfbricking*, to become a full-time member. Then they started auditioning new drummers.

The man they chose to replace Martin Lamble was David James Mattacks, born 1948 in Edgware, north London, who had considerable experience including playing in dance bands in Belfast and Glasgow. He accepted the job but told them: 'I haven't a f***ing clue what you're on about. I can't tell one tune from another."

In the summer of 1969, they convened at a house near Winchester to rehearse their new repertoire – and a number of things began to develop. First, there was the blossoming songwriting relationship between Richard and Swarb, their uncanny ability to compose songs that sounded as if they had been around for 200 years. Then there was Ashley's growing interest – some might say, obsession – with traditional music as he rooted through archives and talked to musicians, cramming as much information as he could into his head.

Despite claiming he didn't understand Fairport until he had been with them a year, Dave Mattacks had worked out how to be a folk-rock drummer, to give the songs and tunes a bit of swing so they didn't sound plodding and old-fashioned. And there was the house itself, in rural secluded Farley Chamberlayne, that provided the healing they needed. Richard said: 'The environment was perfect and the mission kept us sane.'

The album was released just before Christmas – the band's third album that year – and did quite well, reaching No 17 in the charts. But it has grown in stature over the years, being voted Most Influential Folk Album Of All Time and one of the 100 Records The Changed The World. *Liege And Lief* – the title means something like Loyalty And Lord – still stands today as an album of blood and thunder, of courage and conviction, of joy and pain. It is groundbreaking, timeless and never dull. It reels – but it also rocks.

'Come All Ye' (Sandy Denny, Ashley Hutchings)
The perfect introduction to the album, a sort of rocked-up 'calling-on song' of the kind used by morris dancers to introduce their members and encourage the audience to gather around and watch. Acoustic and electric guitars open proceedings, with Swarb's fiddle dancing around like a dervish, while Sandy's voice has swing and power. She gives each band member a nod, including 'our fiddler, who just loves to play' and 'the man who plays the bass does make those low notes that you hear'. Then there's the uplifting chorus as Sandy exhorts all 'rolling minstrels' to 'rouse the spirits of the earth and move the

rolling sky'. It's more than an opening number – it's a statement of intent.
Interestingly, however, it is Sandy's only song written with Ashley and her only
credit on the album.

'Reynardine' (Trad)

A ballad of seduction on a mountainside by a charming rogue, compared
to a wily fox – is he man or animal? It dates back to the 18th century and
has been recorded by practically everyone who has ever made a folk album,
including Swarb and Martin Carthy on their 1969 release *Prince Heathen*.
Sandy's voice soars over a simple, rhythm-less backing similar to that on
'A Sailor's Life' – slow, sensuous chords with Swarb providing restrained
violin. Its weakness is that the song doesn't really change or go anywhere
during its four and a half minutes and is the least effective of all the tracks
on the album.

'Matty Groves' (Trad)

Fairport's attempt to emulate 'A Sailor's Life' has become a staple of the
band's live sets, usually played just before the encore and twinned with an
instrumental performed at breakneck speed. It's a popular morality ballad
dating to the very early 17th century, telling the cautionary tale of little
Matty Groves who is seduced by the wife of Lord Darnell. The cuckolded
husband arrives home unexpectedly and kills Matty and his cheating
missus. Melodically there's not much to it as it alternates between just two
chords, D minor and C. Then it moves into a fast instrumental section,
linked by a fiddle phrase reminiscent of Martin Carthy's version of 'The
Famous Flowers Of Serving Men'. New boy Dave Mattacks pounds away
at the drums, Richard wrenches lead phrases out of his electric guitar and
Swarb saws away valiantly in the background. Future versions would go into
more defined tunes, such as 'Orange Blossom Special' or new reels written
by future Fairporter Ric Sanders. It's better than 'A Sailor's Life' – more
confident and dramatic, with the band flying along together as if possessed.
It's the centrepiece of the album and proof that the folk-rock approach
wasn't just a lucky one-off.

'Farewell, Farewell' (Richard Thompson)

Note how well this newly-written song fits in so perfectly with the
traditional material. That's because the tune comes from the folk song
'Willie O'Winsbury', while the words use the familiar traditional device
of a to and fro dialogue. Some of the lyrics seem to reference the band's
recent tragedy, with the line 'And will you never cut the cloth' suggested
as a reference to Jeannie 'The Tailor' Franklyn. Sandy sings with a
direct simplicity and gentleness that adds greatly to the song's haunting
poignancy, almost breaking in emotion, while the instrumental backing is
mostly low-key.

'The Deserter' (Trad)

A song learned, said Swarb, from an old Victorian broadside, it references the enforced recruitment of young men to fill British ships during the 18th century and the penalty for desertion. In this case, the lucky deserter is sentenced to be shot but is rescued by the timely intervention of Prince Albert. It starts in a leisurely waltz-time driven by simple, strummed acoustic guitar but builds up the rhythm and drama during the 'Court-martial, court-martial' verses, which act a little like choruses. It was said to be Sandy's favourite song on the album, and she certainly does a grand job in telling the story with some drama and emotion.

'Medley: i) The Lark In The Morning ii) Rakish Paddy iii) Foxhunter's Jig iv) Toss The Feathers' (Trad)

The first of the fast and furious fiddle medleys that would become Fairport's calling card reels and rocks like the very devil. At the heart is the dazzling interplay between Swarb's fiddle and Richard's lead guitar, while Ashley and Simon provide solid backing and Dave Mattacks throws in clever little fills, frills and rolls to give the feeling the tunes are almost teetering on the edge before catching their breath and storming on again. First part is a popular jig in three parts, the second a reel from Ireland, the third an Irish slipjig and the final tune a reel, also from Ireland. In future years the band would try to play this at a breakneck speed just to see if they could catch each other out.

'Tam Lin' (Trad)

A magical ballad from the Scottish borders about a young man caught by the Queen of Fairies and the young girl who rescues him through complicated means that we needn't go into here. It has a fairly repetitive tune, so Fairport add interest by playing most of it in waltz-time but adding in the odd bar of 4/4 just to trip up anyone who foolishly tries to dance to it. The guitars play stabbing chords in a style that would be much copied by Steeleye Span, Richard plays a fairly subdued instrumental break, and Dave Mattacks keeps everything together with some clever, inventive drumming. It probably outstays its welcome a bit, but that's folk singers for you – they always sing one verse too many.

'Crazy Man Michael' (Richard Thompson, Dave Swarbrick)

A prime example of the Thompson-Swarb partnership producing something truly wonderful. Like Tam Lin, it's a magical song but many shades darker – its melancholy air may well have been consciously or subconsciously inspired by the recent tragedy. Michael is a sad, disturbed young man who kills a raven he believes is taunting him, only to find he has murdered his own true love. Swarb said: 'Richard had the words set to a trad tune and I thought that the words were great but that the tune weakened it ... He said that if I felt like that, why didn't I write a tune for it – so I did ... Funnily enough, I wrote the piece on the piano, and I don't even play piano!' Richard plays a doubled up Les Paul, giving it a shimmering, ghostly texture that matches the song's grim atmosphere. However, he does obscure some of Swarb's violin, eventually pushing it out of the tune to take over on the instrumental section. Sandy is once again superb, her voice having that little catch to it that suggests something dark and mysterious. A Fairport classic that has been recorded many times since, both in-studio and live, it provides a haunting end to the original album.

2003 Bonus Tracks
'Sir Patrick Spens' (Trad)
A song that turns up on the next album in a slightly faster, sprightlier guise. Perhaps because I know the official version so well, this sounds sedate and a little plodding. Clearly, it wasn't deemed good enough to displace any of the other tracks on the album.

'The Quiet Joys Of Brotherhood' (Richard Farina)
A poem by the US singer/songwriter which he set to the tune of 'My Lagan Love'. Fairport approach it in a similar fashion to 'A Sailor's Life', with Sandy singing over a gentle wash of sound. It was clearly Sandy's choice as she re-recorded it for her first solo album. Richard plays electric dulcimer and Ashley bows his bass.

Full House (1970)

Personnel:

Richard Thompson: vocals, guitar

Simon Nicol: vocals, electric, acoustic & bass guitars, dulcimer

Dave Swarbrick: vocals, fiddle, viola, mandolin

Dave Pegg: vocals, bass guitar, mandolin

Dave Mattacks: drums, harmonium, bodhrán

Recorded at Sound Techniques Studio, Feb-Apr 1970

Produced by Joe Boyd, Witchseason Productions Ltd.

John Wood: engineer

Record label: Island (UK), A&M (US)

Release dates: July 1970

Highest chart positions: 13 (UK)

Running time: 35:08 (2001 reissue 59:00)

Current edition: 2001 reissue with bonus tracks

What do you do after you have survived a terrible tragedy to make the best album of your career? In the case of Fairport Convention, you split up. Sandy Denny was the first to go before *Liege And Lief* had even been released. She wasn't happy with the folk direction the band was taking – after all, she had been there, done that, got the T-shirt – and saw little room for her own songs. She was also missing her boyfriend Trevor Lucas and feared the band's increasing success would keep them apart for long periods. Cue some tears...

A few days later, Ashley Hutchings followed her out of the door. His reasons seemed to be a bit more complicated and probably had more to with the aftershock of the crash. He later said:

Sandy went on to do what she did with her own songs and with Fotheringay. And I got deeper and deeper into traditional music, but they weren't the sole reasons for us leaving. There was something in the air, something strange and weird. And I think we just reacted. In retrospect, it was a silly thing to do. I had a bit of a nervous breakdown, as a delayed reaction to the crash, immediately after I left Fairport.

It must have felt like the end of the road for Simon, Richard and Swarb – and especially for Dave Mattacks, who had only just joined to see everything fall apart. But there was no suggestion that they would throw in the towel – after all, they had gigs to fulfil, including a second US tour. They decided they could share the vocal duties between them but what they really needed was a new bass player.

Enter David Pegg, born 1947 in Birmingham, an old mucker of Swarb's from the Ian Campbell Folk Group days. The rest of the band thought he would be a stuck-in-the-mud old folkie, but at heart he was a rocker who started out on guitar and was in a band with future Led Zeppelin drummer John Bonham.

The rest of Fairport were astounded when they auditioned him. He could play all of Ashley's bass parts – but better! (Now there are three Daves in the band, we shall henceforth refer to them as Swarb, Peggy and DM, to avoid confusion.)

As a five-piece the band lived and rehearsed at a rundown former pub, the Angel in Bishop's Stortford, then went into the studio in February 1970 and cut *Full House*, an album that may not be as important as *Liege And Lief* but is regarded by many as superior. There are, for a start, two astonishing Thompson, Swarbrick numbers that have become firm favourites – the opener, 'Walk Awhile', and the nine-minute epic 'Sloth'. The third new song on the album, 'Doctor Of Physick', is no slouch either. Then there are the works of Mr Trad – a faster, more confident version of 'Sir Patrick Spens' and another rousing medley of dance tunes under the name of 'Dirty Linen'.

It is not perfect. The album suffers from a short running time – just over 35 minutes – thanks to Richard having last-minute collie-wobbles over his vocals and guitar solo on 'Poor Will And The Jolly Hangman' and insisting on the track being pulled. Indeed, some early pressings of the album include the song in the tracklist and had to have a black block overprinted with the correct running order. 'Flatback Capers' – a selection of mandolin tunes played by both Swarb and Peggy – goes on a tad too long and the album's vocals are a little underwhelming compared to what Sandy could achieve.

But the playing is tight and swinging – Dave Pegg, in particular, is a revelation, especially on the instrumentals where he showed he could perform the dance tunes on bass just as quickly and accurately as Richard and Swarb on guitar and fiddle. The 2001 reissue is the one to get – it not only provides extra tracks recorded during the sessions, including the single 'Now Be Thankful', it also juggles the songs into the originally planned running order. The front cover shows the band as playing cards – it would be mimicked on future Fairport album *Myths & Heroes* – and the sleeve notes provide a lot of fun, containing descriptions, by Richard, of spoof folk-games, most of which end with the participants getting badly mauled or killed.

'Walk Awhile' (Richard Thompson, Dave Swarbrick)
Like 'Come All Ye' on *Liege And Lief*, 'Walk Awhile' acts as a 'calling on' song, exhorting the listener to 'walk awhile with me, the better we'll agree'. Confident and swaggering, the song gives every member of the band, except DM, the opportunity to take a verse, exposing some vocal limitations, especially from a clearly reticent Richard, but giving the album a bit of a party atmosphere – everyone can join in. Lyrically it's a bit obscure but, as befits every Richard Thompson song, there are dark references to undertakers, wounded children and people running for their lives. It has become a frequent opening number for live gigs because of the way the guitars open with a bit of a fanfare before settling down into a steady rhythm.

'Dirty Linen' (Trad arr Dave Swarbrick)

A medley of four tunes – 'Last Night's Fun', 'Paddy On The Railroad', 'Drops Of Brandy' and 'Poll Ha'penny'. It reveals from the off that Dave Pegg is more than a match for Swarb and Richard – whereas Ashley would provide a solid beat, Peggy could play the riffs with lightning speed and dexterity. The result is the quintessential Fairport instrumental – fun, fast, furious and deliciously difficult. The first tune is an Irish slipjig in 9/8 with a bit of a call and response to it – Peggy and Swarb play the melody on bass and fiddle, then it's echoed by Richard and Simon on electric and acoustic guitars. That goes into a reel that hails from America, inspired by the Irish who helped build the railroads. Bass and guitar play a fiendishly difficult melody in unison before Swarb joins in on fiddle. 'Drops Of Brandy' is another Irish slipjig and then things end with a hornpipe played by Swarb, with every other instrument joining in until guitars, bass and fiddle are all playing the melody as DM rattles along splendidly.

'Sloth' (Richard Thompson, Dave Swarbrick)

Unhalfbricking has 'A Sailor's Life' and *Liege And Lief* 'Matty Groves'. *Full House*'s epic long track is this powerful anti-war statement. Set to a slow marching beat, it opens with the ominous lines 'just a roll on the drum and the war has begun', lamenting a world turned upside down in which 'the right thing is the wrong thing'. Between each verse, Richard and Swarb trade guitar and violin licks and DM's drumming grows in intensity until the song becomes an outpouring of instrumental rage and violence. Then it's back to the 'just a roll' chorus, ending on a despairing minor chord. After the fun and games of the first two tracks, this is a dark, meaty nine-minute slice of serious music that shows the band's ability to create an ominous, brooding atmosphere. Live, this could render audiences into stunned, impressed silence.

'Sir Patrick Spens' (Trad arr Fairport Convention)

Originally recorded for *Liege And Lief* with Sandy on vocals, this upbeat ballad about a Scottish aristocratic murder plot is taken at a faster pace and is all the better for it. The King of Scotland needs a good sailor to command a ship, so someone suggests the eponymous Sir Patrick. Unfortunately, he's actually a total duffer when it comes to all things maritime and, thanks to his inexperience, his ship is sunk in a storm 40 miles off Aberdeen 'with the Scots lords at his feet'. A stately song that starts slowly before getting into its stride, its emphasis is more on the story than the musicianship, although Richard gets a chance to shine during a brief instrumental section. DM's drumming, in particular, drives everything along with enough inventive frills and stops and starts to keep things interesting.

'Flatback Caper' (Trad arr Fairport Convention)

Another collection of tunes from Swarb, this time played as a twin-mandolin attack. The band performs 'Miss Susan Cooper', a Scottish reel; 'The Friar's

Britches', a jig also known as 'Cunla and The Vicar's Knickers'; Irish slipjig 'The Sport Of The Chase' and 'Carolan's Concerto' by the blind Irish harpist Turlough O'Carolan. Bright and sprightly, at nearly six and a half minutes it goes on a bit too long but shows what a versatile new member they had in Peggy, who learned how to play the mandolin for this set of tunes.

'Doctor Of Physick' (Richard Thompson, Dave Swarbrick)

An overlooked little gem, the good Doctor tends to be overshadowed by the two other originals on the album. But it is a lot of fun, a dark, cautionary tale about an extremely dodgy medic whose bedside manner may be a little more hands-on than most maidens would care to entertain. The ominous chorus line 'Doctor Monk unpacks his trunk tonight' is full of foreboding but in a blackly humorous way. It's another illustration of how Swarb and Richard could create songs that sounded 200 years old, an audio version of a medieval woodcut.

'Flowers Of The Forest' (Trad arr by Fairport Convention)

This ancient lament, usually played as a pipe tune at funerals (it was played at Sandy Denny's), refers to the 10,000 Scottish warriors, many of them noblemen, cut down in the Battle of Flodden in 1513. Words were added in the 18th century by Lady Jean Eliot, daughter of the then Lord Chief Justice of Scotland, Sir Gilbert Elliot of Minto. Fairport provide a respectful reading underpinned by DM's marching drums and Simon on the dulcimer, with the band singing drone-like harmonies.

2001 Bonus Tracks
'Poor Will & The Jolly Hangman' (Richard Thompson, Dave Swarbrick)

A troublesome song inspired by the trial of Harvey Bramham, who was driving Fairport's van at the time of the fatal crash and was subsequently jailed. Richard said: 'It was absolutely no fault of Harvey's, and it gave us an ugly taste of the workings of the British legal system. That was the jumping-off point, anyway.' In the song Harvey becomes Poor Will, 'never a cruel word did say' being hanged on the gallows-tree at the whim of the sadistic, merciless hangman. But he's jolly, this hangman, because he loves his job and will hang you the best as he can. A quintessential Thompson song, it was pulled off the album at the last minute because Richard didn't like the vocals. He said: 'None of us could really sing it, and it sounded like it.' Joe Boyd felt it fit the album perfectly, adding: 'Richard was becoming more and more perverse in the studio.' Richard didn't dislike it that much because he put it on a later solo album with new backing vocals. His vocals here are not great – his voice is a bit thin and reedy and would get a lot better on his solo albums – but it is a tremendous song and deserves to be part of the running order.

'Now Be Thankful' (Richard Thompson, Dave Swarbrick)

A short and sweet song that probably was better as an album track than
a standalone single. Inevitably, it sank without trace and is probably only
remembered today because of its B-side. Swarb sings it beautifully, though – it's
one of his best vocal performances from these sessions. As the title suggests,
the song is a rare optimistic composition, exhorting us to be thankful for all
things below and for our Maker, although some of the lyrics are obscure in
the extreme. It's also a little repetitive – it's just one melody repeated for both
the verses and the chorus. Its lack of commercial success is, therefore, hardly
surprising.

'Sir B. McKenzie's Daughter's Lament For The 77th Mounted Lancers Retreat From The Straits Of Loch Knombe, In The Year Of Our Lord 1727, On The Occasion Of The Announcement Of Her Marriage To The Laird Of Kinleakie' (Trad arr Fairport Convention/Dave Swarbrick)

The flipside of 'Now Be Thankful' was a deliberate attempt to get into the
Guinness Book of Records as the song with the longest title. The studio version
consists of three tunes – 'Biff, Bang, Crash' (Trad), 'The Kilfenora' (Trad) and
'Boston Tea Party' (Dave Swarbrick) – but later live versions mixed things up a
bit so the title really became just an excuse to put together three or four good
folk tunes and play them at 120mph.

'Bonny Bunch Of Roses' (Trad arr Fairport Convention)

A cautionary tale of military over-reach, in the form of a dialogue between
Napoleon Bonaparte's widow and her ambitious son. The roses are said to
symbolise England, Scotland and Ireland, or could be a reference to the British
redcoats. It's a long – nearly 11 minutes – slow ballad with a gentle guitar and
bass backing and slightly martial drumming from DM. Recorded a month after
the *Full House* sessions while the band was in Los Angeles, it could be that it
was never intended for the album. Fairport try hard, but the song doesn't really
come off – it was a lot better when they recorded it for the album of the same
name seven years later. Here, they haven't quite worked out an arrangement
that keeps the listener's interest over its ten verses.

Angel Delight (1971)

Personnel:
Simon Nicol: guitar, bass, viola, dulcimer, vocals
Dave Mattacks: drums, piano, bass, vocals
Dave Swarbrick: violin, mandolin, vocals
Dave Pegg: bass, violin, viola, vocal
Recorded at Sound Techniques Studio, Feb-Mar 1971
Produced by Fairport Convention & John Wood
John Wood: engineer
Record label: Island
Release dates: June 1971
Highest chart positions: 8 (UK) 200 (US)
Running time: 36:46 (2004 reissue 41:58)
Current edition: 2004 reissue with bonus track

By the end of 1970, Fairport Convention were riding high. *Full House* had achieved their highest chart placing to date and they had tasted superstardom with a stint at the Troubadour in Los Angeles, rubbing shoulders with Led Zeppelin – Peggy and Bonzo were old muckers. They had also become a tight, professional band as well as a group of friends who got on well together. How to celebrate? By splitting up, of course.

In January 1971 Richard Thompson shocked the band by announcing he was leaving to concentrate on a solo career. Like Sandy, he felt the band's folk-rock direction had become a bit of a strait-jacket, and there wasn't room for the kind of dark, quirky songs he was now writing (and which ended up on his first solo album *Henry The Human Fly*). In a 1972 interview for *Sounds* he said:

> I wanted independence. Sometimes I think it's very important to think for yourself musically, and at the time with Fairport I didn't do that at all. I was always thinking in terms of the band and in a lot of ways it was holding my musical ideas back a lot.

For Dave Pegg, it felt like the final nail in the coffin for the band. He couldn't see how the others would carry on without Richard's invaluable musical ideas and inspiration. But there were gig commitments to fulfil and pressure from Island Records for a follow-up to *Full House*, as well as a single. Swarb said: 'You get all this spiel from record companies about singles – so we went in and did nine.' Peggy also credits Swarb's discovery of documents that would lead to the *"Babbacombe" Lee* album as another source of impetus, inspiring the band to sit down and start writing.

There are ten tracks on the album, half originals – including two leftover Swarbrick/Thompson compositions – and half by that prolific composer, Trad. Swarb and Simon took over most of the vocal duties, with harmony help from Peggy, and Simon shouldered the responsibility of somehow replicating both his own and Richard's guitar work with just one instrument and one pair of hands. The title track shows that, despite its travails, the band hadn't lost its sense of humour as it paints a merry picture of life at the Angel in Bishop's Stortford, the rundown former pub where they were living a somewhat bohemian lifestyle, brought to a sudden end by a lorry crashing into Swarb's bedroom.

It's fair to say it doesn't quite reach the heights of *Full House* and the guitar/bass/fiddle interplay is not quite as breathtaking as it used to be. Surprisingly, however, *Angel Delight* gave Fairport their highest chart placing ever, thanks to *Top Of The Pops* picking it for their newly-introduced album slot.

The cover shows the band outside an abandoned old building – fans assumed it was the wreckage of the Angel but, as Peggy points out in his autobiography: 'The Angel was a pretty rundown place, but it was never that bad.'

'Lord Marlborough' (Trad arr Fairport Convention)

A confident opener that shows off some of Fairport's strengths: strong vocals, tight-as-a-drum musicianship and the ability to navigate through tricky-dicky time signatures. Swarb, Simon and Peggy's vocals burst through against the backing of Simon's dulcimer before the song jumps up a tone for fiddle, guitar and bass to play the melody in tight unison. Swarb takes lead vocal duties, the instrumental backing ramps up the drama and the whole thing swings along despite being in what appears to be alternating bars of 6/8 and 5/8. Richard who? The Lord Marlborough in the song was Colonel John Churchill, an ancestor of Winston, who was best known for victories against the French and the Duke of Monmouth in the late seventeenth century. The final line – 'I've led my men through fire and smoke but ne'er was bribed by gold' – is a reference to accusations of dodgy dealings that plagued him in later years.

'Sir William Gower' (Trad arr Fairport Convention)

This slower, more ponderous ballad is led by Peggy's fuzz-bass, with Simon taking the lead vocal. His voice improved with age – here it's a bit thin and nasal. There are a lot of repetitive verses so it goes on for nearly five minutes. The story is based on the superstition that having an evil-doer on board ship brings bad luck so best to toss him overboard. In this case, the bad man is the captain, William Gower, and he soon meets his end in the deep. There is, however, no evidence he really existed, and he definitely isn't related to the nineteenth-century physician of the same name.

'Bridge Over The River Ash' (Trad arr Fairport Convention)

Fairport turn themselves into a string quartet for this entertaining medley of two tunes that became a staple of their live show, when they would change the title depending on where they were playing. For example, at an open-air gig in Southport, they renamed it Bridge Over The Manchester Ship Canal. Swarb and Peggy play violins, Simon the viola and drummer Dave Mattacks provides rhythmic bass. It's not the Halle Orchestra, but it sounds surprisingly good. The tunes were collected by John Playford in the 17th century.

'Wizard Of The Worldly Game' (Dave Swarbrick, Simon Nicol)

The first original on the album and a rare songwriting collusion between Swarb and Simon. It doesn't quite reach the melodic and lyrical heights Swarb would achieve with Richard – it is a bit slow and lurching – but it's an accomplished song with a catchy chorus and a nice guitar solo from Simon. They appear to have attempted some obscure Richard-style lyrics here – the song is full of images of a tree sheltering the plants beneath it. If the tree falls, says the song, then 'give it time and it will surely rise again'. But who is the wizard and what is his worldly game? The song refuses to tell us.

'The Journeyman's Grace' (Dave Swarbrick, Richard Thompson)

One of the two compositions left over from the songwriting partnership, this is a thunderously good track with a great chorus that has become a fan favourite. As usual, the apparent simplicity of Richard's lyrics hides multiple meanings – unfortunately, he left before he could tell the rest of the band what it was all about. I'll take a stab and suggest there are references here to a mythical guide who leads you to the afterlife, rather like Charon, the ferryman who takes souls across the river Styx to the Greek underworld. 'When you see your race is run…then you'll find the journeyman with the lantern in his hand, he'll show you a good time for a penny.' Like the ferryman, the journeyman requires payment for his services.

It bears some similarities to 'Walk Awhile' in its lengthy intro that then changes key to settle into the verse, and it has the same driving rhythm and a lengthy instrumental section in which Simon and Swarb trade guitar and fiddle phrases. The 2004 reissue includes a version with Richard recorded in November 1970 for BBC Radio's *Sound Of The Seventies* – the studio rendition, recorded a few months later, is slightly faster with more verses before the instrumental.

'Angel Delight' (Fairport Convention)

Credited to the entire band, the title track is a fun, uptempo ditty driven by Swarb's mandolin and telling of the band's experiences at the former pub, the Angel. Richard Thompson, who was still living at the Angel during this period despite no longer performing with the band, may have chipped in with some lines. Sung from Swarb's point of view, it name-checks the rest of the group plus engineer 'John the Wood' and Fairport's then-manager Robin Gee, who had been dubbed The Mighty Glydd in a Pete (Cook) and Dud (Moore) sketch on *Not Only..But Also*. The sudden end to the band's residency is told in the line 'There's a hole in the wall where a lorry came in, let's split'. It even mentions *Top Of The Pops,* which may have persuaded the show's producers to give it a bit of an airing. One of the highlights of the album, it also reveals some of the band's favourite foodstuffs: Swarb's pulse rate quickens at the sight of a dozen nice fat snails, while Peggy is happy with a couple of kippers and a glass of cider.

'Banks Of Sweet Primroses' (Trad arr Fairport Convention)

A folk standard that practically everyone in the traditional world has had a crack at. Dating back to at least 1892, its true origins are lost in the mists of time. An apparently pleasant, sunny song, it tells a cautionary tale of a young man who hits on a young girl, only to realise that he's already loved and left her, causing her 'poor heart for to wander'. Paradoxically, the final verse is full of hope of a dark and cloudy morning turning into a sunshiny day – it's been suggested that is a later addition as it doesn't quite match the mood of the rest of the song. Fairport's version is a fairly unadventurous slow ballad with some nice harmony work towards the end.

'Instrumental Medley: The Cuckoo's Nest / Hardiman the Fiddler / Papa Stoor' (Trad arr Fairport Convention)

The album's instrumental medley is a more sedate affair than those found on *Full House* and *Liege And Lief* but is no less entertaining – the first tune amuses with Swarb playing cuckoo sounds, while the third has an uncredited tin whistle with bodhran-like percussion. Simon does well in trying to emulate Thompson's contrapuntal guitar playing, although he doesn't quite have the same fiery attack. 'The Cuckoo's Nest' is a popular tune known across the British Isles and in the US – the title may be a cheeky reference to a, ahem, lady-garden. 'Hardiman The Fiddler' is an Irish slipjig, while 'Papa Stoor' is a bridal march named after one of the Shetland Isles.

'The Bonny Black Hare' (Trad arr Fairport Convention)

In contrast to the fellow in the 'Banks Of The Sweet Primroses', the chap roving out here finds a far more willing young lady but discovers he's unable to perform with as much enthusiasm as she would like. Swarb sings the lusty lyrics, which use guns, ramrods and powder as an allusion to the mechanics of lovemaking, with a straight face, accompanied by mandolin and Simon on dulcimer. The rhythm is quite tricky and tends to be dictated by the length of each line. Swarb knew this one well – he recorded it with Bert Lloyd in 1965 and then two years later with Martin Carthy. It is likely to be the only folk song in existence about erectile dysfunction.

'Sickness And Diseases' (Dave Swarbrick/Richard Thompson)

The last of the Swarb/ Richard songs is a jolly discourse on various ailments, illustrating once again Thompson's delight in the grubbier side of life. There's a great singalong chorus plus some hilarious lines, including a reference to a poor fellow who's 'got every known disease and some without a name'.

Swarb takes lead vocals while Simon gets to play some power chords on his electric guitar, overdubbing some lead. The performance is a little looser than one would normally expect from Fairport, with Simon's guitar getting a little random at points, but it's an upbeat and entertaining ending to the album.

"Babbacombe" Lee (1971)

Personnel:
Simon Nicol: vocals, guitar, dulcimer
Dave Mattacks: drums, electric piano, harmonium
Dave Swarbrick: violin, mandolin, vocals
Dave Pegg: bass, mandolin, vocals
Additional personnel:
Trevor Lucas, rhythm guitar on 1974 tracks
Jerry Donahue, lead guitar on 1974 tracks
Sandy Denny, vocals on 1974 tracks
Recorded at Sound Techniques Studio, Aug-Sep 1971
Produced by John Wood & Simon Nicol
John Wood: engineer
Record label: Island
Release dates: November 1971
Highest chart positions: 195 (US Billboard)
Running time: 41:20 (2004 reissue 50:11)
Current edition: 2004 reissue with bonus tracks

For the first time in the band's long and tumultuous career, Fairport recorded two consecutive albums with the same line-up. Not only that, the second album appeared a scant five months after the first – and marked the genesis of a new sub-genre of music, the folk-rock opera.

It's a concept album, the story of Devon-born John Lee, who was convicted on flimsy evidence of murdering his elderly employer Emma Keyse at her home in Babbacombe in 1884. Sentenced to hang, he was reprieved and given life imprisonment after the gallows trapdoor failed to open on three occasions. The album depicts Lee as an innocent victim of legal bungling, although in reality, he was a well-known thief.

Dave Swarbrick came upon a pile of newspaper clippings telling the story – allegedly John Lee's own collection, dated 1908 – while rummaging in an antique shop in Ware, Hertfordshire, and presented it to the band with the suggestion that they make an album out of it. The result was a collection of mostly self-penned songs tracing Lee's journey in and out of the Royal Navy, into the employ of Emma Keyes and, finally, the divine intervention – or it may have been faulty hinges – that saved him from execution at Exeter Prison.

There are only two traditional numbers: a Trumpet Hornpipe instrumental (better known as the theme tune to children's TV series *Captain Pugwash*) and 'The Sailor's Alphabet'. The rest are new tracks credited to the entire band. Some work better than others and there are probably four standouts – the title track 'John Lee', Simon's catchy and witty 'Breakfast In Mayfair', 'The Trial' and the final 'Hanging Song'. All four musicians are on top form with Simon, especially, providing some excellent guitar work as well as assisting John Wood with the production.

Sadly, the album was a commercial flop despite an imaginative PR campaign by the record company but has since been reassessed as a bold and mostly successful attempt to create, if not a folk *Tommy*, perhaps a folk *SF Sorrow*. In late 1974 it was used as the basis for a BBC programme called *The Man They Could Not Hang – John Lee*. Most of the tracks were re-recorded with the then Fairport line-up including Trevor Lucas and Jerry Donahue, with Sandy Denny on vocals for one of them, and two are included in the 2004 reissue. Further tracks can be found on the 2017 compilation *Come All Ye; The First Ten Years*. In 2011 Fairport performed the album in its entirety on live tours to celebrate its 40th anniversary and, a year later, released the Cropredy Festival performance as a digital download.

The original release had no track listings – instead, the songs were grouped together under five narrative descriptions, such as 'John's reflection on his boyhood, his introduction to Miss Keyes and The Glen, his restlessness, and his struggles with his family, finally successful, to join the navy.' In analysing the album I have used the individual titles that appeared on the 2004 CD release. The album cover shows a picture of Lee with his mother after his release from prison in 1907. It is said he then emigrated to the US and died in Milwaukee under the name James Lee.

'The Verdict' (Fairport Convention)
Philip Sterling-Wall, a businessman friend of Dave Swarbrick, plays the judge handing down the sentence to John Lee in a suitably stern tone.

'Little Did I Think' (Fairport Convention)
A rather unsteady opening that doesn't kick off the album as well as it should do. The stop-start nature of the song gives it a lumbering feel and the backing vocals and mandolin instrumental sound as if they come from the bottom of a well. It's heavy on exposition as we learn about Lee's first job nursing a pony for Emma Keyes and his longing to join the navy, and only comes alive when the harmony vocals join in for the final verse.

'I Was Sixteen (Part 1) / John My Son / I Was Sixteen (Part 2)' (Fairport Convention)
What a shame they didn't kick off with this, a sprightly and catchy sequence that opens with some dexterous solo electric guitar work from Simon before the drums kick in and power everything along at a cracking pace. Peggy takes lead vocals, and Swarb's mandolin sings and dances before we enter the slower middle section, sung by Simon, as Lee's father begs him not to join the Navy. Then we get some more Simon guitar before heading back into the main theme again. It's got the spirit and swing of Fairport on top form.

'St Ninian's isle / Trumpet Hornpipe' (Ronald Cooper / Trad arr Fairport Convention)

Lee's out on the briny as a Navy sailor, so this is an excuse for the band to put together some salty sea tunes. The first was composed by Shetland accordion and piano player Ronnie Cooper and named after a small island off the Scottish coast. Mandolin and fiddle play in unison on a chirpy little tune before swiftly moving into the hornpipe which, as mentioned above, would be well known to *Captain Pugwash* fans. It's short and sweet, just 1:14 in length, and could easily have been pushed out a little longer.

'Sailor's Alphabet' (Trad arr AL Lloyd)

Sea shanties – the word is an adaptation of 'chant' – developed to help sailors get a rhythm going together when they were splicing the mainbrace or turning the capstan or whatever it is sailors do. Alphabet songs date back to the early 18th century and exist in many different professions as a way of helping newcomers remember the tools of their trade. This particular incarnation of the 'Sailor's Alphabet' comes from a version Ewan MacColl sang with Bert Lloyd on their 1962 album *A Sailor's Garland*. It goes on a bit – there are 26 letters to cover, after all – but it's a jolly, rousing song with a great singalong chorus of 'Merrily, so merry sail we / No mortal on earth like a sailor at sea'. It captures the myth of a happy life on board ship – the reality was, of course, much, much nastier.

John Lee' (Fairport Convention)

One of the best tracks on the album, it reveals how Lee gets sick and has to leave the Navy, going back to his old job with Emma Keyes. More rock than folk, it opens with a pensive descending guitar figure from Simon before a short two-line verse leads into a fantastic chorus of 'John Lee, you're turning around your fate again' over an unusual but very pleasing chord sequence of C to A-flat minor. This was released as a single but sadly troubled landfill sites more than it did chart compilers. Fairport performed this live on their farewell tour at the end of the 1970s.

'Newspaper Reading' (Fairport Convention)

British folk singer Bert Lloyd reads a report of the Emma Keyes' murder in a lurid style typical of late 19th century newspapers. This leads into…

'Breakfast In Mayfair' (Simon Nicol)

Also known as 'The World Has Surely Lost Its Head', Simon depicts the reaction of a typical newspaper reader to reports of the murder, who makes the assumption Lee is guilty despite being the one raising the hue and cry. This gentle, witty and melodic song consists of just three verses with a lead guitar break before the final verse and includes the hilarious couplet 'This man called

Lee has had his day and soon will be forgotten / So put that paper down before your breakfast goes quite rotten'. In the days before the invention of home-use refrigerators, it may have indeed been possible that your breakfast would go bad if you spent too long with the *Daily Telegraph*.

'The Trial' (Fairport Convention)
Side two of the original LP was book-ended by two fast, frantic songs packed full of narrative. They work thanks to strong, tight performances from the band, catchy melodic hooks in the choruses and lyrics that are thoughtfully and sometimes poetically put together. In 'The Trial' Fairport show Lee as little more than a bewildered observer swept inexorably to his doom by capricious fate and the speed of events. His defence counsel is ill, so the man's brother turns up instead but isn't allowed to say anything. In the end, Swarb sings 'I cannot blame the jury, on the evidence they heard / It seemed that I was guilty, hanged by too many words'.

'Cell Song' (Fairport Convention)
Dave Mattacks plays electric piano on this sad, reflective ballad as Lee sits in his prison cell for three weeks awaiting execution. Swarb sings over simple chords, his voice with a bit of echo on it to suggest the stone confines of Lee's imprisonment. The instrumental break, played on mandolin and fiddle over Simon's dulcimer, is truly affecting, as is Swarb's final verse sung once again over the electric piano.

'The Time Is Near' (Fairport Convention)
Lee's regret and hopelessness are more than adequately expressed in 'Cell Song', and this sad ballad doesn't really add much more. But there are some affecting moments, especially when the band sing together and Swarb adds squealing fiddle in the instrumental to represent Lee's tortured state of mind.

'Dream Song' (Fairport Convention)
Lee's still in that cell, this time having a dream in which 'The hand of a stranger takes hold of his arm / A voice in his ear says 'They'll do you no harm''. To a discordant acoustic guitar backing, spooky vocals drenched in reverb ascend into a banshee scream. It's one sad ballad too many at this point and makes side two feel saggy and slow.

'Wake Up John (Hanging Song)' (Fairport Convention)
At last, we reach the climax of the album. Acapella voices urge Lee to wake up before Simon plays a tasty little acoustic guitar riff. Then three power chords lead us into a fast, rocking little number as Swarb sings of the three failed attempts to execute Lee at Exeter Prison. There's a powerful chorus with the lines 'Shake the holy water, summon up the guard / Dying's very easy, waiting's

very hard' and an instrumental section played on fiddle that's reminiscent of the tune 'Orange Blossom Special'. Finally, Swarb sings 'My life was spared that morning 'cause it wasn't theirs to take', and Lee is spared the noose. It's an exciting song that drives along like a steam train with great drumming from DM and is a worthy end to the album.

2004 Bonus Tracks
'Farewell To A Poor Man's Son' (Dave Swarbrick)
In 1974 Fairport re-recorded some of the tracks for a BBC programme called *The Man They Couldn't Hang – John Lee*, shown on 1 February 1975, and this addition to the story is taken directly from the TV soundtrack. By this time Simon Nicol was out of the band, but he returned for this project, while lead guitar was supplied by Jerry Donahue. The song is a maudlin ballad that adds little to the story and would have made the already slightly saggy second side of the album even saggier.

'Breakfast In Mayfair' (Simon Nicol)
A second track taken from the TV recording, this differs from the album version by having Sandy Denny singing the first two verses and Jerry Donahue recreating Simon's original lead guitar almost note for note. For some reason Sandy's voice sounds strained and unsteady – she had rejoined Fairport by this stage and undertaken a world tour so it could be she was simply tired. Simon takes the last verse and does his usual solid job, but this is not a patch on the original recording.

Rosie (1973)

Personnel:

Jerry Donahue: electric & acoustic guitars, vocals

Trevor Lucas: acoustic guitars, vocals

Dave Mattacks: drums, percussion, piano

Dave Swarbrick: vocals, fiddle, viola, mandolin, acoustic guitar

Dave Pegg: bass, mandolin, vocals

Additional personnel:

Sandy Denny: vocals on 'Rosie'

Linda Peters: vocals on 'Rosie'

Richard Thompson: electric and acoustic guitars on 'Rosie'

Ralph McTell: acoustic guitar on 'Me With You'

Gerry Conway: drums on 'Rosie', 'Knights Of The Road' and 'The Plainsman'

Timi Donald: drums on Matthew, Mark, Luke & John, 'Hungarian Rhapsody' and 'My Girl'

The Swarbrick Brothers (Dave, Cyril & Eric): vocals on 'Me With You'

Recorded at Sound Techniques Studio, Jul-Aug 1972

Produced by Trevor Lucas

John Wood: engineer

Record label: Island

Release dates: February 1973

Highest chart positions: Uncharted

Running time: 36:49

Current edition: 2004 reissue with bonus tracks

Fairport Convention saved John Lee but they couldn't save themselves. At the end of 1971 the only remaining founder member, Simon Nicol, quit to join Ashley Hutchings in The Albion Band. Fairport had toured *'Babbacombe Lee'* during the latter half of 1971 and Simon had found the demands on him as the sole guitarist becoming increasingly more stressful. He told official biographer Patrick Humphries:

> I didn't enjoy going on stage in those days. I was exhausted all the way through that time. I was working at keeping my head above water, in danger of drowning in the music all the time. I was trying to play like Richard, to be Richard and Simon, and I was trying too much. There was a tremendous amount of effort, and that was really the reason I left.

The band tried to carry on with some old friends from the past. Peggy recruited Roger Hill, who had been in Brummie bands The Uglys and The Exception with him but the magic wasn't there and, a few months later, Dave Mattacks jumped ship to join the Albions. Another Brummie, Tom Farnell, was recruited to replace him and they toured the US, supporting The Kinks. Peggy describes the band at this time as 'the worst line-up of Fairport, ever'.

On their return to the UK, Roger quit.

In desperation, the remaining two Daves and Tom went into Richard Branson's Manor Studio with Canadian guitarist David Rea, who they had met at the Troubadour in LA, and laid down early versions of some of the songs that ended up on *Rosie*, along with several instrumentals. The results were deemed unacceptable for release and were scrapped (they were later released on the 2017 compilation *Come All Ye: The First Ten Years* and confirm the wisdom of this decision). Exit David and Tom.

But here came the cavalry... another band had also split up, Sandy Denny's Fotheringay, leaving her soon-to-be husband Trevor George Lucas – born 1943 in Bungaree, Australia – at a bit of a loose end. In 1972 he put together a bunch of musicians, including old and new Fairport members, to produce an album of old rock 'n' roll standards and also worked as an engineer at Sound Techniques Studios.

He offered to produce a new Fairport album and was soon a full-time member. He, in turn, recommended former Fotheringay guitarist Jerry Donahue – born 1946 in Manhattan, USA – and suggested getting some past members back into the studio to record a 'real' Fairport record. That's why Sandy is there, along with Richard Thompson and Dave Mattacks, who were persuaded to join in after The Albion Country Band fell apart.

Trevor also brought with him the backing tracks for two songs intended for Fotheringay's aborted second album, with future Fairporter Gerry Conway on drums. There's also a third drummer, session player Timi Donald, who helped out on some of the tracks while DM was deciding whether he wanted to return to the Fairport fold.

Rosie is not necessarily a bad album, just unfocused and disjointed. There are some great tracks but there's also some forgettable material that Swarb freely admits should have been kept for a solo album. There's not a lot here that one would call folk-rock – indeed, Trevor's influence gives some of the album a definite country and western feel. But it's not the worst album they ever recorded – that calumny was still to come.

'Rosie' (Swarbrick)

Swarb's touching tribute to his then wife, with its chorus refrain of *'rosin up the bow'*, was the first track to be recorded at Sound Techniques. It's truly a 'celebrity Fairport' recording, with Richard Thompson on guitars and Sandy Denny and Linda Peters (soon to be Linda Thompson) on backing vocals. It also marks the first appearance of former Fotheringay drummer Gerry Conway on a Fairport recording – he would later (much later) join as a full-time member. This performance sounds a little tentative, Swarb's voice is a little soft, and the song would grow in stature in later live recordings. But it is sufficiently heartfelt and melodic to become a staple of the band's live repertoire – and Richard's lead guitar makes it even more special.

'Matthew, Mark, Luke & John' (Pegg, Swarbrick, Mattacks, Thompson, Nicol)

The credits come from the original album, but subsequent information pins this rousing, anthemic singalong on just Swarb and Peggy. If the original credits are correct, then it could be a hangover from the old *Full House* days, dusted off to help flesh out *Rosie*. Certainly, the lyrics have a dark, biting edge that's at odds with the upbeat major key musical setting – a typical Thompson device. 'What chance do we have in this game' sings Swarb, as he questions the basis of the Christian religion when everything around appears to be going to hell in a handcart. 'Everything's blacker, we argue with guns, with money we burn and we maim.' Jerry provides some Thompson-like lead guitar – while not quite on the same genius level he does an excellent job. In fact, this powerful, confident performance bodes well.

'Knights Of The Road' (Lucas, Roche)

Sandy's band Fotheringay recorded one self-titled album then fell apart during the sessions for the follow-up. Trevor brought backing tracks for two of the songs, Peggy replaced Fotheringay bassist Pat Donaldson's part, Swarb added fiddle and together they supplied backing vocals. It's not really folk-rock. Indeed, this sounds like it hails from across the pond – a slice of Americana, with an appealing country chug. The subject matter is typically American, being a tribute to long-haul truckers (except these are driving from Carlisle to Lichfield, which doesn't quite have the same romantic ring). Trevor sings in a rich, gravelly voice – if you didn't know he was an Aussie you would swear he's from Texas. It moves at a moderate pace, contains a nice bit of twangy, almost slide guitar from Jerry and, like a truck, disappears slowly into the distance. But is it Fairport?

'Peggy's Pub' (Pegg)

A fun mandolin ditty from Peggy, reminiscent of 'Flatback Caper' from *Full House* but mercifully a lot shorter. It's in two parts – the first suggests Peggy's pub would be a welcoming, buzzing sort of place where the pints are not too fizzy and the pork scratchings are plentiful. Then it changes into something a bit more complicated – did someone just ruin the atmosphere by asking for a cocktail? Anyway, it's a pleasant diversion and the first track on the album to be recorded by the official Fairport line-up listed on the cover. This and 'Hungarian Rhapsody' were Peggy's first compositions for the band.

'The Plainsman' (Lucas/Roche)

The words come from Liverpool poet Pete Roche, the tune is traditional, called 'Tramps And Hawkers'. A ballad in 6/8, the lyrics are firmly rooted in country and western mythology of the rugged loner travelling across the wide-open prairie with only his horse for company. 'If you can't show me how to die, don't tell me how to live' he says in true John Wayne style. Sung by Trevor it's a slice of Americana in the middle of a British folk-rock record (and the second of the tracks originally recorded for Fotheringay). Does it work? Well, it's certainly different, and one could argue that it gives Fairport a good musical kick in the pants. It also ends the strongest side of the original LP.

'Hungarian Rhapsody' (Pegg)

Not long after the recording of *Angel Delight* the then four-piece Fairport toured Hungary on a cultural exchange, playing to 'farmers and soldiers just standing and staring'. They found themselves billeted in pleasant hotels, earning more than twice what they were getting in the UK, eating and drinking very cheap food and wine. The experience was written up by Peggy as comic verse set to a bright tune with a singalong chorus. The song references cimbaloms (a traditional Hungarian instrument rather like a zither) and, rather tastelessly, refers to one of the Hungarian promoters as 'Mr Hilter'.

'My Girl' (Swarbrick)

In my view, Dave Swarbrick is an overlooked songwriter who could pen thoughtful, poetic lyrics and find beautiful melodies to match. But not on this occasion. 'My Girl' – not to be confused with the Temptations hit, and it won't be – is a dull, clunky composition that seems to lurch like a zombie through its overlong five minutes and 14 seconds, the longest track on the album. Timi Donald on drums has little to do but not fall asleep on his cymbals. Even Jerry's lead guitar break is droopingly limp. As Swarb said, some of these songs should have been retained for his solo albums. But this one should simply have been left in a drawer.

'Me With You' (Swarbrick)

Ralph McTell is roped in to play ragtime-style finger-picking guitar as Swarb quotes the sights and sounds of nature to tell us how happy he is. The 'Swarbrick Brothers' are just his triple-tracked voice providing aahs and barbershop quartet harmonies. It's a throwaway little tune lifted by some of his most evocative and amusing lyrics – 'I'm a feather from a black crow beady on the hedgerow', 'Happy as a fox on a midnight raid, happy as a landlord when his rent gets paid'.

'The Hen's March Through The Midden & The Four Poster Bed' (Trad arr Fairport Convention)

The first track recorded with Trevor as producer supposedly has an uncredited Tom Farnell on drums as the band go through a fairly unimaginative rendition of two tunes Swarb used to play with Martin Carthy. Jerry Donahue doesn't attempt any contrapuntal guitar work here, restricting himself to simple chords while Swarb's fiddle takes centre stage. 'The Hen's March' is a slow reel in which the fiddle is scraped by the bow, delivered in a jaunty style that certainly does suggest a hen strutting arrogantly through the farm detritus. 'The Four Poster Bed' is another reel from Scotland.

'Furs & Feathers' (Swarbrick)

A rocking number from Swarb based on the telling of a fairytale about a king who disguises himself as a commoner to find out what his people really think. As you can imagine, it doesn't go well. A flourish of acoustic guitar chords fades in before Swarb leaps into an effective if lyrically nonsensical (to me, at any rate) chorus. Jerry plays some very effective guitar licks while Swarb puts some funky wah-wah on his fiddle and the whole thing is a satisfying dramatic ending to the album.

2004 Bonus Tracks

'Matthew, Mark, Luke & John – Live' (Pegg, Swarbrick)

The live version included as one of the bonus tracks on the 2004 re-issue is taken at a slightly slower pace than the original and comes across as a little uncertain at the start. But it picks up well thanks to some great Dave Mattacks drumming and ends on a rousing note.

'The Hen's March Through The Midden & The Four Poster Bed – Live' (Trad arr Fairport Convention)

Pretty much a carbon copy of the studio track except, once again, Mattacks adds those little offbeat drumming touches that lift everything he plays on.

'Rosie – Live' (Swarbrick)

A slightly ballsier and more confident rendition of Swarb's ballad with excellent guitar from Jerry.

'The Claw – Live' (Jerry Reed)

An absolutely mind-bogglingly fast piece of guitar pyrotechnics written by American country music star Jerry Reed Hubbard and performed with jaw-dropping dexterity by Donahue. At less than two minutes long it's short but oh so sweet.

'Furs & Feathers – Live' (Swarbrick)

Again, a slightly gutsier version than on the album with more confident and interesting guitar licks from Jerry.

Nine (1973)

Personnel:
Jerry Donahue: electric & acoustic guitars, vocals
Trevor Lucas: acoustic guitars, vocals
Dave Mattacks: drums, percussion, keyboards, bass
Dave Swarbrick: vocals, fiddle, viola, mandolin, acoustic guitar
Dave Pegg: bass, mandolin, vocals
Recorded at Sound Techniques Studio, Jul-Aug 1973
Produced by Trevor Lucas, John Wood & Fairport Convention
John Wood: engineer
Record label: Island (UK), A&M (US)
Release date: October 1973
Highest chart positions: Uncharted
Running time: 38:37
Current edition: 2005 remaster with bonus tracks

Fairport's ninth studio album suffered from a lack of imagination in the naming department, but nearly everything else was head and shoulders above its predecessor. Having gigged and worked together for a year, the band – dubbed Fotheringport Confusion after the blending together of Fairport and Fotheringay – was tight and approaching its blend of folk and country-rock with a united front. As Dave Pegg said:

> It was much more of a group because everyone was writing from the word go… It's one of my favourite records; there's a lot of thought in it. I think that five-man band – had it stuck together – would have gone on to do greater things, because we all got on well and there were never any kind of arguments.

For the first time since *Full House,* Fairport now had two guitarists, while Swarb had someone who could take over on lead vocals, as well as a new songwriting partner to replace Richard Thompson. There were traditional songs such as 'The Hexhamshire Lass' and 'Polly On The Shore', but there were also plenty of self-penned country-style rockers that gave the band a slightly more contemporary edge. It's a surprise the album didn't chart in the US as you can hear the American influences in some of the writing.

As well as a lack of naming imagination, the cover wasn't about to win any design awards – just a plain brown with the band's name picked out in gold. The reverse carried a picture of the band at The Brasenose pub in Cropredy, Oxfordshire – a location that was to play a big part in the band's future fortunes. Swarb had moved to the remote village after the Angel pub had been destroyed by a lorry, and Peggy followed suit, moving into a nearby cottage. The rest of the band stayed at The Brasenose when they got together to rehearse at the local village hall and, gradually, Cropredy became Fairport's base.

'The Hexhamshire Lass' (Trad arr Fairport)

We open with a brilliant traditional number, taken from the singing of Bob Davenport, and one that has become a firm fan favourite. Swarb opens acapella with just a drum for company before the band come in with strategically placed chords. Jerry sounds much more confident, playing the fast folk melodies in conjunction with Swarb's fiddle just like Richard Thompson used to do. Hexhamshire was a county in Northern England, now in County Durham, which clearly places the song geographically. The reference in the opening line to the 'buff and the blue' suggests the British Infantry, so the song most likely dates back to the Napoleonic wars.

'Polly On The Shore' (Dave Pegg, lyrics trad arr Dave Swarbrick, Trevor Lucas)

Prog folk anyone? In his trademark gravelly voice, Trevor sings a slow-moving, salty ballad about a valiant sailor who perishes at sea while thinking about his loved one at home (or, as Trevor would introduce it on stage, it's about a pirate who's lost his parrot). The lyrics are traditional, probably from Wiltshire, but the tune is new and gives Peggy a chance to take the lead with some powerful bass playing, with a shimmering instrumental section led by Jerry. The tune goes places you don't expect and has a bucketful of chords in it, but it holds together extremely well and is one of the strongest cuts on the album.

'The Brilliancy Medley & Cherokee Shuffle' (Trad arr Fairport)

We're back to the guitar/fiddle attack as Jerry and Swarb play this superfast melody together twice through before the band come in. Dave Mattacks probably plays bass here and Peggy on mandolin as there are no drums at all. Jerry plays magnificent finger-tying acoustic guitar picking and doesn't miss a beat. Then Peggy takes over on mandolin for the second tune, an old-time bluegrass number that Fairport beef up with some surprise key changes. All in all, this is a marvellous addition to the band's repertoire of instrumentals.

'To Althea In Prison' (Dave Swarbrick, Richard Lovelace)

Lovelace was a 17th century English poet who chose the wrong side in the Civil War and wrote these moving lines while imprisoned in the Gatehouse at Westminster Abbey. No-one is sure who Althea was, and she may have simply been a figment of Lovelace's imagination. Its most quoted lines come from the last verse: 'Stone walls do not a prison make / Nor iron bars a cage'. Swarb sets the poem to a gentle, lilting tune and gives a sensitive, respectful performance that does the moving material full justice.

'Tokyo' (Jerry Donahue)

Another mind-bogglingly difficult guitar tune from Jerry, in a similar vein to 'The Claw' on the *Rosie* re-issue, and an opportunity for the band to emphasise the 'rock' in folk-rock. A reminder that he would have been classified as Fairport's guitar genius if he hadn't had the misfortune to replace someone even better.

Bring 'Em Down (Trevor Lucas)

After a stonking first set, side two of the album gets a little bogged down in somewhat bland country songs. This is one of them, a Dylanesque plod about a meeting with four horsemen, anchored by a chorus that simply repeats the title. Swarb gets to provide some atmospheric fiddle (two of them, in fact, as he overdubbed on himself) but the song goes on a little too long for its own good.

'Big William' (Dave Swarbrick, Trevor Lucas)

Swarb tried this song out with different lyrics during the early aborted recording sessions for Rosie with David Rea. The new words by Swarb and Trevor, about some argument over bread between Joe and the titular large Bill, make little sense and I guess you had to be there. But it does include the great line 'you can stick it where the monkey sticks his nuts' and has a certain appealing bounce to it plus a jolly mandolin break from Swarb.

'Pleasure & Pain' (Dave Swarbrick, Trevor Lucas)

The most overtly country-style song on the album, with its three-quarter waltz time, slide-ish guitar from Jerry, bluegrass-style fiddle from Swarb and the rather preachy lyrics warning us all not to go 'mixing the reds along with the blues'. As if we would. Strangely, the song was covered on a country album by former British wrestling champion Brian Maxine, backed by the Fairports.

'Possibly Parsons Green' (Trevor Lucas, Pete Roach)

A slightly tricksier country rocker that plays about with time signatures and relies on Jerry's guitar licks to provide the hooks. The title seems to be inspired by Bob Dylan's 'Positively Fourth Street', a reference to a residential district of Greenwich Village where he used to live. Trevor and his wife Sandy lived in the Parsons Green area of London when this song was written. The lyrics allude to the strain the relationship was under – Trevor was away touring with Fairport and no doubt sampling some of the perks life on the road was to offer. Sandy, meanwhile, was making good records that no-one, especially her record company, knew what to do with. There were undoubtedly a lot of tears from her direction, as evidenced by the line 'Don't try to use me or cry to confuse me', and her emotional state explains some of the later decisions made by her and the band.

2005 Bonus Tracks
'The Devil In The Kitchen' (Trad. arr Lucas, Swarbrick, Donahue, Mattacks, Pegg)

Is there such a thing as heavy metal folk-rock? Or even orchestral folk-rock? For this frantic and frankly astonishing piece of music embraces both. Originally a single released only in Australia (with 'Possibly Parsons Green' as the B-side) it opens with crashing power chords before Jerry plays searing lead guitar in the style of Scottish bagpipes. Then Swarb leads the band into a fiddle tune at breakneck speed as an entire orchestra tries to keep up! There's a bit of banjo in there too. A cross between folk-rock and something Elmer Bernstein may have written for a hoedown in a cowboy movie, 'The Devil In The Kitchen' is a powerful, cinematic instrumental. A version without orchestra and played mostly on banjo was released on a cassette collection called *The Attic Tracks Vol 1* under the title of 'Fiddlestix'.

'George Jackson – Live' (Bob Dylan)
A straight-forward cover of Dylan's song about the death of Black Panther leader George Jackson as he tried to escape San Quentin prison, performed by the band at The Howff in London in 1973. Of note is Dave Mattacks' drumming and a slow instrumental section in the middle led by Swarb's mandolin but there's nothing much else to write home about. Interestingly, there's a bit of live banter at the end to lead the band directly into...

'Pleasure & Pain – Live' (D. Swarbrick, T. Lucas)
Performed pretty much as on the album but with occasional spoken interruptions from Trevor suggesting a certain ramshackle approach towards stagecraft during this performance!

'Six Days On The Road – Live' (Earl Green, Carl Montgomery)
Dubbed the definitive celebration of being an American truck driver, this three-chord chugging song was first released in 1961 although it is the version two years later by Dave Dudley that became a huge hit. Fairport tackle it with head-on enthusiasm and a few sound gremlins in the recording.

Rising For The Moon (1975)

Personnel:
Sandy Denny: vocals, electric piano, backing vocals, piano, acoustic guitar
Dave Swarbrick: acoustic guitar, viola, violin, backing vocals, vocals, dulcimer, mandolin, autoharp
Dave Pegg: bass, electric guitar, backing vocals
Jerry Donahue: electric guitar, acoustic guitar, slide guitar
Trevor Lucas: acoustic guitar, vocals, backing vocals
Dave Mattacks: drums, tambourine, percussion
Bruce Rowland: drums
Recorded at Olympic Studios, London, Dec 1974/75
Produced & engineered by Glyn Johns
Record label: Island
Release date: July 1975 (UK)
Highest chart position: 52(UK) 143 (US)
Running time: 41:46
Current edition: 2005 reissue with bonus tracks

It must have seemed like a good idea at the time – bring Sandy Denny back into the fold and recreate the classic Fairport Convention of the late 1960s. In fact, there was an inevitability about it – Sandy was waiting for her third solo album to be released and at a bit of a loose end so she virtually smuggled herself on to Fairport's world tour to be close to her husband Trevor Lucas. Before long she was being invited onstage to join in. That's why she appears on *Fairport Live Convention*, released in 1974, on which she is billed as a member of the band. Surely this was precisely what Fairport needed.

The record company saw *Rising For The Moon* as a last chance for the band to really hit the big time. A celebrity producer was brought in – Glyn Johns, who had worked with The Beatles, The Faces, Graham Nash, The Who, The Rolling Stones, to name but a few – and some serious money was spent on promotion and marketing. Island also agreed to absorb the band's debts – Fairport came back from their world tour in early 1974 owing £25,000 to the travel company because all their equipment had been sent as excess baggage instead of freight.

The result is an uneven album that wasn't traditional enough to be Fairport and not good enough to be a Sandy Denny solo release. Sure, it had some special songs on it, mostly from the pen of the great lady herself. The title track, 'Stranger To Himself', 'After Halloween' and 'One More Chance' are among her best-ever compositions.

But some of the other contributions sound half-baked as if they were knocked up in the studio the night before. In fact, they probably were as, by all accounts, Johns had refused to let the band do any covers or traditional material – none of that 'airy-fairy folk bullshit' he said. But give Dave Swarbrick his due, he turns in one of his best-ever compositions, the beautiful 'White Dress', and Sandy sings it sublimely.

Johns gives the album a glossy, pop production, probably the slickest Fairport have ever had. And that's part of the problem. It lacks heart and soul, it sounds like what it is, a deliberate, somewhat cynical attempt to capture the MOR market. Drummer Bruce Rowland said: 'It's the first and only Fairport record that counts as "product". Whether you think that's a good thing or not is another matter.'

Fairport's revolving door was, of course, in full working order. So Sandy came in, but Dave Mattacks left halfway through the recording after clashing with Johns. Apparently, 32 drummers were auditioned before Johns suggested bringing in Rowland – born 1941 in north-west London – who had played with Joe Cocker and the Grease Band. The band was so impressed with his work that they continued using him through the next three studio albums.

Rising For The Moon has been re-issued twice – a remaster in 2005 with three demo tracks and a single B-side, 'Tears', and again in 2013 with a bonus disc of live tracks from the LA Troubadour in 1974. This analysis will concentrate on the widely available 2005 reissue.

'Rising For The Moon' (Denny)
The album kicks off with one of Sandy's best songs on the album, a strong, upbeat number about the travails of touring, but in a positive way 'for that's the way it is, that is our fortune'. Fiddle and guitar open up proceedings before Sandy sings to a rolling rhythm with a slight calypso beat, rather like a packed transit van swaying gently in the wind as it races up the M1. Everyone joins in on the rousing chorus – perhaps it should be called Rousing For The Moon – and there is more good interlocking fiddle and guitar playing from Swarb and Jerry. It's like a modern traditional song and seems to capture exactly the approach the band – and Glyn Johns – wanted. Fairport liked it so much they recorded it again 34 years later.

'Restless' (Lucas, Roach)
This is the sort of country-style strum that Trevor could turn out in his sleep, complete with hoary old clichés about being 'born between the river and the railroad', 'weary in the company of strangers' and 'something in the wind seems to call me like a friend'. It has a certain charm about it, but there is a sense that all Trevor's songs were beginning to sound alike, with their similar sentiments and very simple chord structures. Fairport try hard to make this interesting but its four minutes pass quite slowly.

'White Dress' (Swarbrick, McTell)
Swarb provides one of the best songs on the album – and possibly his best ever composition – in this moving waltz-time ballad that Sandy sings with heartbreaking fragility. Swarb's cunning trick is to add ninths to the opening C and A minor chords, creating a feeling of loss and uncertainty, and then wash it over with celestial autoharp. Then he changes key (A major) for the

instrumental before going back to the C9. Yes, it sounds cheesy, but it isn't. It's a gorgeous piece of music that shows off both Sandy's voice and the band's ability to play sensitive arrangements. It was released as a single with a Trevor Lucas song, 'Tears', on the B-side and was also covered by co-writer Ralph McTell on his 1979 album *Slide Away The Screen*, with the lyrics adapted in a not wholly successful attempt to sing it from a male point of view.

'Let It Go' (Swarbrick, Denny, Pegg)
A bouncy but forgettable number with little in the way of discernible melody – there may have been one there once, but vocalist Swarb pretty much gives up on it halfway through. Despite three verses and two middle-eights but no recognisable chorus, it struggles to reach its paltry two minutes running time. Like 'Night-time Girl', it sounds like a song Swarb, Sandy and Peggy had to knock up during the sessions.

'Stranger To Himself' (Denny)
This is one of Sandy's strongest songs with sharp lyrics and a folky, drone-like backing created by a funereal drumbeat from Bruce Rowland, Swarb's dulcimer, Peggy on fuzz bass and ringing open 12-string guitar chords. Sandy said it was 'very much a song about Swarbrick', adding: 'I began to realise what a complex and odd character he was. Someone – it could have been Peggy – remarked that no one really knew who Swarb was; in fact he doubted if he even knew himself.' That's why she sings about the demon fiddler being 'a stranger to himself, a spy in his own camp'.

'What Is True?' (Denny)
A minor effort from Sandy, in a similar slow style and pace to the later 'One More Chance' but not nearly as successful. She plays electric piano, which jars a bit on my ears, and her voice seems a little hoarse and strained. There's an unusually harsh edge to her vocal here, and it grates on some of the notes, especially when she throws in some clumsy minor chords. By all accounts, she was given a pretty hard time in the studio by Glyn Johns, and it's difficult to believe he would have accepted this as a final attempt. There's also an instrumental section in which no-one plays an instrumental – they just bash out the backing track. Did they forget to complete it? Whatever the reason, 'What Is True' sounds incomplete and unsatisfactory.

'Iron Lion' (Lucas)
The trouble with CDs (and digital, of course) is you no longer get a decent pause between sides one and two as you flip the record over. So a weak Sandy track goes straight into a weak Trevor track. This is 'Restless' and 'Knights Of The Road' all over again – this time Trevor's an engine driver and the 'wheels on the track keep calling me back'. Trouble is, we've heard it all before – same

sentiments, same chords, same rhythm and same gravelly voice. I don't want to be mean, but Trevor's a bit of a one-trick pony, and his work here can't match Sandy and Swarb at their best.

'Dawn' (Denny, Donahue)
A rare collaboration between Sandy and Jerry, this almost brings the album back to the heights achieved by 'Stranger To Himself' and 'White Dress' – but not quite. Based on Jerry's ascending and descending electric guitar figures, Sandy's voice sounds strong and passionate and is a distinct improvement on 'What Is True' (this was one of the earliest tracks to be recorded, with DM on drums). It's perhaps a little bit dreary and overwrought and lacks a decent melodic hook to grab on to.

'After Hallowe'en' (Denny)
At last, a 24-carat gold classic from Sandy, a song she had tried out but discarded for one of her solo albums. 'After Hallowe'en' has a quality and warmth to it – Sandy's voice soars over a gentle acoustic guitar backing with a tiny bit of electric piano in the background and lovely, bubbling basslines from Peggy. Bruce plays with admirable restraint and Swarb's fiddle is appropriately unflashy. When I think of the tragedy of Sandy's early death, this song always comes to mind because of her uncertainty and fragility as she asks herself searching questions about her life and her art. 'But who am I and do we really live these days at all?/ And are they simply feelings we have loved and do recall?' It's heartbreaking and beautiful.

'Night-time Girl' (Swarbrick, Pegg)
Oh dear. Let's be fair to the two Daves – they wrote this lumpen country song overnight in a hotel room before recording it practically the next day. It has a mildly interesting folky fiddle riff but is ruined by risible lyrics and a so-called chorus that does little more than repeat the title ad infinitum. Perhaps it would have worked better as some sort of faux traditional instrumental but, presumably, Glyn Johns would never have let them get away with it.

'One More Chance' (Denny)
Thankfully, the album ends on this high note. It's not very Fairport – it's a piano-led ballad with some searing lead guitar from Jerry, the likes of which we won't hear again until Martin Allcock joins the band in the 1980s. Sandy's lyrics seem to veer between the personal and the global – she opens with the couplet 'Calling all olive branches and laid-off doves' that, as an apparent call for world peace, is clever and evocative. Then, as the song changes from hopeful major to darker minor chords, she cries 'Is it too late to change the way we're bound to go?'. As the ramifications of climate change come home to roost, it's a question that has suddenly become all too relevant. Her singing is just out

of this world, Jerry embraces the opportunity to be a rock guitarist, and the whole thing is eight minutes of some of the most dramatic and powerful music Fairport ever recorded.

2005 Bonus Tracks
'Tears' (Lucas)
Released as the B-side of 'White Dress', 'Tears' is a doleful, somewhat dreary ballad in which people break up, move away and cry a lot. Perhaps it was inspired by Sandy and her ability to turn on the waterworks. Stylistically it owes a lot to Bob Dylan's 'Forever Young' (one of Trevor's favourite songs) except that it lacks that song's positive message. Trevor dominates with strummed guitar and his unmistakable voice, while Sandy on piano and Jerry on lead guitar are pushed way into the background.

'Rising For The Moon', Stranger To Himself', 'One More Chance' (Denny)
These three demos recorded for the album at Sandy's home show just what superb performances she could put in with just a piano or guitar. In structure and rhythm, they differ little from the final versions but, stripped of all the accompanying instruments, they are naked and affecting. Sandy's compositions were frequently swamped by ambitious over-production on her solo albums – these stripped-back recordings reveal the true performer and remind us what a wonderful singer and songwriter she was.

Gottle O' Geer (1976)

Personnel:
Dave Swarbrick: vocals, fiddle, viola, mandolin, mandocello, acoustic guitar, autoharp, electric dulcimer
Dave Pegg: bass guitar, mandolin, backing vocals
Bruce Rowland: drums, percussion, piano, organ, backing vocals
Additional personnel:
Eric Johns: electric guitar
Nick Judd: piano
Martin Carthy: acoustic guitar
Ian Wilson: electric guitar
Jimmy Jewel: saxophone
Henry Lowther: trumpet, flugelhorn
Robert Palmer: harmonica, backing vocals
Bob Brady, Roger Burridge: backing vocals
Benny Gallagher: accordion, backing vocals
Graham Lyle: dobro, backing vocals
Simon Nicol: electric guitar
Recorded at Island Studios and Sawmill Studios
Record label: Island
Released: May 1976 (credited to 'Fairport' in the UK and 'Fairport Featuring Dave Swarbrick' in US)
Producer: Bruce Rowland
Engineer: Simon Nicol (assisted by Dick Cuthell at Island and Tony Cox at Sawmill)[1]
Highest chart position: Uncharted
Length: 30:35 (35:04 on 2007 rerelease)

And then there were three. After all the hopes pinned on *Rising For The Moon*, its commercial failure saw Fairport Convention splinter down the middle like a piece of rotting wood. The Fotheringay trio of Sandy Denny, Trevor Lucas and Jerry Donahue quit, leaving just Dave Swarbrick, Dave Pegg and Bruce Rowland to fulfil Island Records' contractual demand for another album. What went wrong? Peggy said:

> Despite the label's efforts, despite us working, the record sold no more than any of our previous ones, and the tour made very little money for us either – we finished up working hard for six months, going to collect our dosh, and ending up with about three hundred quid each. It was scandalous ... Jerry and Sandy both felt it was too much, too little reward for devoting all their time just to the band, to Fairport. Jerry was much in demand as a guitarist, Sandy always had her own career opportunities beckoning. They felt they had to go. So it was left to Swarb and me again.

Swarb went into Sawmill Studios in Cornwall to make a solo album, and Bruce

was producing. Founder member Simon Nicol, who you may recall had left at the end of 1971, was asked to come in and engineer (and lock up at nights). Peggy provided bass guitar and mandolin, and a swarm of guests was brought in to help out, including Martin Carthy, Robert Palmer and Gallagher and Lyle.

Then Island decided this wasn't a solo record at all – it was the band's final contractually-obliged album. And it was going out with half a name, the snappier (or so the record company thought) one-word moniker of Fairport. Dave Swarbrick later said: '*Gottle O'Geer*, I would like to say once and for all was not ever supposed to be a Fairport album. It was to be my solo album, and I wish, along with most other people, that it had remained that way.'

The result is an album that, most of the time, doesn't sound anything like Fairport (let alone Fairport Convention). There's pop, there's blues, there's an organ, saxophone, flugelhorn and electric guitar so heavily treated it sounds like the honky-tonk piano on The Beatles' 'Don't Pass Me By'. Allmusic called the result 'listless'. Another critic said it was a 'sloppy, ill-focused failure'. It's generally regarded as one of the worst – if not THE worst – Fairport Convention albums and is rarely mentioned in polite company. The songs lack energy, direction and any memorable melodies. The cover seemed to sum it all up – a depressed jester gazing forlornly at his 'marotte' as if desperate for inspiration.

On the reverse is a picture of a six-piece Fairport, one of whom doesn't appear on the album at all. That's the Breton guitarist Dan Ar Braz. who was brought in by Swarb to help complete some tour dates and promote the album. Two others – keyboard player Bob Brady and fiddler Roger Burridge – supply little more than backing vocals.

'When First Into This Country' (Trad arr Pegg)

This piece could have been a strong opening to the album, a song that may have come first from Scotland (some say Devon, which hardly helps to pin it down geographically) but then made its way to America, where it was first recorded in Austin, Texas. A stranger comes to town to woo fair Nancy but steals a horse and ends up banged up in jail. Swarb sings with gusto, and Fairport perform it as a rollicking bluegrass number that almost works save for Eric Johns' horrible 'honky-tonk' electric guitar that sounds like it was recorded underwater and, sadly, has been layered over too many of these tracks.

'Our Band' (Swarbrick)

An affectionate song about Fairport, gently poking fun at the various members' abilities to remember the lyrics, the tour schedule and precisely where they were supposed to be at any one time – 'Someone goes to telephone Joe'. Bluesy piano played by Nick Judd gives this a gentle swinging feel but there are strange, tinny backing vocals from Gallagher and Lyle sounding like something from the 1930s. It's all very strange.

'Lay Me Down Easy' (Swarbrick, Rowland)

A laidback country waltz with hints of Gospel in its backing, which includes what sounds like Nick Judd playing very accomplished piano and a cheesy Hammond organ from Bruce. It's enjoyable in a corny way but, again, bears about as much resemblance to Fairport as The Wombles do to King Crimson.

'Cropredy Capers' (Swarbrick, Rowland, Pegg)

That it took three writers to create something so bereft of content is a puzzle. Bruce lays down a steady beat, Peggy some funky bass, there's Chic-like guitar from Ian Wilson, while Swarb makes some strange noises with his fiddle somewhere in the distance. And, er, that's pretty much it. The tune segues into...

'The Frog Up The Pump' (Trad arr Pegg)

The first set of traditional instrumentals since the Brilliancy Medley on *Nine*, this is bookended by two identifiable tunes, 'Ril Gan Ah' and 'Storka' – the one in the middle is unknown. Undoubtedly the best track on the album, Martin Carthy provides acoustic guitar backing while Swarb kicks up the sawdust on mandolin and fiddle. Bruce is strangely subdued, providing some almost indistinct bodhran. What a shame he didn't get behind the kit and gives this one a bit of welly.

'Don't Be Late' (Swarbrick, Rowland)

A rollicking, piano-led blues (Nick Judd again) with stabs of brass in the somewhat repetitive chorus. Then it transposes into a different key with Jimmy Jewel providing saxophone solo and some wailing harmonica from Robert Palmer. One can imagine Swarb performing this in front of a swinging big band. What it's doing on a Fairport album is anyone's guess.

'Sandy's Song (AKA Take Away The Load)' (Denny)

A morose, maudlin song Sandy supposedly wrote for Swarbrick and his then-wife. Stylistically it bears a strong resemblance to 'One More Chance' but lacks the former's fire and passion. Swarb tries his best to find a tune there, but its funereal pace and lack of any discernible chorus make this a somewhat depressing experience. Peggy also works hard to lift the song with some tasty bass-playing, while Eric Johns produces some Jerry-like licks.

'Friendship Song (AKA Come And Get It)' (Gallagher, Lyle)

Benny Gallagher and Graham Lyle were riding high in 1976 with their mellow pop sound, having scored Top ten hits with 'Heart On My Sleeve' and 'I Wanna Stay With You'. Bruce Rowland had drummed on sessions for them so it may have been this connection that brought them into Fairport's fold. The song they supplied is an uptempo pop tune with Gallagher on accordion and Lyle on dobro, as well as providing enthusiastic backing vocals. It's not a bad song in a repetitive, repeat-the-title-as-much-as-possible way but it comes and goes without making much impact. On a normal Fairport album, it would have been a little throwaway ditty – on *Gottle O' Geer* it was one of the stronger tracks, which tells you a lot about the album.

'Limey's Lament' (Swarbrick, Rowland)

Clearly inspired by Bob Dylan's 'Subterranean Homesick Blues', 'Limey's Lament' is a stream of consciousness song set to a three-chord backing with a monotonous, slightly jaunty beat. The lyrics – telling of Fairport's culture shock when touring in the US – are mainly a list of words such as 'Cowpoke, holy smoke, dumb waiters, alligators, operators...' The whole thing goes on in this vein for nearly five minutes before fading out.

2007 Bonus Track
'Angles Brown' (Pegg, Swarbrick)

It's the same backing track as 'Limey's Lament' but sped up a bit to put it in C instead of the original's B. Different lyrics though – according to Swarb it was 'named after the sort of person who sees an advantage to themselves in every action. In short, a group manager!'. He depicts a slippery character with a fake grin and a nose for money. How sad that Swarb should have become so cynical!

The Bonny Bunch Of Roses (1977)

Personnel:
Dave Swarbrick: fiddle, mandolin, mandocello, vocals
Simon Nicol: electric and acoustic guitars, vocals, dulcimer, piano
Dave Pegg: bass guitar, guitar, mandolin, vocals
Bruce Rowland: drums, percussion, electric piano
Recorded at Island Studios, Hammersmith, August 1976-March 1977
Record label: Vertigo
Release date: July 1977
Producer: Fairport Convention
Highest chart position: Uncharted
Length: 40:24

That should really have been it. Down to a trio with no record deal and only half a name, Fairport (the Convention had been removed by Island Records) should have called it a day. But there's always been something bloody-minded about Fairport Convention (the band put it back again), a stubborn streak that refuses to face reality. Because, amazingly, this wasn't it. Peggy said:

> Bruce, Swarb and I decided that we'd carry on. We'd forget about making records, just do gigs, just get out there and play. Simon was up for that too. By then he was quite keen to get back in the band: he'd had five years doing other things. Well, we had a very happy couple of years then. We had a manager, Phillipa Clare, who was a good hustler, did really well for us and got us a deal with Vertigo, part of Phonogram. So we started making albums again.

It was an optimistic six-album deal, with the band going back into Island's studios in August 1976. The back-to-basics approach extended to the choice of material too – more than half the album consisted of traditional songs and tunes, including a second attempt to record the epic Napoleonic ballad 'The Bonny Bunch Of Roses'. Peggy provided a spirited self-penned jig, Swarb brought a little waltz and compositions from Richard Thompson and Ralph McTell filled the gaps.

The result is a solid, likeable album that was the best thing they had done since *Nine* – maybe since *"Babbacombe" Lee*. It was Fairport back to their traditional roots, working together as a tight, professional ensemble. Bruce provides real power in the drumming department, Peggy's bass shines, Simon's guitar exudes confidence, and Swarb holds it all together with his fiddle and vocals.

Much of the material consisted of songs the band had tried out and discarded in the past or had played on when helping out Fairport friends for albums and gigs. Three of them date back to the *Full House* days. Peggy said: 'We only rehearsed the album for three days, which was mainly spent in the pub playing darts.'

Even the cover is an improvement on some of the past efforts – a black silhouette of Napoleon against a stark white background, with soldiers marching behind him. Fairport Convention were still marching on and hadn't met their Waterloo just yet...

'Jams O'Donnells Jig' (Pegg)
The album bursts into life with this fast, pounding instrumental by Peggy, led by a solid bass riff and power chords from Simon. During future live gigs the band would pump up the volume on this until it came over as almost heavy metal – appropriate as they were now on the same label as Black Sabbath. On the sleeve notes, the tune was dedicated to Irish novelist Flann O'Brien and Scottish folk musician Bert Jansch.

'The Eynsham Poacher' (Trad arr Dave Pegg)
Simon gets the first vocal on the album, his voice having matured into a pleasing baritone. Fairport learned the song from 'John Leslie of Banbury', but it dates back to at least the turn of the century, and the clear geographical references place it firmly in Oxfordshire. Musically it's an upbeat jig of a song celebrating a mild bit of working-class criminality – it's clearly on the side of the poachers. Fairport open with a simple strummed guitar in G major for the first verse before sneakily dropping down to F sharp in the second and then transposing to D for the instrumental section played by Simon on guitar and Swarb on fiddle. The track powers along delightfully and there are superb harmony vocals in the chorus refrain of 'Laddie-i-o, three jolly young fellows as ever you'll know'.

'Adieu, Adieu' (Trad arr Fairport Convention)
Fairport dedicated this to The Who and cheekily open with the two-note riff that starts 'Happy Jack'. Then it's into another celebration of criminality as they tell a tale of a hardened felon meeting his inevitable fate at the hands of implacable justice. Originally started and discarded back in the *Full House* days, the band use all the musical tricks they have to keep the entertainment value up – close harmony singing on a quick, twisty melody, Pegg's busy, walking bass, chord chops from Simon and plenty of key and rhythm changes. The result is two and a half minutes of pure Fairport brilliance.

'The Bonny Bunch Of Roses' (Trad arr Fairport Convention)
This epic, dramatic account of a conversation between Napoleon's widow and his son was, again, first attempted by Fairport for *Full House* and appeared as a bonus track on that album's re-issue. The original showed the challenge the band faced to make this work – it's very long and potentially very boring. Here, Fairport have re-arranged it to provide a variety of instrumentation, moods and pace. One can, therefore, divide this into five distinct sections: The first opens

with Peggy stating the theme on solo bass guitar before Swarb sings the first verse acapella. Then the voice and bass work together before Simon comes in with electric guitar chords on the line 'And I shall raise a terrible army' and Bruce provides some marching drums. Now we have a short pause before Swarb sings over Simon's guitar for section two, the instrumentation building up as the song recalls Napoleon's ill-fated march on Moscow. Section three calms things down a bit as Napoleon's widow, Marie-Therese, warns his son that he's in danger of following his father to an early grave (and he did, dying at the tender age of 21 from a surfeit of aggressive exercise). She also warns him not to be so venturesome 'for England has a heart of oak'. Section four is an instrumental section played at a slightly faster speed by Simon on electric guitar, pretty much following the melody. Then there is a longer pause before Swarb sings the last verse and the band all come in for the dramatic finish. It's a fine track, a tribute to the band's arranging skills as well as its musicianship, and provides an excellent centrepiece for the album.

'The Poor Ditching Boy' (Richard Thompson)

This comes from Richard's first solo effort after leaving Fairport, 1972's *Henry The Human Fly* – supposedly the worst-selling album in the history of the Warner Brothers record company. It's a typical Thompson song – an upbeat, traditional-sounding melody allied to lyrics that would make your blood run cold. The original was acoustic, pretty much just guitar and fiddle. Fairport give it the electric treatment, opening with Simon and his guitar before the band crashes in for verse two and the rousing, harmony-drenched chorus. It loses the dark quirkiness of the original, replacing it with an inappropriate optimism. But it's a well-arranged, well-performed song full of good musical moments.

'General Taylor' (Trad arr Fairport Convention)

A sea shanty from America this time – the titular general is former US president Zachary Taylor and it commemorates his defeat of the Mexican General Santa Ana at the battle of Molina del Ray in Mexico. But it also references 'Stormy', a legendary American sea captain who supposedly stood three feet tall. It is said to be a 'capstan shanty' to be sung while turning the capstan – a giant winch – to pull up the anchor. As Fairport perform it, a solo voice would sing the verse lines and everyone would join in the chorus as they pushed. Fairport used to sing this is in their live set back in 1970, so they knew it well. They perform the first few verses acapella before an electric band accompaniment drives it on.

'Run Johnny Run' (Ralph McTell)

The 'Streets of London' composer was to become a plentiful source of Fairport-style songs – he had helped out musically on *Rosie* but this was the first time the band had recorded any of his solo songs for a studio album. 'Run Johnny Run' first appeared on McTell's 1974 album *Easy*, and it's clear that Fairport had long expressed an interest in covering it. It certainly fits in with a general theme on this album of celebrating criminals – Johnny is a jail-breaker, running from the law, burrowing through woods and splashing across streams to evade the guard dogs. Fairport give the song the frantic, breathless quality it deserves, driven by Swarb's thrashing mandolin and strong vocals.

'The Last Waltz' (Dave Swarbrick)

The only song from Swarb on the album is a gentle waltz written as a thank-you to the fans for supporting them over the years. Its lyrics suggest the demon fiddler, who was suffering from increasing hearing problems, was thinking about calling it a day. 'The party's all over, and it's time to go' he sings, as every member of the band takes a turn with a verse. It's a pretty, insignificant little song that would barely merit a mention if it wasn't for the fact that, for Swarb, it was indeed time to go, just one album later.

'Royal Seleccion No13' (Trad arr Fairport Convention, Leon Jessel)

This was the sort of thing Fairport could do in their sleep, but it's still irresistible, opening with a few lines of doggerel discovered by Simon and then powering into four exciting tunes. Three are traditional – 'Haste To The Wedding', 'Clarke's Hornpipe' and 'The Dashing White Sergeant' – and one written in 1897 by German composer Leon Jessel, 'The Parade Of The Tin Soldiers'. They play 'The Dashing White Sergeant' last, at a considerable dash, with Simon on guitar keeping up with Swarb's fiddle every step of the way. It's a great end to a fine album.

Tipplers Tales (1978)

Personnel:
Dave Swarbrick: fiddle, mandolin, mandocello, vocals
Simon Nicol: electric and acoustic guitars, vocals, dulcimer, piano
Dave Pegg: bass guitar, guitar, mandolin, vocals
Bruce Rowland: drums, percussion, electric piano
Recorded at Chipping Norton Studios, Oxfordshire, February 1978
Producer: Fairport Convention
Record label: Vertigo
Released: May 1978
Highest chart position: Uncharted
Length: 36:26

The theme of *Tipplers Tales* was drinking – but it was really all about endings. It was the last studio album with the line-up of Simon, Bruce and the two Daves – indeed, the last to feature Swarb as part of the band. He had been diagnosed with tinnitus, which this author can confirm is a pain in the, er, ear, and he had been warned to either stop playing with an electric band or go deaf. It was also the last time Fairport Convention would record any studio material for seven years, certainly under that name.

Paradoxically, it would lead to the members making more money than at any time in their history. Their manager Philippa Clare had booked them plenty of gigs and was organising their finances, so every bit of cash they earned went into their pockets. But the record company, Phonogram (which owned Vertigo), was falling out of love with the band. The kudos of having Fairport Convention was outweighed by the fact that their albums never sold more than 15,000-20,000 copies, no matter how good or bad they were. So the record label said 'no more albums, please'. Peggy explains:

> We said, "Sorry, we're going to send you another four; one a month if necessary". In the end, they paid us not to make any more. It wasn't a great deal of money. It was about £30,000. It was the first time we had ever made money out of music. We got like £7,000 each. It was more money than we'd ever had in our lives.

Tipplers Tales was recorded in just ten days and, considering the frictions that had started to sour the studio process, it is surprisingly sprightly and strong. Six of the ten tracks are traditional, and the vague drinking theme does seem to link a number of them, such as 'Ye Mariners All', 'Three Drunken Maidens', 'John Barleycorn' and two segued instrumentals, 'The Hair Of The Dogma' and 'As Bitme'. This extends to the cover, what looks like a child's painting of wine bottles with a castle in the distance. And there's the 11-minute centrepiece on the story of legendary fiddler Jack O'Rion that allows Swarb to 'rosin up the bow' and show off his prowess on the violin.

Sadly, there was one more ending as tragedy once again struck the Fairport family. On 21 April 1978, shortly before *Tipplers Tales* was released, Sandy Denny died of an embolism three weeks after a fall at her parents' home. Her beautiful songs and breathtaking voice had been both a blessing and a curse to the band. Without her, Fairport may not have lasted more than two or three early albums and ended up as a footnote in 1960s music history. And without her, perhaps the *Nine* line-up would have gone on to even better things, and the band would not be considering bringing down the curtain. Dave Pegg said: 'We had already been thinking about what might happen to Fairport; with Sandy gone, it felt like a piece of the jigsaw would always be missing.'

'Ye Mariners All, including Bottom of the Punch Bowl/East Nuke of Fyfe' (Trad arr Fairport Convention)

Tipplers Tales starts as *The Bonny Bunch of Roses* ended – with a rollicking fiddle tune (a very similar one in fact to the final instrumental on 'Royal Seleccion No13'). 'Punch Bowl' is a Scottish reel, while 'East Nuke (sometimes Neuk) of Fyfe' (sometimes Fife), is a hornpipe played here on mandolin. Both are in major keys before the track changes to A minor for the main event, 'Ye Mariners All'. Also known as 'A Jug Of This', it's a salty drinking song first recorded by Swarb with Martin Carthy on the latter's first solo album in 1965. It spends most of its time exhorting all sailors to part with their money in exchange for an inebriating beverage and a pretty girl, although it has a slightly surreal penultimate verse in which the singer asks to be transformed into a fish so he swims in a jug of ale. Fairport's version became one of the four live favourites from this album and found its way on to the band's 50th-anniversary release in 2017.

'Three Drunken Maidens' (Trad arr Fairport Convention)

Fairport perform a fairly straightforward version of this cheerful 18th Century drinking song, unusually chronicling the drunken escapades of the fairer sex rather than men. The first line places this geographically in the Isle of Wight, which was a popular haven for smugglers of intoxicating liquor. Swarb probably knew this one better than the rest of the band as he recorded it with Bert Lloyd back in 1966 (although as 'Four Drunken Maidens') and this version takes a similar approach in tempo. Unusually for a Fairport traditional song, this has a modern fade-out at the end.

'Jack O'Rion, including Turnabout/Tiree/Miss Stevenson's/Do It Again/March of the Last/Turnabout' (Trad arr Fairport Convention except tunes by D. Swarbrick)

Like the title track on *The Bonny Bunch of Roses*, this is the long song on *Tipplers Tales*, the story of lecherous fiddler Jack O'Rion and his even more lecherous (and deceitful) young boy Tom. Swarb had recorded this twice before, with Bert Lloyd in 1966 and Martin Carthy two years later.

The titular fiddler could, it seems, persuade young women to be biologically accommodating simply by applying bow to string, and in the song makes arrangements to fiddle about with a young countess. But his young boy Tom, an even superior player, lulls his master to sleep and then enjoys the lady's charms in his stead. Unfortunately, this little bit of saucy subterfuge ends badly for the lad – Jack finds out and strings him up for it.

Like 'The Bonny Bunch of Roses', we can divide this track into distinct sections as the verses are interspersed with Swarb's self-penned tunes. It opens with Peggy's bass and a fragment of Swarb's 'Turnabout' before the first few verses set up the assignation in a bouncy D minor. Then there is a pause in proceedings for section two, a slow air from the Western Hebrides called 'Tiree' that then goes back into a more spirited 'Miss Stevenson's', which ends up in a major key. Then we slow down and return to D minor for section three, as the Countess lays out the plan for Jack's return and the fiddler trots home to his young boy Tom 'as fast as he can go'. On those last lines, the song breaks into a fast Swarbrick jig, 'Do It Again', played as a fiddle and mandolin duet.

Another pause – it's a bit stop/start, this one – then more story. Jack tells Tom to wake him at cock-crow so he can enjoy his assignation with the Countess. Tom sends his master to sleep with a fiddle tune and then goes off to lay with the lady in Jack's stead (doing the deed on the hard cold floor, the cad). He returns home to wake his master, who then grabs his fiddle and heads off for his assignation. With me so far?

Now we are into another tune, 'March of the Last' – slower and slightly darker, because we all know what's going to happen, don't we? Swarb, unaccompanied, sings the next verse as Jack announces his arrival at the lady's door, then there's some gentle electric guitar from Simon as the Countess, quite understandably, says: What, back for more? Finally, we return to Peggy's bass intro as an angry Jack discovers the subterfuge and goes back to take revenge, and we play out on 'Turnabout'. It is a bit episodic and fractured, but there's jazz there as well as folk as Swarb gets to show off his fiddle chops, and it's nice to know he got to do this song before quitting the band.

'Reynard The Fox' (Trad arr Fairport Convention)

Songs about foxes and foxhunting were very popular in Britain, while the character of Reynard – a trickster who was both man and animal – is common to British, Dutch, German and French folklore. What is unusual about this song is it is written partly from the fox's point of view and thus could be seen as early anti-foxhunting propaganda. Sandy Denny certainly knew this song – she sang it live in the early 1970s and there are suggestions Fairport tried to record it with her, presumably for *Liege And Lief*. The *Tipplers Tales* version has become a staple of the band's live act and was re-recorded by a later line-up in 1987. Bruce's drums fade in before the band sets up a swinging, driving rhythm. The first verse is acapella with excellent close harmonies before the instruments kick in again. It's a joyful, upbeat song – despite the fact that, in the end, the dogs catch poor Reynard 'by the slabs and will not let him go'. Ouch!

'Lady Of Pleasure' (Allan Taylor)
Members of Fairport would have undoubtedly bumped into singer/songwriter Allan Taylor in the London folk clubs during the mid-1960s. This shanty-sounding waltz number would have fitted well in *"Babbacombe" Lee* – it's all about a dockside prostitute who's 'a sailor lad's port in a storm'. Fairport's version is pleasant but brief, just two and a half minutes. Simon takes lead vocal and Swarb adds some restrained jigs between some of the verses.

'Bankruptured' (D. Pegg)
One of three instrumentals that last less than two minutes each, giving the second side of the album a rather disjointed feel. It is, however, a pretty, sprightly mandolin tune that one could imagine as the theme for a children's TV series. Postman Pegg, perhaps. A jazzy feel is provided by Bruce gently stroking his drums with brushes and I believe I'm right in thinking it's Peggy playing the acoustic guitar fiddly bits too – he certainly did live with PJ Wright.

'The Widow Of Westermorland' (Trad arr Fairport Convention)
Usually entitled 'The Widow of Westmorland's Daughter', this is a saucy tale about an innocent young girl who is fooled into thinking she can gain back her maidenhead by lying the opposite way round on the bed. However, she wins the day by stealing her young man from his more worldly-wise bride-to-be. Swarb originally recorded it with Bert Lloyd in 1966. Fairport give it a thundering good treatment, going along like the clappers, interspersing the verses with a three-part fiddle tune called 'The Random Jig'.

'The Hair Of The Dogma' (D. Pegg)
A short but sweet instrumental driven by Peggy's bass and with Swarb playing fast fiddle arpeggios over the top. Simon also gets a chance to play some rock star-like lead guitar. It segues via Bruce's cymbals into…

'As Bitme' (D. Pegg, B. Rowland)
Very similar to 'Cropredy Capers' – slightly faster but with the same lack of any real tune or anything, just a driving rhythm from Bruce with a repetitive Peggy bassline. This is turn segues into…

'John Barleycorn' (Trad arr Fairport Convention)
The final track on the album is a traditional singalong tribute to the humble corn crop. A popular song recorded by practically everyone who has ever put their hand behind their ear, it is usually performed in a minor key, as are

the versions recorded by Mike Waterson, Martin Carthy and Traffic. However, Fairport set it to the much more upbeat and triumphant tune by Johann Schultz known as 'We Plough The Fields And Scatter', and the result makes a very satisfying ending to the album. In live performances, the band would attempt to hold the note on the 'ley' of the final 'John Barleycorn' for as long as their oxygen would last out.

Gladys' Leap (1985)

Personnel:
Simon Nicol: vocals, electric and acoustic guitars
Dave Pegg: bass guitar, mandolin, bouzouki, double bass, vocals
Dave Mattacks: drums, drum machine, keyboards, percussion
Additional personnel:
Ric Sanders: violin ('Bird From The Mountain', 'The Hiring Fair', 'Instrumental Medley')
Richard Thompson: electric guitar ('Head In A Sack')
Cathy Lesurf: vocals ('My Feet Are Set For Dancing')
Harold Wells: spoken intro to 'Bird From The Mountain'
Recorded at Woodworm Studio, Barford St. Michael, Oxfordshire
Record label: Woodworm
Released: August 1985
Produced by Simon Nicol, Dave Mattacks and Dave Pegg
Highest chart position: Uncharted
Length: 38:01
Current edition: 2001 Talking Elephant reissue with bonus tracks

But it all comes round again… Despite being officially 'dead' for seven years, Fairport Convention managed to release a single and three live albums between 1979 and 1985. They also built the foundations for what has become the largest annual folk festival in Britain, the reunion concert in Cropredy, which in 2019 celebrated its 40th anniversary.

The break gave the members a chance to make some real money. In particular, Dave Pegg got a lucrative billet as bass player for progressive rock giants Jethro Tull, a job he held until 1995 when Fairport's growing popularity and demands on his time forced him to quit. The money meant he could build his own recording studio (as well as buy a Porsche and a property in France!).

Simon returned to The Albion Band, toured with Richard and Linda Thompson and formed a duo with Dave Swarbrick. Dave Mattacks also slotted in some Albion Band while working as a session musician with practically everyone who's anyone in the music industry, including Paul McCartney, George Harrison, Jimmy Page and Chris Rea.

Back in 1979, the band did a mammoth 36-date farewell tour that ended with Fairport supporting Led Zeppelin at Knebworth. They wanted to go out with a live memento of those final shows but, having ended their record deal with Phonogram, had no label willing to release anything for them. So Peggy and his wife Christine started Woodworm Records and pressed up 3,000 copies of a posthumous live album called *Farewell, Farewell*, selling them from their home. It was later re-released on Simons Records – a short-lived label based in East Ham in London and nothing to do with Mr Nicol – and received another lease of life in 1997 as Encore, Encore on Folkprint. That release included a 1980 single called 'Rubber Band'.

Ah, a single. In a triumph of hope over experience, Fairport recorded Mike Waterson's amusing 1972 ditty and released it in 1980, with 'Bonny Black Hare' from *Farewell, Farewell* on the flipside. The title and lyrics seemed to fit Fairport to a T – after all, they were the ultimate rubber band, bouncing back time and time again. Except, ironically, they weren't bouncing back on this occasion. The song includes the immortal line 'just like margarine our fame is spreading' but Fairport's fame appeared to be melting away like a tub of Flora left out in the sun.

The farewell tour ended in August with Fairport playing in a farmer's field near the historic village of Cropredy, scene of a major civil war battle in 1644 and four miles north of Banbury, Oxfordshire. Cropredy was special to the band – at one time both Peggy and Dave Swarbrick lived in the village – and they had been playing private performances there since 1976. On this occasion, 4,500 cheered when Fairport promised to be back the following year.

Which they did, making the reunion a two-day event with special guests. In 1981 it was held in the grounds of Broughton Castle, and Fairport's performance was recorded for release through Woodworm Records as *Moat On The Ledge*. The festival returned to a field in Cropredy the following year and live recordings were issued as a limited edition cassette tape called *AT2*, while 1983's performance came out as *The Boot*.

By 1985 Peggy, Simon and DM realised they needed to add some new material to their Cropredy repertoire. Peggy says Swarb wasn't interested in being involved, thanks partly to his hearing problems. Swarb, however, saw things a little differently., claiming he didn't know they were working on an album until he was presented with the backing tracks and asked to overdub his fiddle. He said:

It would have been the first Fairport album since ***Unhalfbricking*** that I would have played on as a virtual session musician. I lived nearby; in fact, I had a home visit from Peggy and Simon. Why didn't they pop round with a cassette or post it? I was given no choice of keys to play in, no choice of material, or songs to sing. I thought then, 'They clearly don't want or need me'.

The absence of Swarb left Fairport with no band songwriter, so they cast about for compositions from their friends. One of their first ports of call was Ralph McTell, who had a long association with the band – they had known him since the late 1960s, he played on the *Rosie* album, and the Fairports had frequently helped him out on his recordings. Ralph supplied three songs: 'Wat Tyler', a historical epic about the 1381 Peasants' Revolt, co-written with Simon; 'Bird From The Mountain', a celebration of poaching; and a song destined to become a fan favourite, 'The Hiring Fair', written with Dave Mattacks.

Other numbers came from Cathy Lesurf and Dave Whetstone, who had both been in The Albion Band with Simon; a Richard Thompson composition that he had demoed at Woodworm Studios but done nothing with; a song by

John Richards of Maurice and the Minors that Peggy heard while they were recording at Woodworm Studios; and three instrumental tunes put together by Dave Pegg. The only composition by our old friend Trad was one of the three instrumentals, 'The Wise Maid'.

The album title came from the story of postwoman Gladys Hillier, who used to jump a 3ft stream on her rounds in the village of Cranham, near Stroud in Gloucestershire. The spot was eventually named Gladys' Leap in her honour. The album cover picture, however, suggests a leaping dancer rather than a postwoman – she is barefoot and watched by a crowd of onlookers.

Fairport turned to another Albion Band friend, Ric Sanders, to provide fiddle on three tracks. Richard played electric guitar on the closing track (his gag was that he'd left the band in 1970, and played with them ever since) and Cathy Lesurf sang her own composition. The result was welcomed as a strong comeback album that also set the precedent of Fairport showcasing the work of contemporary composers alongside traditional material.

'How Many Times' (Richard Thompson)
A seemingly upbeat, positive start to the album, with strong drums from DM, a twin guitar and mandolin attack from Simon and Peggy, and the repeated refrain of 'How many times do you have to fall before you end up walking?'. Of course, like many Richard Thompson songs, there's a dark side to the lyrics that belies the apparently cheerful three-chord tune – it was written around the time of his break-up with wife Linda in 1980 and, inevitably, there are lines that seem to reference that traumatic time. But it's a good opening track with fine vocals from Simon.

'Bird From The Mountain' (Ralph McTell)
A waltz-time celebration of poaching from Ralph that opens with a local friend, Harold Wells, speaking lines from the first verse. Peggy sings with his gentle, hesitant Brummie brogue and Ric Sanders provides understated fiddle backing. The tune relies on well-worn chord sequences with a loping, descending bass line but the lyrics are quite evocative, conjuring up images of setting out before dawn with gun, rod and line and a dog by your side. It's a pleasant song but not one of the standouts.

'Honour And Praise' (John Richards)
Richards (not to be confused with Richard!) hails from the Black Country and, like many of the Fairport members in the 1960s, played in pop and rock bands as well as folk clubs. During Fairport's interregnum, he was a founder member of Maurice And The Minors and was recording at Woodworm Studios when Peggy heard this song and asked if Fairport could use it. The result is this fine, traditional-sounding track about a trading ship lost in a storm, told from the point of view of the sole survivor. Simon sings two verses and the chorus over gentle guitar finger-picking before the rest of the band come in and attack the

stirring chorus with vigour: 'Fight for honour and for praise/Sailed the seas throughout the days/In cold ground I'll never lay/I'd rather die on the ocean.' It pointed the way for the new Fairport – find contemporary songs with a traditional bent and present them with powerful, dramatic arrangements and intricate harmonies.

'The Hiring Fair' (Ralph McTell, Dave Mattacks)

The highpoints continue with a song that takes a similar approach to 'Honour And Praise' – written in the 1980s but harking back to the 1580s. Hiring fairs dated back to Edward III and were a common way for farmers to hire short-term agricultural workers to bring in the harvest. Both men and women would attend these yearly gatherings and – in this song – a chap takes a fancy to 'a maid in the very next row'. To his delight, they are both employed on the same farm and, as they toil under the hot sun, his fancy turns almost into an obsession until, finally, they consummate their relationship with a roll in the hay. What could have been a rollicking 'I said dear maid do you come here often' type of jolly romp is actually, in the hands of Fairport, passionate, romantic and quite beautiful. Simon plays finger-picked guitar in E minor and C before telling the story in his simple but affecting baritone (what a fine voice he had developed by this stage), while DM adds some sensitive keyboards and Ric provides soaring, sensual fiddle in the instrumental section (which changes key to G minor). The result is a 24-carat Fairport classic to rank alongside anything from *Liege And Lief* and *Full House,* and one that can still reduce a 20,000 festival audience to complete, transported silence.

'Instrumental Medley '85: The Riverhead (Dave Pegg), Gladys' Leap (Dave Pegg), The Wise Maid' (Trad arr Simon Nicol and Dave Pegg)

It wouldn't be a Fairport album without an instrumental medley played so fast the fiddler's bow melts. It starts with some very loud drums from Dave Mattacks that, live, would turn into a bit of a solo tour de force. Then Peggy comes in with a run on the bass and some clever harmonics before settling into a self-penned drum 'n' bass jig. The second tune is a faster jig for the entire band with Ric on fiddle and DM playing practically everything within reach, including what sounds like a metal bathtub. Then Ric and Simon take centre stage for a lightning-fast, finger-twisting reel, 'The Wise Maid', one of the most popular Irish folk tunes (even though it seems to only date back to the 1970s!). Sadly, it fades out instead of coming to a triumphant end, but the entire piece makes a resounding statement that Fairport are back and as good as ever.

'My Feet Are Set For Dancing' (Cathy Lesurf, arr by Bill Martin)

The only mis-step on the album. Fairport do disco? Noooo!!! Those horrible, tinny 1980s syn drums! And is that Peggy attempting slap bass? It's a shame because Cathy has a beautiful voice with the purity of Maddy Prior. She was a member of Fiddler's Dram when they had a 1979 hit with 'Day Trip To Bangor (Didn't We Have A Lovely Time)' and then joined Simon Nicol in The Albion Band. Cathy frequently sang Sandy songs at the Cropredy festival and always did them justice. But this misguided attempt to be modern and relevant falls flat on its face and now sounds dated and out of place.

'Wat Tyler' (Ralph McTell, Simon Nicol)

From the ridiculous to the sublime. This soon-to-be fan favourite is a modern folk epic that references the Peasants' Revolt of 1381. Back in the late 14th century England was ruled by Richard II, who had ascended to the throne at the tender age of 10 after his grandfather, Edward III, died with no living legitimate sons. Thanks to the social upheaval caused by the Black Death and the Hundred Years War, in which the former Norman kings fought to recover lands in France, the English people were being heavily taxed and didn't like it one bit. All it would take was one spark...

That was supplied in May 1381 when a royal official attempted to collect unpaid poll taxes in Brentwood, resulting in violent uprisings that spread across south-east England. Groups of rebels from Essex and Kent marched on London to seek redress for their grievances – the Kent contingent was led by Walter, the roof tiler. In London the rebels went on a rampage of destruction and murder, ending only when King Richard agreed to meet them at Smithfield, just outside the city walls.

Wat Tyler and the king met face-to-face, with Tyler being a bit over-familiar with the 14-year-old monarch. Then he called for a flagon of water, rinsing out his mouth in a disgusting fashion that caused the king's men to insult and abuse him. One thing led to another and Tyler ended up attempting to stab the Lord Mayor of London, who fought back with his sword. Another of the king's servants also weighed in with a knife. Tyler was eventually captured and decapitated, his head placed on a pole and carried through the city before being stuck on a pike at London Bridge to glare down at all the tourists. The revolt collapsed in the wake of his death and the king revoked all the concessions he had made to the people.

The song Ralph and Simon conjured up captures the drama of the event with its marching beat, chopping guitar chords and rousing chorus – 'And on the field at Blackheath/Us commons covered the earth/More men than ever I did see/Poor honest men from birth'. You can tell whose side Ralph and Simon are on – the lyrics rewrite history a bit to make Tyler more of a hero than he actually was. The reedy synth backing sounds dated now, but it's held together by Simon's strong, heavily reverbed singing and DM's powerful drum sound. In a live setting, Fairport would create a powerful wall of sound with this track, with rumbling bass that would shake the ground under your feet. 'Wat Tyler' shows off Fairport's arranging skills – frequently down to an uncredited Dave Mattacks – and their ability to shift from gentle ballads to almost heavy rock.

'Head In A Sack' (Dave Whetstone)

An upbeat, driving rock number ends the album with Richard Thompson appearing on a Fairport studio recording for the first time since *Rosie* in 1972. Accordion-player Dave Whetstone performed in folk groups in the mid-70s and, along, with Jean Pierre Rasle on the bagpipes, was drafted into a reformed Albion Band along with Simon Nicol and Dave Mattacks. Later he formed Waz with Martin Allcock and Pete Zorn (and was Simon Nicol's neighbour!). Lyrically there are plenty of interesting images to play with – 'Dancing on a tightrope with my head in a sack' – and a catchy chorus but ultimately the song appears to be completely meaningless! Never mind, it's an energetic way to end a mostly successful comeback album.

Bonus Tracks
'Angel Delight' (Swarbrick, Pegg, Nicol, Mattacks), 'Polly On The Shore' (Music D. Pegg, Lyrics trad arr Lucas, Swarbrick), 'Lucky Old Sun' (Beasley Smith, Haven Gillespie)

Three songs recorded at the 1982 Cropredy reunion concert and originally released a year later by Woodworm Records on *AT2*, a limited edition cassette. The first two tracks have been covered before – 'Angel Delight' is the title track of Fairport's 1971 album and 'Polly On The Shore,' comes from *Nine* (1973). 'Lucky Old Sun' was first recorded and released as a single by Frankie Laine in 1949 and has been covered by dozens of performers in the years hence. A slow, ruminative number sung here by Trevor Lucas, it has similarities to 'Ol' Man River', the 1927 song by Jerome Kern and Oscar Hammerstein II from the musical *Showboat*, in that it contrasts the singer's hard life with the apparently easy time the natural world has. In this case, that lucky old sun 'just rolls around Heaven all day' – neglecting to mention, of course, that it does so at 5,505C.

Expletive Delighted! (1986)

Personnel:

Simon Nicol: electric & acoustic guitars

Martin Allcock: acoustic, slide & electric guitars, bouzouki, mandola, mandolin, double bass

Ric Sanders: electric & octave violins, keyboards

Dave Pegg: bass, mandola, lead acoustic guitar

Dave Mattacks: drums, percussion, keyboards

Additional personnel:

Jerry Donahue: guitar on 'Hanks For The Memory'

Richard Thompson: guitar on 'Hanks For The Memory'

Recorded at Woodworm Studios, Barford St. Michael, Oxfordshire

Record label: Woodworm

Released: August 1986

Producer: Fairport Convention

Highest chart position: Uncharted

Length: 38:01

Current edition: 1994 re-issue on Terrapin Trucking Record Co Ltd

With Dave Swarbrick unwilling to tour again – and refusing to play at Cropredy on the new songs recorded without him – Fairport Convention realised they needed to sign up some permanent replacements if they were to go out and promote new recordings. Filling the fiddle slot was pretty straightforward – there was Ric Sanders, who had guested on *Gladys' Leap* and was champing at the bit to join one of his favourite bands.

Ric – born December 1952 in Birmingham – had learned his first fiddle tunes from Dave Swarbrick's hugely influential 1967 album *Rags, Reels & Airs*. But he had a more diverse musical background, having played with Japanese classical/rock percussionist Stomu Yamash'ta, jazz pianists Johnny Patrick and Michael Garrick and Canterbury jazz/rock group Soft Machine. He also formed short-lived fusion outfit 2nd Vision with jazz guitarist John Etheridge. His Fairport connection came about thanks to The Albion Band album *Rise Up Like The Sun*, which contained a cover of John Coltrane's 'Afro Blue' suggested by Ric. When the call came from Dave Pegg to play on *Gladys' Leap*, he leapt at the chance.

Fairport could have carried on as a four-piece, as they had done twice in their career so far. But with Simon taking over as frontman and lead vocalist – and bearing in mind the more adventurous arrangements the band was attempting – it was agreed that a second guitarist was required. He came from a somewhat unusual source.

Martin (later Maartin) Allcock – born January 1957 in what is now Greater Manchester – first met the band at Lancaster University when he was a 17-year-old music student and Fairport fan. He and Peggy became great drinking buddies – he was invited to join the band thanks to his ability to play virtually any instrumental in existence AND read and write those dots on music sheets.

Fairport still suffered from a lack of band songwriters – an issue that wouldn't really be resolved until Chris Leslie joined in 1997 – but both the new boys brought some self-penned instrumental pieces with them. In an effort to 'catch the moment' and show off their musical chops, it was decided to make the next album entirely instrumental, using five new tunes plus some old Fairport material that could be given a shot in the arm. There was also a composition from John Kirkpatrick, a beautiful air penned by the blind Celtic harpist Turlough O'Carolan and, finally, a spirited (and totally out of place!) tribute to Hank Marvin and the Shadows featuring the twin twang of guitarists Richard Thompson and Jerry Donahue.

For a lot of Fairport fans, the instrumentals show the band at its fast and furious best, so *Expletive Delighted!* is, indeed, a delight. It has been criticised for having an over-loud drum sound, but I disagree – DM's drums were part of what made Fairport unique so, for me, the louder, the better! It's also a bit short at just over 35 minutes. But packed within that truncated running time are some stonking tunes played with verve, style and skill. And Ric excels here with two compositions – including the exquisite 'Portmeirion' – that became staples of the live set.

The cover shows the band with gags on their mouths and, as an additional joke, contains the claim 'Lyric sheet enclosed'. It didn't chart and was later coupled with *Gladys' Leap* as one release on Folkprint.

'The Rutland Reel/Sack The Juggler' (Ric Sanders)

Swarb who? Ric Sanders lays his claim to be the new demon fiddler with this medley that kicks off at 100mph then goes into overdrive. It's at least as fast and entertaining as anything Dave Swarbrick did with the band and, on stage, became the instrumental ending to 'Matty Groves'. Yes, it sounds like a couple of traditional tunes, but Ric throws in dramatic jazzy phrases, plus a few bars of the blues, to produce something utterly unique. The first tune is, as the name suggests, a no-nonsense, 4/4, hard-driving reel with Ric playing something like 20 notes to a bar. Then it powers into 'Sack The Juggler,' an even faster display of fiddle virtuosity with Dave Mattacks pounding away as if performing a drum solo. Some serious echo is stuck on the end, so Ric's final fiddle notes bounce away into the ether.

'The Cat On The Mixer/Three Left Feet' (Martin Allcock)

The first tune is a fiendishly difficult composition mostly in 7/4 (I think!) but with various bars of different time signatures thrown in. Guitar and fiddle play a minor key jig while lead guitar wails over the top. It must have been a real challenge to learn, but Fairport were no doubt helped by the fact that it had been previously released on Button Records as the B-side of a single in October 1983 by a band called Tied Logs. The A-side was a traditional tune, 'The Bluebell Polka', and Martin is listed as the producer of the single as well as composer. Second tune here is a more straight-ahead gallop, repeating the four chords of D, A, C and F that pop up occasionally during 'The Cat' but take over at the end. A combination of jazz, rock and folk, it suggests Martin was going to help Fairport take things in a more proggy direction.

'Bankruptured' (Dave Pegg)
Peggy's sprightly tune from *Tipplers Tales* is resurrected and extended to sound more like the Quintette du Hot Club de France than Fairport. Ric gets a chance to channel his inner Stephane Grappelli while Peggy out-Djangos Django Reinhardt on acoustic guitar and Martin plays double-bass. The result is a distinct improvement on the original and evidence, once again, of Fairport's new jazz influence.

'Portmeirion' (Ric Sanders)
Ah, what a beauty this is. 'Portmeirion' must be Ric's most beloved composition, a lyrical, flowing waltz-time tune (in D major, for you musicians out there) in which he produces enthralling, bitter-sweet melodic lines. Martin provides tasteful acoustic lead guitar, Ric adds gentle keyboard chords, and Simon and Peggy bring unobtrusive guitar and bass support. Ric's inspiration here is the pretty and quirky Italianate village of Portmeirion in Gwynedd, North Wales – designed by Sir Clough Williams-Ellis in 1925 and made famous as the setting for the 1960s spy fantasy *The Prisoner*. Apparently, Ric's fiddle solo here was the first, improvised take – he then had to learn it to reproduce it live. It's a rare tour when 'Portmeirion' isn't played and, like 'The Hiring Fair', is guaranteed to be listened to in delighted and appreciative silence.

'Jams O'Donnells Jig' (Dave Pegg)
Another old Fairport tune, this time from *The Bonny Bunch Of Roses*. As stated earlier, Fairport would sometimes perform this almost as a heavy metal band and this is where they start cranking up the volume and distortion. DM gets more to do here, kicking things off with a drum intro and then hitting what sounds like a metal tray throughout (perhaps this is why some reviewers complained he was too loud!) while Martin has his guitar effects pedal on 'heavy metal' setting. Live, this would grow an ending that channelled King Crimson's '20th Century Schizoid Man'.

'Expletive Delighted' (Ric Sanders)
A short, under two minutes piece composed deliberately as the title track of the album. It's mostly solo Ric but triple, maybe quadruple, tracked, playing a haunting tune rather like the 'Thaxted Horn Dance' in the way it drifts towards you. Then DM and Peggy come in with slow, loud, pounding drums and bass to bring things to a dramatic end.

'Sigh Beg, Sigh Mor' (O'Carolan)

A lyrical Irish air usually attributed to the late 17th-century blind harpist and singer Turlough O'Carolan and said to be his first composition – the title translates as 'Big Fairy Mound, Little Fairy Mound'. Simon and Dave Swarbrick played it when they toured as a duo in the early 1980s during Fairport's break but here it is a showcase for Ric to play long, languid notes on his violin, accompanied by guitars, bass and DM on slightly clunky keyboards. At more than seven minutes it probably goes on a bit long and is perhaps a little too similar in style to 'Portmeirion' (to be fair, it's 'Portmeirion' that's similar to 'Sigh Beg Sigh Mor'). In 1987 it was re-recorded and released as the B-side of the 'Meet On The Ledge' single.

'Innstuck' (Martin Allcock)

Martin's second track on the album is a short, cheerful bouzouki-led tune in 5/4 time with a distinctly Eastern European feel to it. Opening with acoustic guitar chords from Simon, there's not a lot to it – the same eight-bar melody is repeated again and again, relying on the build-up of mandolins, fiddle and occasional drum to provide interest. On stage, this would be coupled with the song 'There Once Was Love' by Paul Metsers.

'The Gas Almost Works' (John Kirkpatrick)

Melodeon player and accordionist John Kirkpatrick has a long association with the Fairports, beginning in 1970 when he met Ashley Hutchings at a showing of a film on Morris dancing at a London folk club. He played in early incarnations of both The Albion Band and Steeleye Span and in 1982 formed Brass Monkey with Martin Carthy. This tune began life in the early 1970s as a hornpipe in 4/4 time called 'Fulham Gasworks' and gained its new title when Kirkpatrick changed the time signature to 5/4. Peggy and DM played it in the Richard Thompson Band live in 1980. Fairport's version opens with a drum roll, and dramatic chords as Ric's fiddle slowly fades into view before the band pick up the complicated 5/4 rhythm. On stage, this would be tacked on the front of 'The Cat On The Mixer/Three Left Feet' to create a medley of tricky instrumentals.

'Hanks For The Memory' (Various, arr Jerry Donahue)

Richard Thompson and Jerry Donahue return to Fairport for the last track on the album, a tribute to the Shadows guitarist Hank Marvin. They power their way happily through 'Shazam!' (Duane Eddy, Lee Hazlewood), 'Pipeline' (Bob Spickard, Brian Carmen), 'Apache' (Jerry Lordan) and 'Peter Gunn' (Henry Mancini), with Thompson providing little lead guitar moments that leave you asking 'How the hell does he do that?'. It's a bit out of place on an album of folky, jazzy instrumentals and can only be described as fun but forgettable.

In Real Time: Live '87 (1987)

Personnel:
Simon Nicol: vocals, electric & acoustic guitars
Martin Allcock: vocals, electric & acoustic guitars, bouzouki, bass
Ric Sanders: violin, keyboards
Dave Pegg: bass, mandolin, drums, vocals
Dave Mattacks: drums, keyboards
Recorded at The Mill Studio, Farnham, Buckinghamshire
Producer: Dave Mattacks
Record label: Island
Released: December 1987
Highest chart position: Uncharted
Length: 40:10
Current edition: 1990 Island Records reissue

Fairport Convention returned to their old record label for an album with a title that, shall we say, is a little economical with the truth. For this is not live at all – instead, it was recorded in the studio and audience responses were dubbed on later from a John Martyn concert in Leeds. To continue the masquerade, everything has a bit of concert hall echo on it and the album cover shows the band performing at the Cropredy festival.

This harmless bit of subterfuge was entered into thanks to Island Records celebrating their 25th anniversary and choosing – out of their long and extensive catalogue of hugely successful artists – the band they had dumped a decade earlier as commercially unviable to mark the occasion with new recordings. Island wanted a live album, but the band didn't have time to record one. Instead, Fairport went into the studio to record highlights from their current live set.

Fairport also produced a new version of 'Meet On The Ledge' – a song that, on its first release in 1968, only managed to struggle to No 52 in the UK charts – and issued it as a 7" and 12" single, backed by an authentically live version of 'Sigh Beg Sigh Mor'.

While *In Real Time: Live '87* is no-one's idea of an essential Fairport Convention album, it nevertheless provides a snapshot of what the band could achieve with its still fairly new line-up and doubled as a celebration of its twentieth anniversary. The performances are confident and robust (with some reviewers complaining the recording was too loud; just turn your stereo down then!), although the three slow ballads in the middle of the set drag it down a bit, especially on the CD version. 'Matty Groves' has turned into a nearly 11-minute monster, thanks to a new Dave Pegg opening tune and Ric's medley from *Expletive Delighted!* tacked on the end. And there's a song that only previously appeared on a Simon Nicol and Dave Swarbrick album.

Needless to say, it didn't chart and wasn't as interesting as that year's live recording from Cropredy, released on cassette tape in 1988 as *The Third Leg*.

'Reynard The Fox' (Traditional)

The foxhunting song from *Tipplers Tales* is given a faithful reproduction here except with extra oomph from DM on drums (the original drummer was Bruce Rowland), while vocal harmonies from Simon, Martin and Peggy are tight and effective.

'The Widow Of Westmoreland's Daughter/Random Jig' (Traditional/James Hill)

Like Reynard, this comes from *Tipplers Tales*, although the original title put the spotlight on the widow, not on the daughter. This version has a slight change in the order the band play each of the three parts of 'The Random Jig' between the verses.

'The Hiring Fair' (Dave Mattacks, Ralph McTell)

The standout track from *Gladys' Leap* is almost a minute longer than the original, thanks to a short keyboard intro, a slightly extended instrumental section and a longer outro. It's also taken at a slightly more languid pace, with tasteful acoustic guitar licks between verses from Martin.

'Crazy Man Michael' (Richard Thompson, Dave Swarbrick)

Originally sung by Sandy Denny on *Liege And Lief* and performed by guest female vocalists at Cropredy, this is the first recording of Simon tackling the Richard and Swarb classic, and he does a fine job. His voice has matured into a warm baritone and he sings with feeling and character – although without the fragility that Sandy gave it. It's slightly slower than the original (and 20 seconds longer) with the bass more to the fore and Martin playing electric guitar without the wobbly, doubled-up effect Richard Thompson used. Ric's fiddle is far more prominent in the instrumental section than Swarb's was, but Martin's guitar solo lacks the ghostly shimmer of the original.

'Close To The Wind' (Stuart Marson)

Marson, a schoolteacher who sang around the Nottinghamshire folk clubs, wrote this for a Radio Northampton songwriting competition, which he won. It tells the true story of a gang of housebreakers and highway robbers who had their headquarters in the village of Culworth and preyed on the surrounding area. Eventually most of the gang were arrested and hanged opposite the White Elephant public house in Northampton in 1787. Sung from the point of view of one of the gang waiting to be executed, the song attempts to generate some sympathy for the villains. The chorus of 'for the wild sea, we'd sailed upon it/ Too close to the wind' suggests some sort of nautical theme but in fact, is simply figurative – sailing close to the wind means to do something risky or dangerous. Simon Nicol and Dave Swarbrick first recorded this for their 1984 duet album of the same name, with Peggy on bass and DM on drums and keyboards. Fairport's version is a carbon copy of that recording – a slow ballad that opens with acoustic guitar, picked violin strings and fretless bass before keyboards and drums enter halfway through. The biggest difference between the two versions is Simon's voice – a little thin and reedy on the original, it is much warmer and richer on the Fairport recording.

'Big Three Medley (The Swirling Pit/Matty Groves/The Rutland Reel/Sack The Juggler/) (Dave Pegg/Traditional, Ric Sanders)

Matty Groves was always – and still is – a changeable beast. By 1987 it had become a bit of a monster with no fewer than four parts to it. 'The Swirling Pit' was a Peggy-penned mandolin tune in the style of a traditional jig that he played live with Jethro Tull (accompanied by mock vomiting sounds). No prizes for guessing that the swirling pit is the toilet bowl that has been the end-of-the-night destination for many a reveller. Electric guitar and drums lead into the driving rhythm of 'Matty Groves', with Ric generating agonising screaming sounds from his fiddle and Martin playing accomplished slide guitar. That, in turn, crashes into Ric's instrumental medley that opened the *Expletive Delighted!* album. Now an 11-minute epic, it dominates this album and justifies its existence. It may not be 'live', but it's certainly kicking.

'Meet On The Ledge' (Richard Thompson)

According to the tracklisting, this is a 'studio version', but of course, they all are on this album. By 1987 it had become the traditional encore number, but it wasn't always – a few years after Fairport first recorded it for *What We Did On Our Holidays* the band had stopped playing it. The song was only inserted back into the live set for the 1979 farewell tour because Fairport wanted to provide a bit of a historical overview for what they thought would be their last ever performances. That's when they realised what a powerful, emotional number it was, especially after the death of Sandy Denny, and it slowly it made its way to the end of the set where it remains even today. Originally sung by Ian Matthews (when he was MacDonald) and Sandy, this newly-recorded version hands the vocal duties to Simon and inserts an instrumental verse in the middle. It has a more stately, respectful air to it as befits a song that has grown in meaning and stature across the years. This is the version that was released as a 7" and 12" vinyl single in 1987 to celebrate both Island Records 25th anniversary and the band's 20 years. It didn't chart, leading to Ric joking at the time: 'We're going to release it every 20 years until it's a hit.'

Red & Gold (1988)

Personnel:
Simon Nicol: guitars, vocals, dobro
Maartin Allcock: guitars, bouzouki, mandolin, accordion, keyboards, vocals
Ric Sanders: violin
Dave Pegg: acoustic & bass guitars, vocals
Dave Mattacks: drums, percussion, keyboards, harpsichord
Recorded at Woodworm Studios, Barford St Michael, Oxfordshire
Producer: Simon Nicol
Record label: Rough Trade
Released: December 1988
Highest chart position: 74 (UK)
Length: 40:32
Current edition: Unknown

The band signed a deal to release its next two albums on Rough Trade, better known for the somewhat un-folk-like Stiff Little Fingers and The Smiths. This helped to give the new Fairport line-up a modest chart placing of No 74, albeit for just a week. *Red & Gold* was the first proper studio album of songs and tunes by the comeback band and the last to be released on vinyl until the format was recently resurrected. It's also – fanfare please! – the first time the same Fairport line-up has released three studio albums in succession.

The album shows how far Fairport had moved from their old 'folk/rock' label – compared to *Tipplers Tales*, which in terms of running time was about 70% traditional, *Red & Gold* had just one song by Trad. Everything else came from contemporary writers, including the nearly seven-minutes-long title track composed by Ralph McTell. There were also compositions from former Albion Band colleague Dave Whetstone and Welsh singer/songwriter Huw Williams, who along with brother Tony would tour with the band as the support act. Just three tracks were penned by band members, all of them instrumentals, and they returned to plundering Bob Dylan's back catalogue for the first time since *Unhalfbricking*.

Critics generally welcomed the album as 'assured and enjoyable', particularly singling out for praise Simon Nicol's vocals on the title cut. A few of the tracks are a little bland and forgettable, but there are an equal number of gems such as 'Red And Gold' (the album title differs in having an ampersand) and 'Summer Before The War'. It also shows how important Cropredy had become to the band – 'Red And Gold' was the first of a string of songs written about the festival and the village in which it takes place.

The album has been re-released no fewer than 12 times, with the HTD Records version in 1995 adding a live version of 'Close To The Wind' from the previous year's festival. The most recent issue was on Talking Elephant in June 2001 but, at the time of writing, it appears to be difficult to get hold of any copies of the album at a reasonable price.

'Set Me Up' (Dave Whetstone)

As in 'you have set me up, you bugger'. Mr Whetstone's second appearance on a Fairport album after 'Head In A Sack' on *Gladys' Leap* is in a similar vein although not quite as interesting – a medium-paced rocker with fairly nonsensical lyrics and a somewhat plodding melody, lifted by Ric Sanders' fiddle solo. It appeared briefly in the live set when Fairport promoted the album but disappeared soon after that.

'The Noise Club' (Maartin Allcock)

No, it's not a typographical error – Mr Allcock did indeed put an extra 'a' in his first name, presumably as a joke after being referred to by his bandmates as Maart with a long 'ah'. He even released a solo album in 1990 with the same name. 'The Noise Club' – apparently titled after his daughter's bedroom – is a cheerful little jig mostly in 5/4 featuring his midi-guitar sound and a brief drum solo from DM. Thanks to Fairport's musicianship they handle its shifting time signatures with ease, especially towards the end during which the band plays in 5/4, but the drummer's in 4/4 – and they still end together.

'Red And Gold' (Ralph McTell)

Ralph continues his most generous practice of giving his best songs to his Fairport friends. This was inspired by the history of Cropredy, where in June 1644 one of the many battles during the English Civil War was fought between the Royalist army and the forces of Parliament led by Sir William Waller. Ralph said inspiration came from listening to the band at the fifth festival, 'watching the sun go down and the colours in the field changing from green and brown to red and gold'. The story of the battle is told from the viewpoint of a local, William Timms, who sees the clash from a hidden position after accidentally injuring himself. McTell claimed to have invented the name – there is no W. Timms in the Cropredy churchyard – but the similar name Timmins appears in Flora Thompson's trilogy *Lark Rise To Candleford*, which was made into two plays at London's National Theatre with music by The Albion Band.

'Red And Gold' is a stately epic ballad, opening with a stirring chorus that cleverly uses colour comparisons to make its point – red and gold for the wealth and power of the ruling classes but also red for the blood that was spilt and gold for the fields of harvested wheat. Meanwhile, green and brown are 'peasant colours' but also represent the brown earth and the green of the corn when it's growing. McTell creates evocative images of weeping willows overhanging the Cherwell flowing through the Oxfordshire landscape, contrasting the peace of nature with the blood-lust of mankind. Fairport perform it with reverence and respect, alternating sombre, acoustic-guitar-led moments with the power of the full band, and Simon does it justice, singing with passion and commitment. No wonder this has become one of the growing list of Fairport classics – and probably can only be truly appreciated while sitting in a field at Cropredy while the sun is setting.

'The Beggar's Song' (Trad arr Allcock)

The only traditional song on the album is a jolly singalong proposing the controversial premise that being a beggar is a happy pursuit so long as one is suitably inebriated.Maartin's irony-free arrangement opens with sprightly mandolin and fiddle before the band take a verse each and then join together for the beer-spilling chorus. Its three and a half minutes pass pleasantly enough but, like 'Three Drunken Maidens' from *Tipplers Tales*, it's too straightforward a rendition to make much of an impact.

'The Battle' (Ric Sanders)

Like the title track from *Expletive Delighted!* this is a short interlude from Ric playing a fast fiddle tune in 5/4 (rapidly becoming Fairport's favourite time signature) with heavy drums accompaniment that ends with stabs of dramatic strings that could have come from the soundtrack of an action movie. But surely this would have worked better just before or after 'Red And Gold'?

'Dark Eyed Molly' (Archie Fisher)

Scottish folk singer Archie Macdonald Fisher famously didn't like what Fairport did to his gentle ballad, first released on his 1976 album *The Man With A Rhyme*. It's difficult to see why as it follows the lyrics and tune most faithfully, replacing the original finger-picked acoustic guitar accompaniment with the full band treatment. Perhaps he didn't like the Jethro Tull-inspired keyboard intro – and to be honest neither do I as it sounds clunky and bit, erm, Casio, if you get my meaning. But for the rest of the time, Fairport provide a sensitive, sometimes moving, account of this tale of a man drowning his sorrows in drink as he thinks of his unrequited love for the titular lady. Fisher was an elder statesman of the folk scene, born in Edinburgh in 1939 (and, at the time of writing, still with us). Dave Swarbrick would have known him, and by the time Fairport recorded *Red & Gold* he was hosting a folk programme on BBC Radio Scotland. Archie's live act included 'All Around My Hat', later to become a big hit for Steeleye Span.

'The Rose Hip' (Ric Sanders)

A pretty fiddle tune inspired by the blind Irish harpist Turlough O'Carolan. Gently-picked acoustic guitar opens proceedings, and Ric joins in by plucking the strings of his fiddle before settling down to a sweet, lilting melody in G major. Ric double-tracks his violin parts so was never able to perform this live as on the record until fellow fiddler Chris Leslie joined the band. Like O'Carolan's music, it contains melody lines that climb up and down as if walking the hills of Ireland.

'London River' (Rod Shearman)

Folk singer Rod was in the Merchant Navy in the 1950s so many of the dozens of songs he penned have a salty, seafaring theme. The simple but affecting lyrics tell of his joy at returning to the Thames after time spent in other parts of the globe drinking rum and avoiding the attentions of affectionate seamen. Fairport perform it in the spirit in which it is no doubt intended, as an upbeat, rumbustious shanty-style singalong, with Maartin taking an accordion solo during the instrumental verse.

'Summer Before The War' (Huw Williams)

I saw guitarist Huw and his bass-playing brother Tony support Fairport on tour around the time *Red & Gold* was released and bought two of their CDs on the strength of their performance! Huw writes thoughtful, bitter-sweet songs with simple but affecting melodies, many of them set in or around the Second World War. Simon Nicol covered 'Rosemary's Sister' – about a young girl killed in the Blitz – on his 1987 solo album *Before Your Time* and 'Summer Before The War' is in a similar style, a gentle ballad led by finger-picked acoustic guitar evoking memories of warm, innocent summers but with the dark clouds of conflict on the horizon. Simon's direct, naive vocals are perfect for songs like this, letting the lyrics do the talking as the band provide a subdued waltz-time backing. Along with the title track, 'Summer Before The War' is one of the highlights of *Red & Gold*.

'Open The Door, Richard' (Bob Dylan)

This is the first Dylan song to appear on a Fairport studio album since they filled up *Unhalfbricking* with no fewer than three of his compositions back in 1969. Like one of those cuts, 'Million Dollar Bash', it comes from *The Basement Tapes*, a collection of unreleased demos recorded around 1967 that circulated as bootlegs before getting an official release in 1975. On Dylan's album, the song is titled 'Open The Door, Homer' but he clearly sings 'Richard' and it has been suggested that 'Homer' was a nickname for American folk singer and poet Richard Farina, who died aged just 29 in a motoring accident in 1966. The title may also have been inspired by a 1947 song of the same name recorded by saxophonist Jack McVea. The lyrics don't help much – they mention Jim, Mouse and Mick, whoever they are, and seem more concerned with playing little linguistic tricks rather than saying anything profound.

Melodically, Dylan is all over the place, so Fairport take inspiration from Thunderclap Newman, who recorded a much slower version in 1969 but pinned the melody down. I'm going to be controversial here and suggest that most Dylan songs are better performed by anyone other than Bob Dylan, and Fairport do a fine job creating a swinging, uptempo version that polishes up the original as much as they can. But it could never be described as classic Dylan and is a slightly obscure way for Fairport to end the original *Red & Gold* album.

1995 Bonus Track
'Close To The Wind' (Stuart Marson)

The 1995 HTD Records release of *Red & Gold* contains this bonus track, recorded live at the Cropredy festival in 1994 and included for no apparent reason – Fairport played 'Red And Gold' as part of their festival set, surely a more appropriate choice. In any event, this doesn't improve on the original studio recording release on *In Real Time: Live 1987* (which you will know, if you read the preceding chapter, wasn't live at all) – Simon's voice is too distant, and the drums are too loud and busy.

The Five Seasons (1990)

Personnel:
Simon Nicol: vocals, acoustic guitar, 12-string guitar
Maartin Allcock: accordion, acoustic 6 and 12 string guitars, backing vocals, piano, banjo, bodhran rim, electric guitar, mandolin, string synthesizer, double bass
Ric Sanders: violin
Dave Pegg: bass, mandola, vocals, double bass, mandolin,
Dave Mattacks: drums, organ, keyboards, percussion, clavinet, bass synthesizer
Recorded at Woodworm Studios, Barford St Michael, Oxfordshire
Engineered by Tim Matyear
Mixed by Barry Hammond with Simon Nicol and Dave Mattacks
Record label: Rough Trade
Released: December 1990
Highest chart position: Uncharted
Length: 49:02
Current edition: 2001 Talking Elephant re-issue with bonus track

A fourth album from the same Fairport Convention line-up? Unheard of! Until now, of course. Even though Maartin Allcock kept inserting, then removing, then inserting again an additional 'a' into his first name, this is the same line-up that gave us *Expletive Delighted!*, *In Real Time: Live 1987* and *Red & Gold*. Sadly, the band is a little disparaging about this release, and some reviewers suggested the musicianship was let down by a poor selection of material.

True, 'Claudy Banks' is long and a bit dull, 'All Your Beauty' a forgettable mock-country song and there's one too many Dave Whetstone compositions (two too many on the 2001 re-issue). But there are some fabulous instrumentals, a slice of jolly trad fun in 'The Card Song' and an absolutely gorgeous rendition of Peter Blegvad's 'Gold'. And there's 'The Wounded Whale', a brilliantly put-together slice of progressive folk-rock which, for an old proggie like me, is one of the most ambitious things they've done.

The album title seems to be a reference to The Four Seasons and the cover a re-enactment of the sort of poses Frankie Valli and the Four Seasons would create on the front of their LPs. It was the second and last Fairport album on the Rough Trade label.

'Claudy Banks' (Trad arr Fairport)

A sailor returns home in disguise to test the fidelity of his true love, going so far as to suggest he's dead in order to gauge her reaction. It's a story that goes back to Homer's Odyssey and features in many traditional folk songs. It's been suggested 'Claudy Banks' (or 'The Banks of Claudy') comes from Northern Ireland – there is a village called Claudy in Co Londonderry and it does indeed have some banks as it lies in a valley where the river Faughan joins the Glenrandal. But it's also been argued the most likely location is Caldy on the banks of the River Dee in Cheshire.

Geographical arguments aside, this is a hugely popular traditional song first collected by Vaughan Williams in around 1908 and recorded by many folk artists including George 'Pop' Maynard, The Copper Family and The Young Tradition. The Fairport connection is probably the version performed by Shirley Collins and The Albion Country Band on the 1971 album *No Roses* – the tempo and melody line are very similar. Fairport perform it as a straight-ahead 4/4 rock number, attempting to create interest out of the repetitive verses by changing the instrumentation from strummed and picked acoustic guitars to accordion and organ. The problem is, it does go on a bit, even with a key change for the instrumental section. Simon does his best, vocally, to put a bit of passion into the thing, but the song as a whole fails to really take off and, at nearly six minutes, is a bit too long for an opening number.

'All Your Beauty' (Barry Lowe, Martin White)

Put them together and do you get Barry White? Well, not exactly... Barry Lowe was a songwriter from the New Forest who once appeared on a 1990s reality TV series called *The Village* in which he helped Dave the Plumber get a record deal. 'All Your Beauty' is a corny country song about a cheatin' woman that's horribly cliché-ridden both musically and lyrically. Thankfully, Fairport appear to perform it with their tongue in their cheek and, at 2:55, it's mercifully short.

'Cup Of Tea!/A Loaf Of Bread/Miss Monahan's' (1 & 2 Martin Allcock, 3 trad arr Martin Allcock)

Three tunes written and arranged by Maart that seem to channel his inner Jimmy Shand, the former miner turned button accordionist whose music epitomises Scottish country dancing. 'Cup Of Tea!' is a fast but stately reel in D major with Maart on piano and accordion. Then there's a minor key interlude with Peggy and Ric playing intricate mandolin and fiddle before Fairport go into 'Miss Monahan's' (usually spelt Monaghan's), an Irish reel commonly played on the tin whistle. The three tunes together actually sound more folk than rock, especially with DM's very traditional drumming, but it is a fun three-minute instrumental.

'Gold' (Peter Blegvad)

Prog rock fans like myself know Mr Blegvad as a founding member of Slapp Happy, the avant-garde pop group that briefly merged with Henry Cow in the 1970s, so to find him on a Fairport album is quite a surprise. But maybe not – dig deeper into his catalogue, and you find songs like this, sheer poetry set to exquisite melodies and frequently performed with just acoustic guitar accompaniment.

Blegvad's version of this came out in the same year as Fairport's, and I'm not entirely sure which one is the best. Fairport's performance certainly irons out the idiosyncratic wrinkles and, in that respect, enables the listener to concentrate on the story. A gold miner and his woman set out to find the elusive yellow metal – they are trapped in the snow and she is struck by a fever in a prospector's shack. In the end, the gold that they'd found 'would not crown a tooth'. But it's more a rumination on the nature of what constitutes value in our topsy-turvy world. As the lyrics say 'If gold could be found lying round everywhere it'd be the lowliest of metals, too soft for serious use'. It would be worthless if it didn't require 'such heartbreak to seek, to find it and mine it'.

Fairport open with Simon's voice over solo piano played by Maart in D major. Then there's a pause before the entire band comes in on A minor – the melody lines of the five verses are pretty much the same, but the chords shift about beneath, with copious use of heart-wrenching major sevenths. Simon's vocals are lovely, with excellent harmonic support from Peggy and Maart, unobtrusive organ from DM and sensitive violin bowing and plucking from Ric. One of the two standout tracks on an otherwise undistinguished album.

'Rhythm Of The Time' (Dave Whetstone)

The best Whetstone song Fairport have covered, an atmospheric and evocative tune that conjures up images of workmen with their scythes harvesting the wheat in the early morning with a whistle on their lips. The song itself has a gentle, swinging motion to it – you can almost feel the scythe heavy in your hands as it swishes back and forth. It's an idealised image, of course – Whetstone says 'there was in the beginning and there will always be a whistle on the breeze in the morning', but these days it's more likely to be sound of a diesel engine. It's a bit on the long side – you think it's finished at 5:12, but no, there's another 40 seconds to go.

'The Card Song/Shuffle The Pack' (Trad arr Fairport/Ric Sanders)

A chug-a-lugging drinking song that dates back to the 1850s and was popular among soldiers in India. Ewan McColl and Peggy Seeger recorded it, as did the Ian Campbell Folk Group (but after Swarb's departure and before Dave Pegg's arrival). The verses start with the king and then work their way down the pack before ending with the ace. The fun of the song would be trying to remember which card comes next while becoming increasingly inebriated.

The chorus is usually sung as 'Here's to you, Tom Brown' but in practice, singers would nominate the next person to take a verse, who would then be expected to drain their glass halfway through. Fairport's version name-checks friends of the band including Ralph May, the real name of Ralph McTell; Jonah Jones, who was Fairport's manager for many years; and Neil Cutts, former landlord of the White Bear in Masham, Yorkshire. Fairport's version is a jolly romp, ending with a jig penned by Ric and featuring, if you listen carefully, sampled quotes from a T-shirt seller Maart met during a tour with Jethro Tull.

'Mock Morris '90 (The Green Man/The Cropredy Badger/Molly On The Jetty)' (Ric Sanders)

Well, it starts like a morris tune. But Ric throws in some tricky time signatures guaranteed to put a knot in your hankie and tangle your bells, then Maart plays heavy rock power chords, so it's more like morris meets Black Sabbath. By the end, Metal Maart has pretty much taken over, and the whole thing ends in a cacophony. It's fun, it's furious, and it's unlike any morris dance tune you've ever heard.

'Sock in It' (Dave Whetstone)

Another of Whetstone's rather pedestrian and forgettable rock numbers that Fairport insist on doing. It powers along, the chorus of 'put a sock in it for me' is mildly amusing and the bass synthesizer gives it a bit of a funky backing. But, ultimately, this is a meaningless, throwaway bit of fluff that is really beneath this band.

'Ginnie' (Huw Williams)

Another gentle little bitter-sweet number from Huw Williams about a young lady who, well, is not always quite with us all the time – 'locked up in that little world of her own'. But sometimes, when the music is right and people are singing the old songs, she will suddenly come to life and 'dance the jig tonight'. As usual with Huw, it tugs at your heartstrings just as much as it vibrates your cochlear and is a reminder of how music can reach people when all other methods of communication fail. Simon sings with finger-picked acoustic guitar backing, with the rest of the band giving it a bit of swing.

'The Wounded Whale' (Archie Fisher)

Archie wasn't happy with what Fairport did with his 'Dark Eyed Molly' on *Red & Gold*. Was he happier with their treatment of 'The Wounded Whale'? This is a nearly seven-minute epic from the band, who take a 10-verse traditional song about the capture of a mighty leviathan and turn it into a prog-rock tour de force. Archie sang this on the same 1976 album that gave Fairport 'Dark Eyed Molly' and he appears to have collated it from two versions taken from the logs of the nineteenth-century whaling ships Maria and the Uncas, reproduced in Gale Huntington's book *Songs The Whalemen Sang*. The lyrics are truly evocative and moving, depicting the whale 'high, wide and swimming, great flukes gently driving, stately and slowly he sinks in the main'. But this isn't just a tribute to the power and majesty of the whale, it also lauds the bravery and strength of the whalers: 'Now row hearties row for the pride of your nation, spring to your oars, let the reeking blood flow.' And, finally, there is the kill: 'Watch him as he dies, see the blue signal flies, here he goes "fin out", and the contest is o'er.'

Fairport's version opens with a string synthesizer fading in a long, low major chord as Simon sings the first verse, then the band crashes in on the lines 'a whale there she blows' with heavy drums, bass and electric guitars on the Metal Maart setting. The song drives forward like a boat propelled through the sea by a double line of oars before a more reflective section over acoustic guitar chords. Then we're back to the band treatment as cetacean and homo sapien meet in mortal combat.

The song ends with lovely, moving strings playing a repetitive, rising phrase as Maart wrenches wailing – even whaling – lines from his lead guitar, like cries of pain. What a powerful finish to an album.

2001 Bonus Track
'Caught A Whisper [Live]' (Dave Whetstone)
A bonus track on the Talking Elephant re-issue, it's the third Dave Whetstone song, making him and Bob Dylan the only composers outside the band to ever have three tracks on a Fairport album. Like 'Close To The Wind' on *Red & Gold* it comes from the 1994 Cropredy festival – unlike that track it was never recorded for a Fairport album. Instead, you'll find it on Simon Nicol's 1987 solo release *Before Your Time*. Apart from its slight reggae rhythm, there is not a lot about the song to stick in the mind and it has clearly been included simply to promote the festival.

Jewel in The Crown (1995)

Personnel:
Simon Nicol: vocals, acoustic guitars, 12-string electric guitars
Maartin Allcock: electric guitars, backing vocals, bouzar, accordion, tambourine, bodhran, acoustic guitars, talking drum, triangle, mandola, fretless bass, keyboard strings, tinkly bits, keyboard woodwind, electric piano, lap steel guitar, pub piano
Ric Sanders: violin
Dave Pegg: bass, backing vocals, mandolin, acoustic bass, fretless bass, electric guitar
Dave Mattacks: drums, percussion, organ, glockenspiel, crotales, electric piano
Recorded at Woodworm Studios, Barford St Michael, Oxfordshire
Engineered by Mark Tucker and Tim Matyear
Mixed by Mark Tucker, assisted by Fairport, except 'Jewel In The Crown', 'Diamonds And Gold', 'The Naked Highwayman', 'The islands', 'Red Tide' and 'Closing Time' mixed by Gus Dudgeon and Tim Matyear.
Produced by Fairport Convention.
Executive producer: Dave Pegg
Record label: Woodworm
Released: 9 January 1995
Highest chart position: 86 (UK)
Length: 60:36
Current edition: 2004 Talking Elephant reissue

Five years passed since *The Five Seasons*, during which the members of Fairport Convention kept themselves busy with tours, the annual festival and their own projects. For Ric, the time was also spent recovering from an almost career-ending accident after falling through a plate glass window, cutting all the extensor tendons in his arm. It took two operations over the course of seven months to save his hand, the second one because one of the repairs snapped, and Chris Leslie stepped in for him for the 1993 Cropredy Festival.

When Fairport reconvened at the end of 1994 to record their nineteenth studio album it was with a renewed sense of purpose, leading to what is generally regarded as their best release since *Nine*. In his autobiography *Off The Pegg* the bass player says:

> There was something about making that album. We knew it was going to be a good one. It was 1995 and the year had something about it for Fairport. We were getting renewed attention in the press – there was even a big article in **Mojo**...*Jewel In The Crown* is an important album in Fairport's history for a lot of reasons. We put special care into tracking down the songs that would go into it.

The title track came from Julie Matthews, who was in The Albion Band with Simon. Ralph McTell offered 'The Islands', which he had penned for a TV series, while 'Red Tide' arrived via Beryl Marriott, who had been sent the song for her considered opinion. Nigel Schofield, a long-time friend of the band and Dave Pegg's co-author, brought to their attention 'Slipjigs And Reels' and 'The Naked Highwayman' from the Steve Tilston and Maggie Boyle album *Of Moor And Mesa* (1992). There were original tunes from Maart and Ric and a closing number – appropriately called 'Closing Time' – by Leonard Cohen and the first of his songs to be recorded by the band since the departure of Ian Matthews.

Recording kicked off with Tim Matyear at the mixer before he quit Woodworm Records and was replaced by Mark Tucker, with famous Elton John producer Gus Dudgeon helping out on a few of the tracks. The result is a confident, assured album packed full of great songs – there are 15 tracks, over an hour of music, more than any previous Fairport album before the bonus tracks are added. There's no denying the quality of songs such as the powerful and darkly ironic title track, 'Slipjigs', Maart's 'A Surfeit of Lampreys', 'Highwayman', 'London Danny', 'Travelling By Steam' and Ric's instrumentals.

The packaging has a somewhat mixed theme. The front cover, inspired by the lyrics in the title track, shows a map of the world at the height of the British Empire when it ruled a quarter of the Earth's total land area. But the reverse is a little more light-hearted, with the tracklist displayed as if on an Indian restaurant receipt surrounded by the remains of a takeaway curry. Inside there's a picture of Maart, DM, Ric and Simon looking through the window of the Jewel In The Crown tandoori restaurant in Bridge Street, Banbury, Oxfordshire. It is, perhaps, an example of quite insensitive cultural stereotyping but the mid-90s were more naive times. Oh, and the CD carries a picture of a poppadum. Do not attempt to eat it.

'Jewel In The Crown' (Julie Matthews)

Simon was in The Albion Band with Yorkshire-born singer/songwriter Julie, and she recorded her own version of the song on her solo album *Such Is Life*, released a year later. At first sight, this is an uncomfortable glorification of the British Empire bringing 'hope and inspiration' to 'lesser nations', liberating them from their dictators, dividing everyone up into their appropriate social classes and tearing down and reshaping their borders – all for 'a small slice of your oil wells'. Of course, the song must be taken with a large bucket of searing irony, because what Julie is doing here is skewering grand old British racism, arrogance and military bullying – all done with 'God' on our side.

Fairport kick it off with aggressive acoustic guitar strumming from Simon before he launches into the first verse with gusto. Then drums, electric guitar, fiddle and bass enter sparingly before coming together for the rousing chorus – 'We are Britannia, jewel in the crown'. Vocal harmonies are strong and powerful, Ric's fiddle soars and swoops and the whole track is a classic example of what Fairport can do when they emphasise the rock over the folk (and have a damn good song to do it with).

'Slipjigs And Reels' (Steve Tilston)

The first of two excellent Tilston cuts on the album – he would be a
composer Fairport would turn to again and again for his ability to create
traditional-sounding contemporary songs with strong narratives and a sense
of humour. The Liverpool-born singer/songwriter and guitarist first recorded
this with his then-wife Maggie Boyle on their 1992 album *Of Moor And Mesa*.
It was inspired by a photograph of a 19th century immigrant to America
named Evil Murdoch who led a wayward life before being killed by Mescalero
Apaches.

In the song, he takes a ship to New York (probably from Ireland – 'slipjigs'
are a form of Irish dance music) with nothing to his name bar a 10 shilling
note sewn into the lining of his coat for safe-keeping. He mixes with some
bad people, commits a murder, gains a reputation as a cold-hearted killer
called The Kid and finally is ambushed by 'wild mescaleros' near Santa Fe.
From the subject matter, you would think this was a dark, depressing ballad
but in fact, it's a sprightly waltz that takes its inspiration from the more
optimistic chorus about his love of the ladies, gambling and, most of all, the
slipjigs and reels.

Tilston's original rendition contained a lot of clever fiddly-diddly on
acoustic guitar, but Fairport create a more simplified version, based mostly
on Simon's acoustic guitar and Ric's fiddle. Maartin adds accordion and also
some fast runs on his bouzar – a hybrid of a bouzouki with a guitar body
made for him by Stefan Sobell of Hexham. The song swings and sways rather
like a dance and there are great vocals in the choruses. A class number, this
one.

'A Surfeit Of Lampreys' (Maartin Allcock)

You have to hand it to Maart – not only can he play most instruments human
hand has fashioned, but he has a particular way with titles. As he said, you
have to call these tunes something to tell them apart. This is a jig that starts
with Peggy slapping and plucking his bass before Maart plays a fiddly little
tune in D minor on his bouzar (although he keeps ending up in B minor,
which is a nice little transition that helps add a bit of interest to the tune).
Later, Maart wrenches some lead lines out of his electric guitar on top of
Ric's fiddle. The title comes from the death of Henry I, 4th son of William
the Conqueror, who succumbed to dysentery in 1135 after eating too many
lampreys, an eel-like, bottom-feeding fish considered a delicacy in the Middle
Ages.

'Kind Fortune' (Trad arr Fairport Convention)

One of two traditional songs on the album, this came to Fairport through
close study of *Folk Songs From Newfoundland*, a book by Maud Karpeles.
Maart said: 'This song must be almost unique in folk music. There are very
few songs of any type that I know of where the drummer gets laid, but here

Above: The first Fairport Convention line-up (or second if you include Shaun Frater's single gig on drums) with Martin Lamble, Richard Thompson, Ashley Hutchings, Judy Dyble, Simon Nicol and Ian Mac-Donald. *(Polydor)*

Right: The wonderful Sandy Denny, who replaced Judy Dyble in the band in May 1968. *(Island Records)*

Left: That mysterious and eclectic first album – 'for an insignificant minority of seekers'. *(Polydor)*

Right: *What We Did On Our Holidays*, the stunning second album that included future classics 'Fotheringay' and 'Meet On The Ledge'. *(Island Records)*

Left: The band can barely be seen in the background of the cover of *Unhalfbricking*, shot in the garden of Sandy Denny's parents. It lent an air of mystery to the album, which shows the first flourishing of Fairport's folk-rock leanings in 'A Sailor's Life' and includes Sandy's classic 'Who Knows Where The Time Goes?' *(Island Records)*

Right: From tragedy to triumph... the band's classic fourth album that gave birth to British folk-rock while allowing Richard Thompson to blossom as a powerful, original songwriter. *(Island Records)*

Left: Goodbye Ashley and Sandy...but hello Dave Pegg on bass as Fairport release *Full House* in 1970. Later versions restored Thompson's 'Poor Will And The Jolly Hangman'. *(Island Records)*

Right: Fairport's highest-charting album in the UK (so far!), *Angel Delight* was the first release without guitarist Richard Thompson. The wreck of a building on the cover is NOT the Angel pub in Little Hadham – it was never that bad. *(Island Records)*

Right: A press report of the tragic van crash that killed drummer Martin Lamble and Jeannie 'The Tailor' Franklyn.

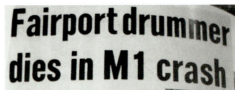

Fairport drummer dies in M1 crash

FAIRPORT CON-VENTION drummer Martin Lamble, and an American girl known as Jeanie The Tailor were killed when the group's van overturned and crashed on the M1 at Mill Hill on Monday morning.

The group were on the way back to London after a gig at Mother's Club in Birmingham.

Martin (19) and Jeanie, whose real name was Franklin, girl friend of Fairport guitarist Richard Thompson, both died instantly. Group members Thompson, Simon Nicol and Tiger Hutchins were all taken to hospital in Stanmore with cuts and bruises. Richard suffered cracked...

LAMBLE
died instantly

the death crash.

'WO KILLED IN M1 MINI-BUS CRASH

...year-old girl was killed and a youth man died of ... injuries when a mini-bus ... a pop group careered ... the M1 and overturned at ... Hill today.

... other youths were in... two of them seriously. ... her vehicle was involved ... man who died was a mem... able ...

Fairport Convention pop gro... of Hadrod Road, Harrow. After died in multiple ... after doctors had ... two hours to ... The girl to ... Jean...

Left & Below: The band on Top Of The Pops, miming to their single 'Si Tu Dois Partir', with Dave Mattacks not entirely sure what he's doing on washboard.
(BBC, Island Records)

Above: The *Liege And Lief* line-up with Dave Swarbrick. Sadly, a break-up was just around the corner. *(Island Records)*

Below: The band in 1969 before their Top Of The Pops appearance, looking suitably moody in the BBC dressing room. *(Island Records)*

Left: The first folk-rock opera? Fairport's concept album *"Babbacombe" Lee* failed to make any impact when it was released in 1971 but has grown in stature since. *(Island Records)*

Right: Fairport members came and went in the months leading up to the release for Fairport's patchy 1973 album *Rosie*, which contains some of Dave Swarbrick's best - and worst - work. *(Island Records)*

Left: The simple but striking cover of *Nine*, Fairport's 1973 album. *(Island Records)*

Right: And then there were four... Richard quits, leaving the remaining quartet to record *Angel Delight* and *"Babbacombe" Lee*. *(Island Records)*

Left: The 1973 line-up with Trevor Lucas and Jerry Donahue pose outside The Brasenose pub in Cropredy on the back cover of *Nine*, a welcome return to form. *(Island Records)*

Right: Well, it was a good idea at the time... Sandy rejoins Fairport for 1975's *Rising For The Moon* as Island Records make one last attempt to propel the band into the big time. But, sadly, it failed to rise... *(Island Records)*

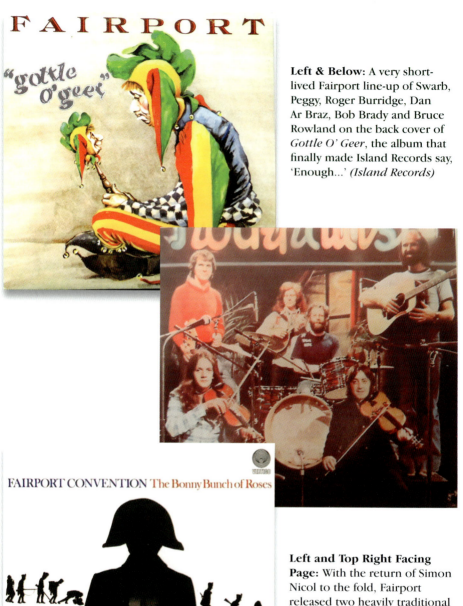

Left & Below: A very short-lived Fairport line-up of Swarb, Peggy, Roger Burridge, Dan Ar Braz, Bob Brady and Bruce Rowland on the back cover of *Gottle O' Geer*, the album that finally made Island Records say, 'Enough…' *(Island Records)*

Left and Top Right Facing Page: With the return of Simon Nicol to the fold, Fairport released two heavily traditional albums in the late 1970s, *The Bonny Bunch of Roses* and *Tipplers Tales*, later available as a single, tuneful CD package. *(Vertigo)*

FAIRPORT CONVENTION

FAIRPORT CONVENTION

Gladys' Leap

Left: *Gladys' Leap*, the 1985 comeback album, saw Dave Mattacks rejoin the band but Ric Sanders replacing Dave Swarbrick on violin. *(Woodworm Records)*

Right: No talking at the back! The band is gagged for 1986's all-instrumental *Expletive Delighted!*, despite a sticker on the cover cheekily claiming a lyric sheet was included. *(Woodworm Records)*.

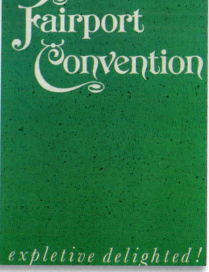

Fairport Convention

expletive delighted!

FAIRPORT CONVENTION

"In Real Time"

Live '87

Left: 1988's *In Real Time* included shots of the band at Cropredy to give the impression the album was live. But it's all lies! *(Island Records)*

Right: The Battle of Cropredy Bridge (29 June 1644, history fans!) is depicted in the striking artwork for 1988's *Red & Gold*. *(Woodworm Records)*

Fairport Convention

RED
&

Includes Bonus Track

Fairport Convention THE FIVE SEASONS

Left: The 1986 *Five Seasons* Fairport line-up, with Ric and Martin Allcock, lasted ten years and six albums. They were a band once again. *(New Routes)*

Right: The highpoint of the Martin Allcock years, 1995's *Jewel In The Crown*. *(Woodworm Records)*

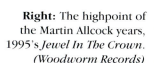

Left: When Dave's away the band still play… An acoustic gig in Banbury provided the bulk of the material for the excellent *Old New Borrowed Blue* (1996). *(Woodworm Records)*

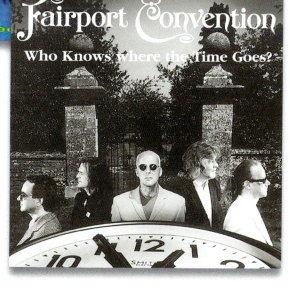

Right: Named after the evergreen Sandy Denny song, Fairport's 30th-anniversary album was the first with new boy Chris Leslie - and the last with old boy Dave Mattacks. *(Woodworm Records)*

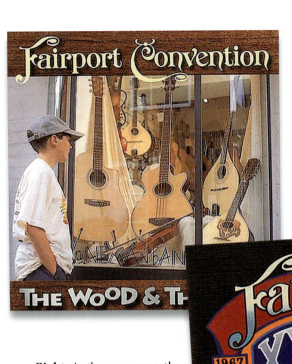

Left: Chris Leslie's son Sam gazes wistfully through the window of a Banbury music shop on the cover of 1999's *The Wood And The Wire*. *(Woodworm Records)*

Right: As the cover says, the 35th-anniversary album was, appropriately enough, *XXXV*. Chug-a-lug! *(Woodworm Records)*

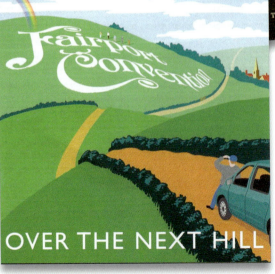

Left: Fairport's almost non-stop touring is commemorated in the title of 2004's *Over The Next Hill*, the band's first album on a new record label. *(Matty Grooves Records)*

Right: The band share a 40th birthday feast on the cover of 2007's *Sense Of Occasion*. *(Matty Grooves Records)*

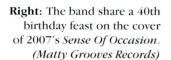

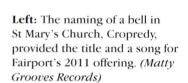

Left: The naming of a bell in St Mary's Church, Cropredy, provided the title and a song for Fairport's 2011 offering. *(Matty Grooves Records)*

Right: Forty-five years after their first tentative steps, Fairport put together a re-recorded 'greatest hits' package, cunningly disguised as a 45rpm single (look them up on Wikipedia, you young people). *(Matty Grooves Records)*

Left: Who could replace talented multi-instrumentalist, Martin Allcock? Step forward talented multi-instrumentalist Chris Leslie. *(Matty Grooves Records)*

Below: Fairport at Cropredy, the annual festival that now draws more than 20,000 to the little Oxfordshire village. *(Matty Grooves Records)*

Top: After 50 years on the road, nothing beats a good sit-down. *(Matty Grooves Records)*

Above: The band on stage in Belfast during their 2019 acoustic tour. *(Kevan Furbank)*

Right: The current Fairport line-up (although that could always change!): Gerry Conway, Ric Sanders, Chris Leslie, Simon Nicol and Dave Pegg. *(Matty Grooves)*

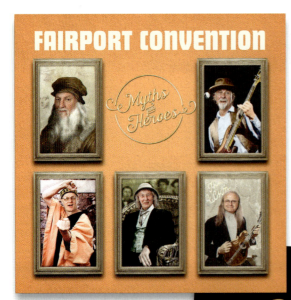

Left: The cover of 2015's *Myths & Heroes* mimicked the band's 1970 album *Full House*, but with the members appearing as their personal heroes. *(Matty Grooves Records)*

Right: Fairport go back to the *Nine* cover for inspiration as they release their 50th-anniversary collection in 2017. *(Matty Grooves Records)*

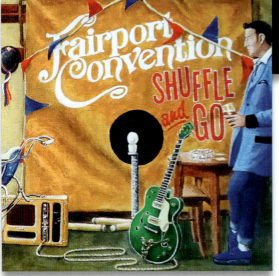

Left: Fairport hit their 30th... album, that is. Mick Toole painted the cover of *Shuffle And Go*, released in 2020. *(Matty Grooves Records)*

at least he has to threaten suicide to get his own way.' Yes, a simple tale of a regiment's drummer who spies a comely young maiden and tries his luck only to find she is the daughter of a captain and considers him far beneath her. He threatens to kill himself, which does the trick and they saddle a horse and head off to Plymouth to get married. As you can guess by the geography, this clearly didn't originate in Newfoundland. The tale is told over a cheerful jig with the last line repetition of 'and it's oh, kind fortune'. Simon sometimes has trouble fitting all the words into the line (and we haven't even got to 'The Naked Highwayman' yet), but the result is a charming and pretty little song.

'Diamonds And Gold' (Ben Bennion, Maartin Allcock)

At the time of writing, Bennion is a member of a country-blues-rock band called Freeway Jam and a close friend of Dave Pegg. He and Maart penned this rather depressing song about a young girl with dreams of wealth who ends up a drug-addled centrefold. DM's organ chords give it a funereal feel, exacerbated by the funeral march pace of the song. It's not my favourite track on the album as it recycles well-worn power ballad chord sequences, coming to life only through the dramatic middle-eight. It's one of the songs mixed by Dudgeon and Tucker, and it has an open, powerful sound in which every instrument feels separated. But it's also one of the tracks that could have been left in the vaults.

'The Naked Highwayman' (Steve Tilston)

A mock traditional song by the already-mentioned Mr Tilston about a highwayman meeting his match in a deceitful woman who strips him naked, steals his pistols and then holds up the coach from Bristol to London. There were female highway, er, persons back in the day, most notably Lady Katherine Ferrers, a young orphaned heiress who turned to a life of crime with her lover after being forced into a marriage of convenience. Very few went around stealing other criminals' clothes, however, and this begs the question of what she did with her own apparel. Perhaps The Cross-Dressing Highwayman could be a good follow-up...

Anyway, what's notable about this particular composition is the sheer breakneck speed at which the lyrics have to be sung – even the chorus is ridiculously fast. Fairport once tried to get the audience to sing along at Cropredy by putting the lyrics up on the big screens like some giant karaoke. According to Peggy, people were keeling over through lack of breath. A mostly acoustic number, it powers through its nine verses like a runaway train – apparently, it was even longer before Gus Dudgeon took some scissors to it – with some short instrumental interludes featuring Ric. At the end, the shivering naked highwayman vows never to rob again, so some good came out of it. All together now: 'All you roving fellows, listen while you can, of the time that I became the naked highwayman.' Excuse me; I feel faint...

'The Islands' (Ralph McTell, Maartin Allcock)

Ralph and Maart wrote this for the soundtrack of BBC TV series *World Tour of Scotland* with Billy Connolly. Inspiration came from the grounding of the oil tanker Braer in 1993, when a massive spillage threatened to cause havoc. But the sea dispersed the oil, protecting the islands from harm. The song compares the arrival of the Braer to the coming of the Vikings to the same shores around 800AD, and how the islands soaked up their language and culture. So the sea protects and guards the Shetlands, while the land absorbs invaders and turns them into locals. Ralph's song is a mystical, haunting number that opens with the sound of the sea and Maart's keyboard strings, with Simon singing over acoustic guitar. To be honest, there's not much going on here melodically and it is a bit of a clunky number relying a little too much on echo and effects. Even Simon's voice begins to grate after a while and, despite some string interludes and Maart playing no fewer than seven instruments, it overstays its welcome.

'The Youngest Daughter' (Trad arr Maartin Allcock)

A short and sweet Irish reel that begins with some sequenced tinkly bits and DM on glockenspiel before Maart plays the tune ridiculously fast on acoustic guitar and then the band come in for about a minute of the sort of folk-rock instrumental madness Fairport do so well. Maart had known this tune for 15 years and, in the liner notes, dedicated it to his daughter Jane, born in November 1993.

'London Danny' (Jez Lowe)

Jez is a songwriter and novelist who has worked with Archie Fisher and Steve Tilston, among others, so they can all sit down and discuss how Fairport have treated their songs! He recorded 'London Danny' for his 1988 solo album *Bad Penny,* and it's said to be his favourite composition, even though it took him two years to write. The title refers to a bit of a Flash Harry, a fellow with money, charm and wit who's catnip to the ladies but will never settle down. One of his conquests ends up married to another man, but she still sighs in the night for the flashy rogue she lost.

The beauty of the song, and what gives it a bittersweet magic, is that it's told from the viewpoint of the husband who knows full well that his wife yearns for another – he knows he has little to offer in comparison, so he begs London Danny not to take her away from him. There are some lovely, touching lines here – all he asks is 'to let her heart beat me to sleep at night in bed'. You would think from the subject matter and the writing that this is a sad, maudlin ballad but you would be wrong – it's in D major and Fairport's version rolls along brightly with a bit of a swing to it. Simon's voice fits this style of song perfectly – it has a sense of naive yearning to it.

'Summer In December' (Ric Sanders)

Here's one of Ric's gorgeous tunes, opening with keyboard woodwind and acoustic guitar and then settling down into a gentle waltz – similar to 'The

Rose Hip' on *Red & Gold*. Ric can turn out these sort of tunes in his sleep, but they always provide a welcome interlude of peace and contemplation amid the perils and passions of a folk-rock album. Actually, this one builds up into quite the drama queen towards the end, with DM providing those loud drums some critics keep carping on about.

'Travelling By Steam' (Huw Williams)

Huw was really born after his time, as all his nostalgic songs prove. At least this one isn't about the war. Instead, we're on the right side of the footplate and travelling on a steam engine in a song originally commissioned by the BBC for a programme about railway workers. In the liner notes, Huw says: 'They asked if I had a suitable song; 'yes' I replied, before spending the rest of the day in Cwmbran Library researching the subject. Next morning I delivered the completed song!' I know nothing about steam engines so I can only assume the references to 'traps', 'Tommy-boxes' and standing in 'the bite' are accurate. It sounds good though, and the song travels along at a gentle gallop like a moderately-fast steam train through the English countryside. Simon and Ric played this as part of a duo before recording it for Fairport. Here they attach a little morris tune at the end that Ric always knew as 'Swaggering Boney' but, he discovered later, has the alternate and most serendipitous title of 'Travel By Steam'.

'She's Like The Swallow' (Trad arr Maartin Allcock)

Another traditional number dug up by Maart from the same book that gave him 'Kind Fortune'. Like that song, this originated in the British Isles before crossing the North Atlantic – versions were collected by Cecil Sharp and Ralph Vaughn Williams. Some say it is likely Irish or Scottish, others that it hails from Cornwall. In Canada, it is a popular choral song, but even the Canucks consider it English. In Fairport's hands, this is similar in tone and style to 'The Islands' – a doomy minor key, dominated by electric piano and keyboard strings with a touch of lead acoustic guitar (from Simon, unusually). It doesn't have the most attractive melody, and the backing really drags the track down – it will be one you will want to skip after a few minutes. Unusually, only Maart, Simon and DM appear on this, Peggy and Ric clearly having gone out for a curry.

'Red Tide' (Rob Beattie)

Rob Beattie is a freelance writer and a member of tribute band The Alter Eagles who was a magazine editor when he penned this song and sent it to folk pianist Beryl Marriott for her consideration. She, in turn, passed it on to Fairport (she had a long association with the band, being the one who spotted Swarb's talent in the early 1960s and steered him away from guitar to fiddle). Coming straight after 'She's Like The Swallow' and not long after 'Diamonds And Gold', this completes a trio of thoroughly depressing songs on the album.

The red tide of the title is despair and depression and, later, drunkenness, lust and, finally, death. As the author himself admits, not many laughs, really. Gloomy keyboard strings again open proceedings in E minor, then Simon sings over acoustic guitar and an ominous electronic wash of sound. The whole band doesn't come in until the second verse – Peggy's bass is deep and heavy, DM's drums as powerful as anything on the album and Maart playing rhythmic notes and then sustained lead on his electric guitar. Ric lets rip on a driving instrumental ending section in which DM's drums seem to get even louder, if that's humanly possible, before the violin echoes away into the distance. It is, without doubt, the heaviest track on the album, sort of Fairport meets Blue Oyster Cult, marred by a dreary melody and the utterly depressing subject matter.

'Home Is Where The Heart Is' (Clive Gregson)
A bit of light relief now, at last, with a relatively gentle and upbeat number about how nice it is to come home. Gregson was a member of 1980s rock band Any Trouble before working with Richard Thompson through mutual friend John Wood. This song comes from Gregson's first solo album *Strange Persuasions* with Christine Collister on vocals – he saw her singing at a Cheshire folk club and formed a musical partnership that continued through five albums. Gregson says he wrote the song in about 10 minutes on a piano in his parents' front room, although he had the title – a generally well-worn cliché – in his notebook for some years. It's an unremarkable, country-style uptempo ballad – strummed acoustic guitar and gentle violin notes lead into Simon's warm baritone on lyrics that are simple but affecting. Ric both plucks pizzicato-style and bows his violin while, strangely, it's Peggy who provides tasteful country guitar licks while Maart is busy on electric piano. The total effect is pleasant but a bit cheesy.

'Closing Time' (Leonard Cohen)
'Suzanne' and 'Bird On A Wire' were part of Fairport Convention's repertoire back in the pre-trad late 1960s, but they never got round to officially putting any Leonard Cohen songs on their albums until now. 'Closing Time' comes from the Canadian singer, songwriter, poet and novelist's ninth studio album *The Future*, released in 1992, and it's that rare thing, an uptempo, optimistic, even euphoric Cohen song. It's about the end of a wild party, the drink has been flowing, inhibitions torn down like the Berlin Wall and no-one's entirely sure if they are leaving with the same partner they came in with. The bitter-sweet lyrics are full of humour, yearning and sexual longing and the song chugs relentlessly along as if the night is never going to end.

Fairport's version actually gives the song more fight and aggression – it opens with barmaid Tracey Bullard ringing a bell and calling last orders at The George in Barford St Michael before the band thumps in with solid bass and drums. Ric plays the same three-note fiddle phrase as the original and

Simon does his best Cohen impersonation – he can't achieve the same deep, tuneless, leering growl as Cohen so the Fairport version is strangely sexless but he does a creditable job. But it certainly retains the humour and spirit of the original as Maart and Peggy provide frequently amusing backing vocals. No yearning or regret for them – just get the pints in. Chug-a-lug!

Old New Borrowed Blue (1996)

Personnel:
Simon Nicol: vocals, acoustic guitar
Dave Pegg: Vocals, acoustic bass, mandolin
Maartin Allcock: acoustic guitar, bouzar, accordion, mandocello, bodhran
Ric Sanders: violin
Recorded at Woodworm Studios, Barford St Michael, Oxfordshire
Engineered by Matt Davies
Mixed by Mark Tucker, assisted by Matt Davies
Live tracks recorded and mixed by Mark Tucker from a concert at Banbury Mill
Theatre on 30 December 1995
Produced by Fairport Convention.
Record label: Woodworm
Released: May 1996
Highest chart position: Uncharted
Length: 70:40
Current edition: 2007 Talking Elephant Records

Dave Mattacks was busy playing in the Richard Thompson band and drumming for Mary Chapin Carpenter, so the band toured the UK, the US and Australia as a four-piece under the name of Fairport Acoustic Convention. To promote the American leg, they released this half-studio, half-live hybrid featuring Simon Nicol, Dave Pegg, Maartin Allcock and Ric Sanders unplugged (the Australian tour was known as 'Unplugged & Half-Cocked'). The result is an overlooked little gem, an unpretentious album brimming with great songs, absolutely brilliant ensemble musicianship and a rich sense of humour. Seven of the sixteen tracks are studio renditions with a surprisingly high number of band-penned compositions, while three of the live numbers recorded at a Christmas concert in Banbury are new to the repertoire. There are instrumentals from Ric, Peggy and Maart, plus a song with lyrics an' all from Mr Allcock and Chris Leslie, a future Fairport member.

The acoustic line-up allowed the band to play smaller venues and more intimate gigs. I recall seeing them at the Red Lion in Birmingham when Maart played stonking slide guitar during 'Matty Groves' by sinking his pint and then stuffing the empty glass on to his left hand to stroke up and down the strings. In fact, so successful was the drumless experiment that the band decided to do an acoustic tour every May, as well as open the Cropredy festival on a Thursday evening.

The album was both a first and last – the first acoustic collection by a band that had been led down a pretty rock road by Maart but also the last to feature him as he quit soon after. Luckily, there was someone waiting in the wings to take over...

'Woodworm Swing' (Ric Sanders)
A jazzy opening from Mr Sanders as he takes inspiration from the Hot Club de France for a fast and furious number paying tribute to the guitar and

violin attack of Django Reinhardt and Stephane Grappelli. Similar to Peggy's 'Bankruptured', Ric and Maart play fiddle and mandocello in unison over chopping chords from Simon and DP's walking bass before everyone except Simon gets a chance to take a little bit of the improvisational limelight. Fast, fun and played to perfection.

'Men' (Loudon Wainwright III)

Fairport learned this from the US songwriter and folk singer's 1992 album *History*, an album about the death of his writer father. To modern ears, this is a bit of an anti-feminist whinge about how men have to fight the wars, provide for their family and go down with the sinking ships. 'Have pity on the general, the king and the captain,' whines Mr Wainwright, 'they know they're expendable, after all, they're men.' There is some belated recognition that perhaps the world wouldn't be so full of horrors if men didn't have the power and every man didn't think he's right. But there are undoubtedly some readers who, upon listening to this maudlin, self-pitying ballad, will have little sympathy with his sentiments. Fairport's version is a little slower than Loudon's original but more instrumentally dense with strong vocals from Simon.

'Aunt Sally Shuffle' (Dave Pegg)

A double act from Simon on acoustic guitar and Peggy on mandolin on a short but sweet tune in which DP runs up and down his instrument's fretboard over the unusual chord sequence of B flat and A major. It's very closely related to 'Peggy's Pub' and 'The Swirling Pit'.

'There Once Was Love/Innstuck' (Paul Metsers/Maartin Allcock)

Originally from New Zealand, Metsers was active in the English folk scene for about 20 years before deciding to give up touring and playing in public to start his own wooden board game manufacturing company! Well, a fellow's got to earn a living... 'There Once Was Love' is a sprightly, bluegrassy ballad in 6/8 (with one or two interesting rhythmic hiccups) with a catchy chorus and a very interesting middle eight that slips into a different key and allows the band to beef up their harmonies on the soaring line 'empty tracks and the driving rain'. It segues rather effortlessly into Maartin Allcock's 5/4 instrumental first exposed to the public on *Expletive Delighted!*

'Frozen Man' (James Taylor)

This is, to my knowledge, the only folk song about cryogenics, inspired by a picture Taylor once saw of the frozen body of John Torrington, a Leading Stoker on Captain Sir John Franklin's ill-fated 1845 Arctic voyage to find the Northwest Passage. Taken from Taylor's 1991 album *New Moon Shine*, it tells the rather sad (but totally fictitious) story of nineteenth-century sailor William James McPhee, whose frozen body is brought back to life in the modern age.

But the process has not been entirely perfected – in fact, so bodged is the job that children cry when they see his ravaged face. There's a particularly touching verse in which he visits the graves of his wife and daughter to find they both died of extreme old age. 'Lord, have mercy on the frozen man,' sang James Taylor, adding: 'When I die, make sure I'm gone.' Fairport do a fine job, keeping fairly close the original but more clearly delineating some of the instrumental touches with fiddle and bouzar, giving the ballad a bit more body and drama. James Taylor, of course, needs no introduction – the only surprise is that Fairport have never before drawn from his extensive back catalogue of fine compositions.

'Mr Sands Is In The Building' (Maartin Allcock)
Maart wrote this after buying an Ovation mandocello in New York and wanting to show it off on the album. The result is a funky, tricky little jazzy, sometimes folky, tune with snapping fingers and bodhran carrying the rhythm. There are supposed to be references to two pop songs here, but damned if I can hear them! What I can hear are frequent references to the opening of the old British blues band standard 'Cat's Squirrel'. According to the liner notes, Maart wanted to call the tune 'F*** Off!' but Peggy thought it wouldn't get much airplay. He settled on a title that's used in theatres and the London Underground as a coded reference to a fire or bomb alert, because 'Sands' would be used to put a blaze out.

'Lalla Rookh' (Chris Leslie. Maartin Allcock)
I first heard this as an instrumental on a compilation album called *Master Craftsman*, dedicated to Coventry guitar-maker Rob Armstrong. At that point, it was called 'Our Ship Is Sailing' and was written by Maart while on tour with Jethro Tull. He asked Chris Leslie to provide some words, which led to this stirring ballad about the figurehead of an old sailing ship. In the liner notes for *Old, New, Borrowed, Blue* Maart says there is a figurehead in the Cutty Sark collection at the Royal Museums in Greenwich from an 1856 ship called Lalla Rookh that used to trade between England and Shanghai. But back to the song – it's a fine, powerful ballad with strong acoustic guitar strumming from Simon and superb harmony vocals during the middle eight. 'Please think of me when I am on the deep,' they sing, 'and keep me safe within your heart.'

'Foolish You' (Wade Hamsworth)
'Spontaneously, they arrive on stage…' 'Foolish You' opens the live half of the album, a song by Canadian folk singer Albert Wade Hemsworth but probably best known from the singing of Kate and Anna McGarrigle. It's a medium-paced country-style song, lyrically ploughing a well-worn furrow – one partner has gone off to find fame and fortune, leaving some poor sap home alone. Foolish you for thinking you can find fortune, and foolish me for being left behind.

Great harmonies from Simon, Maart and Peggy and confident acoustic playing make this a strong opening number.

'Crazy Man Michael' (Thompson, Swarbrick)

This needs no introduction, being the third time it's turned up on a Fairport album. Performed by the acoustic quartet, it sounds even more like a traditional old folk song, instead of being written in 1969.

'Widow Of Westmoreland's Daughter' (Trad arr Fairport Convention)

Another Fairport standard that's already turned up a few times. On *Tipplers Tales* it was 'The Widow Of Westmorland' (no daughter, no middle 'e'). It's basically an acoustic copy of the version on *In Real Time: Live 1987*.

'Genesis Hall' (Richard Thompson)

Thompson's bitter rant at the forces of law and order gets a rare airing here – and would go on to make frequent appearances in the Fairport live repertoire. Another fine rendition from Simon on vocals, with stalwart harmony support on the emotional chorus.

'The Deserter' (Jon [probably John!] Richards)

Not to be confused with 'The Deserter' on *Liege And Lief*, this is a contemporary song by Black Country folk singer John Richards – his first name is misspelt in the liner notes – who also provided 'Honour And Praise' for *Gladys' Leap*. The traditional song, originally sung by Sandy Denny, was a bit of a humorous romp, with the titular reluctant soldier deserting, getting caught, being pardoned, deserting again and so on. However, Richards' song takes a much more sombre view of illegal pacifism, asking the listener 'don't despise the deserter who ran from the war' and giving as his reason not necessarily cowardice but his bewilderment at being sent by his government to kill someone just like him in a foreign land. Simon originally recorded this for his 1987 solo album *Before Your Time* with Sheila and Sheryl Parker on backing vocals. This performance, with vocal support from Peggy and Maart, stays faithful to his studio version, a gentle waltz-time ballad with a strong message.

'The Swimming Song' (Loudon Wainwright III)

A classic Wainwright number that first surfaced on his 1973 album *Attempted Mustache*. It's almost a nursery rhyme, sung from the point of view of a child learning how to swim for the first time. He might have drowned, he says, but 'I held my breath and I kicked my feet, and I moved my arms around'. By the end of the summer, he's swimming breaststroke, butterfly and doing swan dives. Not bad for an amateur. Fairport attack this with appropriate uptempo gusto, diving in with some deliberately out of tune strumming for comic effect before settling into the simple, repetitive chords of the sung. Sanders' violin solo is introduced with 'Here's Ricky!', while 'Here's Marty!' allows Allcock to play a guitar solo that references the riff of The Beatles' 'I Feel Fine'.

'Struck It Right' (Huw Williams)
The full title of this song is 'Struck It Right This Time', and you will find the original on Huw and Tony Williams' 1991 album *Junction Twenty-Six*, while Simon covered it for his second solo album *Consonant Please Carol*. It's an optimistic, uptempo number about the power of positive thinking. An old man digging for oil, a girl hoping for a happier year, an athlete striving to win a race, a songwriter searching for the elusive lost chord – the naysayers warn of things that can go wrong but they reply 'I don't worry, I don't mind cos I know I've struck it right this time'. Huw and Tony perform it with finger-picked acoustic guitar and stand-up bass – Fairport's version follows that performance pretty faithfully with, of course, the full acoustic band treatment, along with 'humorous' out of tune moments in the final verse.

'The Hiring Fair' (Ralph McTell, Dave Mattacks [uncredited in liner notes])
A third outing for this one, too. Shorn of its keyboard flourishes, it works just as well, helped by some sensitive bouzar solos from Maart between verses and imaginative bass runs from Peggy.

'Matty Groves/Dirty Linen' (Trad arr Fairport Convention)
A classic Fairport track that has been through so many different incarnations and still had a few more to come. After electrifying 'Matty Groves' so much it became Metal Matty, the acoustic quartet take it back to its traditional routes. This is not the version I saw them perform in Birmingham – Maart's solos on the bouzar are relatively sedate. But it livens up considerably when it launches into 'Dirty Linen' from *Full House*, with the crowd clapping along in support. It ends a short live set that shows Fairport at the top of their game, singing and playing beautifully with swing, wit and sheer jaw-dropping musicianship. But nothing stays the same...

Who Knows Where The Time Goes? (1997)

Personnel:

Simon Nicol: vocals, electric guitar, acoustic guitars

Dave Pegg: bass, backing vocals

Dave Mattacks: drums, percussion, electric piano, psaltery, organ, harpsichord, glockenspiel

Ric Sanders: violin

Chris Leslie: vocals, violin, mandolin, electric guitar, bazouki-strat

Richard Thompson: lead vocals on 'Heard It Through The Grapevine'

Maartin Allcock: keyboards on 'Heard It Through The Grapevine'

Roy Wood: guitar & brass arrangement on 'Heard It Through The Grapevine'

Sharron & Michelle Naylor: backing vocals on 'Heard It Through The Grapevine'

Sue Hughes & Helen Miller: trombone on 'Heard It Through The Grapevine'

Penny Hughes: baritone sax on 'Heard It Through The Grapevine'

Henzie Miller & Karen Blackmore: trumpet on 'Heard It Through The Grapevine'

Recorded at Woodworm Studios, Barford St Michael, Oxfordshire, except 'Heard It Through The Grapevine' at the Cropredy Festival 1995 and 'Who Knows Where The Time Goes?' at Marlow Theatre, Canterbury, March 1997.

Produced and mixed by Fairport Convention & Mark Tucker

Record label: Woodworm

Released: June 1997

Highest chart position: 86 (UK)

Length: 56:00

Current edition: 2000 release on Mooncrest under new title of Wishfulness Waltz

It had been the most stable line-up in Fairport Convention's history, spanning 11 years and six albums. But in 1996 Maartin Allcock quit the band, wanting to spend more time with his family and feeling he had 'moved on musically'. The decision seems to have taken the band by surprise – promotional material for the winter tour included Maart in the line-up. The decision shocked fans who had come to love not only his versatile musicianship but also his quirky Mancunian humour. Who on earth could replace Maart?

Step in someone who already had strong links with the band – indeed, had been a Fairporter for the 1993 Cropredy festival after Ric's attempt to punch a hole in a plate glass window. Christopher Julien Leslie was born in Banbury, Oxfordshire – virtually Fairport's spiritual home – on 15 December 1956. Like Ric, he modelled his playing on Dave Swarbrick and began his career as a duo with his brother John. Later he was one-quarter of Swarb's band Whippersnapper, formed in 1984, and continued in the line-up until 1993. His other credits include The Albion Band (appearing on *Demi Paradise* with Simon Nicol), All About Eve and Steve Ashley.

He played at Cropredy virtually from the beginning of the festival – in 1980 he was part of the opening act, billed as Captain Coco's Country Dance Band. A few years later, Peggy called on Chris and John when he needed some help putting together a soundtrack for a film about Adnam's Brewery called *In One End And Out The Other.*

So when Fairport were looking for a replacement for Maart, and one who was already familiar with the band and its repertoire, Chris seemed to fit the bill (despite being a teetotal vegetarian Buddhist!). Like Maart, he can play virtually any instrument thrust into his hands, including guitar, bouzouki, mandolin, banjo and tin whistle.

He is also no mean songwriter and, as time was to prove, he would be a major asset to Fairport in that department. In fact, he made his songwriting and vocal presence felt right from the off – the album opens with his stirring composition 'John Gaudie' and he has a credit on 'Spanish Main', written with Maartin. His arrival also seemed to excite Ric Sanders, who wrote 'The Bowman's Retreat' for the both of them to play – and, for the first time, the band could perform 'The Rose Hip' live as it sounded on *Red & Gold*. Other material on *Who Knows Where The Time Goes?* comes from Anna Ryder, who supported Fairport on a tour; the ever-reliable Steve Tilston; and, for the first time, Peggy borrows a song from his other band, Jethro Tull.

The result is a mostly successful album with only one or two tracks that don't quite work as well as the rest. Some fans feared the band would lose its hard edge with the departure of Maart but there seems to be a conscious effort to keep the rock quotient up – Simon has a chance to get out his 1962 Fender Stratocaster electric guitar and, along with Chris playing a 'bazouki-Strat', turns the aforementioned 'Spanish Main' into one of the noisiest tracks Fairport have ever recorded. Oh, and Maart still has a presence, playing keyboards on one of the two live tracks at the end.

The title – taken, of course, from the Sandy Denny song of the same name, which closes the album – is a discreet reference to the fact that this release marked 30 years of Fairport Convention and the cover, shot at Barford St Michael post office, is superimposed with a clock face, just to drive home the message.

'John Gaudie' (Chris Leslie)

Chris Leslie makes an instant impact with a song he originally wrote for Dave Swarbrick's band Whippersnapper, recording it their 1985 album *Promises*. It was inspired by one of the tunes at the end, a traditional reel from the Shetlands called 'Jack (or Jock, or John) Broke Da Prison Door', written about a fiddler who suffers some behavioural problems thanks to a bang on the head when he was young. Acting up one night, he is detained by the local constabulary but escapes by smashing down the cell door (and then writing a tune about it).

The Whippersnapper version is slower and heavy on the mandolin but, as befits a song about a mad fiddler, Fairport's opens with violin and solo voice before harmonies and bass come in for the chorus. Drums enter for verse two, followed by Simon on electric guitar power chords and then the entire band go into an instrumental section based on the tune 'Jack Broke Da Prison Door' before heading into verse three. Three repeats of the chorus end the vocal section of the song and we're back into John's (or Jack's or Jock's) tune again. That leads into two more Shetland tunes, 'Donald Blue' and 'The Bonnie Isle O' Whalsay', all played ferociously by Fairport and providing a rousing finale to the opening track.

'Sailing Boat' (Anna Ryder)

Or, as she prefers to be known, annA rydeR, a multi-instrumentalist who supported Fairport on tour in 1999 and released one of her six solo albums on Woodworm Records. Dave Pegg called her Fairport's favourite singer/ songwriter – the band would record two more of her compositions, and she would make frequent appearances on the Cropredy Festival stage. 'Sailing Boat' is from her 1993 album *Eye To Eye* and has a fairly simple theme – she wishes she had a sailing boat and, were she in possession of such a vessel, she would travel far and not come back. The RNLI may have something to say about that.

A slow ballad in C major, it is pleasant if unremarkable – there are too many songs in the world with a similar style and chord sequences, although Anna (sorry, annA) puts in the occasional discordant note in the verse to make the listener sit up and take interest. Simon sings it convincingly – let's face it, he's at an age now when sailing off somewhere in a boat probably holds a lot of attractions – Chris provides a lilting mandolin instrumental, and the whole thing slips along like, say, a catboat on a calm sea with a gentle but steady wind.

'Here's To Tom Paine' (Steve Tilston)

A man who could argue HE is Fairport's favourite singer/songwriter provides his third composition for the band, a stately but bright ballad about the eighteenth-century English-born writer and human rights activist Thomas Paine (originally Pain – he added the 'e' when he was in his 30s). While in America Paine wrote the pamphlets *Common Sense* and *The American Crisis* in 1776, inspiring patriots to declare their independence from Britain. His pamphlet *Rights Of Man* (1791) supported the French revolution and argued political violence was allowed when governments fail to protect the natural rights of the people.

King George III no doubt considerrd him a bit of a pain but Tilston is in no doubt about Thomas's place in British history. Originally recording the song for his album *All Under The Sun*, with Maggie Boyle, he sings a chorus that proclaims Paine as 'never a better-born Englishman' and compares the longevity of his thoughts and words to a pigeon-poo covered statue of the king. Fairport follow Tilston's template fairly closely, giving a solid, confident reading with a positive, uptempo feel. Violin, acoustic guitar and mandolin work closely together and DM provides subtle organ support. Unusually, most of the song is in D major but shifts into D minor for the middle-eight. By the way, the song is the adopted anthem for the Tom Paine Society of America.

'The Bowman's Retreat' (Ric Sanders)

Ric wrote this collection of three tunes to celebrate Chris coming into the band – it's a powerful, driving instrumental number played as a twin fiddle attack by the two violinists. The title is a little misleading – the bowmen are not retreating but rather advancing on all fronts with fiddles flying in a cloud of rosin dust. In a live setting, this would frequently be linked with 'Matty Groves' or 'John Gaudie' and is guaranteed to get the fans on their feet.

'Spanish Main' (Allcock/Leslie)

One of the heaviest tracks Fairport have recorded on any of their studio albums (although some live versions of 'Matty Groves' with Maart would make it seem like a Daniel O'Donnell ballad in comparison). Simon kicks things off with powerful alternative G and F chords on his Fender Stratocaster while Ric doubles up Chris's lead electric guitar lines. Maart's lyrics tell a tale as old as time – a sailor falls in love with a young, dainty girl, not knowing she has already given her love to a haughty lord who runs them through with his sword and leaves them lying dead together. So a little bit like 'Matty Groves', then. Simon sings with enough of a baritone growl to give the song real menace and it ends with Chris giving it loads on his Telecaster and Ric providing screaming violin.

'The Golden Glove' (Trad lyric/Tune Sally Barker)

Also known as 'The Squire of Tamworth' and 'Dog And Gun', the words date back to at least 1777 and are said to be based on an actual event during the reign of Queen Elizabeth I. A woman disguises herself to find out what a young farmer thinks of her. She gives him a golden glove – claiming she found it – then goes home and says whosoever finds my glove shall have my hand in marriage. Up trots the farmer with said accessory in hand, they marry, and there are happy endings all round.

The tune, however, is not traditional – it was written by Sally Barker for her 1992 album *Tango!* Sally is a Leicestershire-born singer/songwriter notable for being a member of The Poozies, an all-female folk group, and a 2014 contestant on the BBC One talent show *The Voice*, becoming runner-up to Jermaine Jackman. She also supported Fairport on tour in 2017. The band's version of 'The Golden Glove' is a 6/8 ballad led by Simon's Eggle acoustic guitar, with Chris on mandolin and DM playing almost inaudible harpsichord as well as drums. From its gentle opening, it grows into an exultant band production as true love triumphs over all. This is a gorgeous song, performed and arranged with sensitivity and imagination.

'Slipology' (Ric Sanders)

A jazzy slipjig from the fiddler with, he says, a be-boppy title. He's referring here to Charlie Parker, one of the leading exponents of the 1940s jazz style known as bebop, who wrote and recorded a tune called 'Ornithology'. Slippery minor chords in 6/8 from Simon's Strat open proceedings, with DM playing his drums with brushes and Chris on mandolin. It is dedicated to 'our hero' Spike Milligan who, as well as being a British comedy giant, was no mean jazzman himself – he started on trumpet then moved to guitar, playing in a post-war trio.

'The Wishfulness Waltz/Midnight On The Water' (Alan Franks/ Benny Thomasson)

If it wasn't for songs such as 'John Gaudie' and 'Spanish Main' you might think there was a bit of a twilight age theme going on here – a sort of wishful, sailing away, we're too old for this sort of thing kinda vibe. Luckily, this is a gorgeous song, so we'll forgive them. Alan Franks is a writer and musician who composed and recorded this for a 1995 album with Patty Vetta called *Will*. As the title suggests, it's a wistful waltz with a gentle, flowing melody sung beautifully by Mr Leslie, with lyrics painting a sort of 'Who Knows Where The Time Goes?' picture. It is followed by a waltz instrumental credited to Texan fiddler Benny Thomasson, but other sources suggest it was actually composed by his father. Listen carefully, and you will hear phrases that sound uncannily like the chorus of 'Pleasure And Pain' on *Nine*.

'Life Is A Long Song' (Ian Anderson)

Peggy was probably inspired to include this because, at the time, he was playing bass for Jethro Tull and it is one of Ian Anderson's most popular acoustic songs. Originally released as an EP in 1971 – and later included on the compilation album *Living In The Past* – it is a sprightly tune with somewhat depressing lyrics suggesting that life is, indeed, a long song but 'the tune ends too soon for us all'. Fairport's version smooths out all the kinks and idiosyncrasies of Anderson's original and, in my considered opinion, thoroughly ruins it in the process! Ah well, never mind. It doesn't last long, just 2:38, and it gives Peggy, Chris and Simon a chance to take turns at singing a verse each and joining in on the chorus repeat of the title. Peggy and his son Matt had recorded this once before for tribute album *To Cry You A Song*, released in 1996. Like many tribute albums, it proves that nothing beats sitting down and listening to the originals.

'Dangerous' (Kristina Olsen)

The second misstep on the album is this clumsy number by US folk singer and instrumentalist Olsen. A woman falls in love with a wild adventurer who courts danger, but it is she who ends up as this song's corpse by, er, forgetting to put her seatbelt on. Essentially, this is a way of saying 'clunk-click every trip' in four and a half minutes. The band tries hard to put some life into what is a bit of an uninspired chug, with Simon playing a semi-acoustic Gretsch, Chris on 'bazouki-strat' (surely bouzouki?) – basically a Stratocaster converted to take sets of two bouzouki strings, like a 12-string – and DM condemned to endless two-in-a-bar drumming. The problem is, there are no highs or lows in this song – it goes along at the same pace and the same emotional level until, mercifully, it fades out.

'Heard It Through The Grapevine [Live]' (Whitfield/Strong)

Recorded at the 1995 Cropredy Festival, this old Marvin Gaye number by the celebrated Motown songwriting team of Norman Whitfield and Barrett Strong is packed full of goodies. There's confident keyboards from Maartin Allcock, Richard Thompson growls the lyrics with passionate abandon and the Roy Wood Big Band, coupled with Ric and Chris on strings, give the song a dramatic, cinematic backing. It's performed with such gusto and enjoyment, and also respect, that it fully deserves the roar of audience approval at the end.

'Who Knows Where The Time Goes?' (Sandy Denny)

Fairport chose to use this live recording of Sandy's heartbreaking classic instead of producing a studio version. Perhaps they thought they wouldn't be able to top what is a stunningly beautiful performance from the band, captured in March 1997 at the Canterbury Marlowe Theatre. Ric and Chris's twin fiddles provide warm string support while Simon's gentle baritone cradles the lyrics that every Fairport fan has etched on their heart. The band does the song full justice and ends an album that fully deserves to bear Sandy's words on the cover.

The Wood & The Wire (1999)

Personnel:
Simon Nicol: vocals, acoustic and electric guitars
Chris Leslie: vocals, mandolin, bouzouki, didgeridoo, violin
Dave Pegg: bass, backing vocals
Ric Sanders: violin
Dave Pegg: bass, backing vocals, gargle
Gerry Conway: drums, percussion
Recorded at Woodworm Studios, Barford St Michael, Oxfordshire
Engineered and mixed by Mark Tucker
Produced by Dave Pegg, Simon Nicol and Mark Tucker
Record label: Woodworm
Released: November 1999
Highest chart position: Uncharted
Length: 60:45
Current edition: 2005 release on Talking Elephant Records with bonus tracks

Perhaps this album should have been called 'Who Knows Where Our Band Members Go?', for it heralded yet another departure from the ranks, this time by someone who had made two previous attempts to escape. It was third time lucky (unlucky for the listener) for Dave Mattacks, who had left after *"Babbacombe" Lee* but rejoined to finish off *Rosie*, then quit after *Gottle O' Geer* and returned for *Gladys' Leap*.

For 13 years after Fairport's comeback, he had successfully combined the band's recording and touring commitments with being an in-demand session musician, but by 1998 it had got too much. Two years later he moved to Boston, New England, where he started teaching a summer course at Berklee University as well as giving private drumming lessons. A quiet, polite but matter-of-fact man of few words, he was asked in an interview how hard it was to leave Fairport after all those years. His response was: 'Not very.' He also said it was 'not very likely' he would come back yet again.

DM's contribution to the Fairport sound cannot be overestimated. He virtually invented folk-rock drumming – there was no template when he replaced Martin Lamble in Fairport in 1969 just as the band was changing its direction, certainly not for the rocked-up jigs and reels. His solid, powerful but inventive drumming always added something special to a song and his keyboard skills – he was originally a pianist before turning to drums – frequently proved invaluable and helped create some Fairport classics, such as 'The Hiring Fair'.

To replace him Fairport turned, as they frequently did, to an old friend – Gerald Conway, born September 1947 in King's Lynn, Norfolk. He had already played on a Fairport Convention album, albeit by accident – as a member of Fotheringay he was on the two recordings Trevor Lucas brought to the band for *Rosie* and was then asked to drum on the title track.

Gerry also played on albums by Steeleye Span and Sandy Denny, further strengthening his folk-rock credentials, and had two stints with Jethro Tull, playing alongside Dave Pegg on bass. And he was Cat Stevens' drummer from 1971 to 1978.

The Wood & The Wire has been hailed as one of the best AND worst post-comeback albums. *AllMusic* gives it four stars, but some fans say this is where Fairport began to lose the rock in folk-rock. It really depends on how much Chris Leslie you like, as he dominates this album like no other songwriter before him save our old friend Trad. Nine of the fourteen tracks are written or co-written by Chris, and he takes lead vocal on seven of them, leaving 'frontman' Simon Nicol with six. Chris has a gentle tenor voice reminiscent of Ian (now Iain) Matthews that works well on the wistful songs, but some fans felt his dominance softened the band, sandpapering off the hard edges provided by Maart.

Gerry's drumming here is more laidback than DM's, although he does introduce more uncommon percussion instruments. The title refers to the chief components of musical instruments and how they can take over your life and the cover shows Chris Leslie's son Sam looking through the window of the One Man Band music shop in Banbury.

'The Wood And The Wire' (Chris Leslie, Nigel Stonier)
Like *Red & Gold*, the album title appears to use an ampersand while the song title spells out 'and' in full (although it's in full on the CD spine). Not that I'm being pedantic or anything. 'The Wood And The Wire' opens strongly with a jig-like figure displaying a slight eastern feel played on acoustic guitar and violin. Simon sings the first few verses about a young man seduced by the lure of a musical instrument, with sparse acoustic backing and Gerry on dhumbek, an Egyptian/Arabic drum shaped like a goblet. The band's trademark close harmonies come in for a very effective and memorable chorus – the vocals are particularly impressive when they sing a long B note on the word 'fire'. Bass and unobtrusive electric guitar come in, and Chris strums mandolin for the third verse, while Ric gets to improvise during a brief instrumental section.

The song ends on a minute and half of instrumental based on the jig intro that gives Ric, Chris and Simon a chance to shine – Simon especially gives us a bit of classy electric guitar. 'The Wood And The Wire' is a fairly spirited opening for the album – not as manic as 'John Gaudie' on the previous release but still with plenty of fire in its belly. By the way, Chris Leslie's co-writer on this and six other songs on the album is Nigel Stonier, a record producer, writer and musician chiefly known for his work with Thea Gilmore.

'The Dancer' (Chris Leslie)
A tribute to those who try to keep the old songs and dances alive in a world that appears to despise and ridicule any music not performed by pimply

teens on *X Factor*. In the liner notes, Chris says it was inspired by 'three old Oxfordshire characters' – two morris dancers from Bampton and a singer who was also a shepherd from Church Enstone – and it talks about passing the traditions down from father to son. The violin and finger-picked acoustic guitar opening suggests a gentle ballad, but Simon picks things up with quite aggressive rhythmic chords, and the entire band comes in fairly forcefully after the first rendition of the chorus. After the middle eight, Chris slips in the opening line from 'The Holmfirth Anthem' – also known as 'Abroad For Pleasure', 'Pretty Flowers' and 'Through The Groves' – a traditional song, as the title suggests, from Holmfirth in the Southern Pennines. The song's 'hook' is in the repetition of the line 'It was written in the stone', with accompanying ascending guitar chords. A pleasant song with a bit of life to it.

'Wandering Man' (Chris Leslie, Nigel Stonier)
Dedicated to everyone who has to travel for a living, Chris and Nigel's contribution to the rich folk-rock tradition of travelling songs is this gentle but rhythmic number notable for having an extra line of lyric at the end of each verse, making them nine bars instead of the usual eight, and also for Chris playing didgeridoo at the end. Gerry brings out his collection of unusual percussion instruments, playing Nepalese and Moroccan hand drums and tingshaws. The 'clip-clop' rhythm of the song suggests this particular wandering man is thoroughly enjoying his travels.

'The Heart Of The Song' (Pete Scrowther)
Four songs in and this is the first non-Chris Leslie track, penned by a County Durham singer/songwriter who moved to Switzerland in 1978 and recorded albums with Swiss bands Legal Tender and Rusty Nugget. He didn't release his own version of this until his second solo album in 2003. Scrowther describes this as 'abstract musings on the power of song' – like 'Wandering Man' it has a travelling theme but one that calls on all weary plodders to stop for a moment and join together in listening to music. A waltz-time number with a bit of a stomp, it gives Simon his second lead vocal on the album while Chris and Ric play harmonies on mandolin and violin.

'A Year And A Day' (Ric Sanders)
In the liner notes, Ric says 'When you miss someone you really love, every day can seem like a year.' So this is a bitter-sweet tune in slow three-quarter time, a bit of a cross between 'Portmeirion' and 'The Rose Hip', with both Ric and Chris playing a moving string arrangement on their violins. Simon provides acoustic guitar-picking support and takes over the melody for one of the verses. There's definitely a sense of loss running throughout the track, but there's also some optimism there that Ric will soon be reunited with whoever it is he is missing as the two violins soar up the scales.

'The Game Pieces' (Chris Leslie, Nigel Stonier)

A tale about a set of chess pieces from the Isle of Lewis that somehow contrive to get themselves moved to a museum in Edinburgh, where they can have a nice rest from all that checkmating. It opens with acapella harmonies from Chris, Simon and Peggy then the bass leads the band into a sprightly jig-rhythm as Chris tells tall tales about the journey of the chess pieces. A velvet bag is found by the survivor of a shipwreck – he is murdered by a robber who is then compelled to bury the contents of the bag – yes, the chess pieces – in the ground because that is where they want to stay. Eventually, they are dug up by a crofter who sells them at auction, and they end up in the museum, 'silent air around, no-one to touch them'.

'Close To You' (Chris Leslie)

The fifth Chris Leslie song on the album is a medium-paced ballad about a lonely lighthouse keeper yearning for his loved one as he watches an approaching storm. It is a pleasant enough number with a gentle, lilting tune in A major – Ric plays ethereal violin, like the distant cries of seagulls, while Gerry keeps the rhythm going with rim shots and woodblock. The middle eight melody containing the lines 'Ships pass. Tall masts. Out in the sound' may remind you a little of Cyndi Lauper's 'Time After Time'. The chorus is not particularly distinctive but Fairport, as usual, know how to use their harmony voices to great effect to give it a yearning feel.

'Still A Mystery' (Chris Leslie, Nigel Stonier)

The accusation from some fans is that Chris softened the band from the days of Maartin Allcock, steering them more down the middle of the road. The trouble is, this attempt to write something more aggressive and harder really doesn't work at all, sounding clumsy and forced. Simon plays slashing electric guitar chords and sings in his angriest tone, but it's thoroughly unconvincing, similar to some of the Dave Whetstone songs the band attempted on previous albums. Lyrically, it's a clichéd story about someone who keeps their real self hidden – who is 'still a mystery'. Even Gerry's 'dhumbek ensemble' at the end can't hide the air of desperation around this song and the band quite rightly put it out of its misery at the 2:40 mark.

'Banbury Fair' (Chris Leslie)

The area around Banbury in Oxfordshire was Fairport's adopted home, but Chris Leslie was born and bred there and has frequently been inspired by the sights and memories of his home town. This is an unashamedly nostalgic depiction of the famous street fair from his childhood, in which he and a pal enjoy the big wheel, the rifle range, the coconut shy and finally win on a horse-racing game (as predicted by a gypsy fortune-teller). The images are explored through a spirited, 6/8 song with a singalong chorus that mentions 'The Talk of the Town' – this was a tent containing a stage for strippers. The 400-year-old fair still takes place in the town every Michaelmas.

'The Lady Vanishes' (Chris Leslie, Nigel Stonier)

Simon takes lead vocals on this gentle ballad about a woman hiding a trauma from the past – when reminded of it 'the lady vanishes – the child returns'. His warm baritone is perfect for these sort of songs, although it's fair to say this is not the most memorable track to be graced by his voice. The reference to a 'trick' in the lyrics compares the titular's lady's change of demeanour to the famous illusion created by English magician Jack Hughes in which a playing card showing a queen is made to disappear before your very eyes.

'The Good Fortunes' (Ric Sanders)

Four tunes that Ric thought were good. See what he did there? The two fiddlers race through 'Coleraine', a minor key double jig from Northern Ireland that also crossed the Atlantic and became popular in New England; 'Trip To Yorkshire', an Irish slipjig also known as 'An Turas Go Yorkshire', with Spike Jones impressions from Gerry and 'popping' noise from musician Sam Dunkley; 'Bonny Breast Knot', a barn dance reel possibly from Sussex (there are three different tunes with that name); and, finally, 'Durham's Bull', a fast reel named for US radio fiddler Buddy Durham. Ric dedicates it to Fairport fan and veteran film actor Don Backhurst, who was known as The Indian Chief and had just died aged 74.

'Western Wind' (Trad arr Nicol, Pegg, Sanders, Leslie, Conway)

The only traditional song on the album is possibly the oldest Fairport have ever recorded – the opening verse dates back at least to the early 16th century although the words are believed to be fragments of medieval poetry from a couple of hundred years before. It is usually sung to a tune that Henry VIII stole for his own 'Pastime In Good Company' (Note to Ed: He's dead, so he can't sue). This version, however, is actually two songs shoehorned together – 'Western (or Westron) Wind' and 'Now Westlin' Winds', composed by the Scottish poet Robert Burns. You can see from the lyrics they are different animals – the opening section yearns for the sweet winds of spring when the author will be in bed with his love, while the rest extols the joys of hunting with guns. Fairport learned this version from Dublin folk singer Susan McKeown, who released it on an album called *Bones* in 1996. It opens with the 'Western Wind' verse sung acapella by Simon, Chris and Peggy before a swiftly-strummed acoustic guitar takes us into the Burns section. Gerry provides ethnic percussion accompaniment on dhumbeks while Peggy plays both electric bass guitar and double bass, one of them following the melody beneath Simon's voice. Chris and Ric provide moderately fast harmonic solos before the song goes back into its acapella opening verse again to end. It's a lively rendition with exquisite harmonies and is one of the high points on the album.

'Don't Leave Too Soon' (Chris Leslie, Nigel Stonier)
A gentle, touching parting song that does what it says on the tin. It's not about romantic loss – rather, this is addressed to a friend or someone the author admires. A musical friend, too, because it ends with the repeated line 'Haven't we still got songs to sing...' It's played with respectful restraint – Simon's acoustic guitar and Chris's bouzouki blend together and Gerry's percussion is laid-back and unobtrusive, while Ric does little more than support the song with long violin notes.

'Rocky Road' (Steve Tilston)
In the hands of the dour Steve Tilston and performed on his 1998 album *Solarubato* this is a song with a bitter taste as he laments the 'rocky road' he is on and the 'traps' that time will set for 'fine young bloods who think yourselves immune'. In Fairport's hands, it becomes almost a celebration. Simon opens with a folky little riff on electric guitar before launching into the first verse, then the band comes in with pounding drums and strong harmonies. Chris takes a verse, there's a mandolin/violin instrumental, then Peggy's Brummie brogue warbles through verse three. Just to show how seriously Fairport are taking this song, they change the last line of the chorus 'Not any more' to 'Not Demi Moore'. The wags. The track then lurches quite dramatically, and for no thematic reason, into 'The Quaker', a fast Cotswold Morris tune led by Chris on mandolin.

2005 Bonus Tracks
'The Good Fortunes [Live]' (Ric Sanders)
As the title suggests, this is a live version of the studio recording that gives Gerry a bit more to do on his dhumbeks before launching into the four good tunes.

'Now Be Thankful [Live]' (Richard Thompson, Dave Swarbrick)
Another live version, this time of the band's 1970 single penned by Swarb and Richard from another Fairport era. It's a gentler version with Chris on lead vocals and a mandolin/violin instrumental section to pad it out a bit – the original was a bit short. Some of the vocal harmonies are a little dodgy here! A studio recording of this turns up on their next album...just over the page...

XXXV (2002)

Personnel:

Simon Nicol: vocals, guitars

Chris Leslie: vocals, mandolin, Fender electric 5-string mandolin, violin, tenor banjo (borrowed from Peggy!)

Ric Sanders: violins, electric piano

Dave Pegg: bass, backing vocals, gargle

Gerry Conway: drums, percussion

Additional personnel:

annA rydeR: vocals, six French horns, accordion, pennywhistle on 'The Crowd'; penny whistles, accordion, piano on 'My Love Is In America'; accordion on 'Madeleine.'

Chris While & Julie Matthews: vocals on 'My Love Is In America'

Ian Anderson: flute on 'Portmeirion.'

Mark Tucker: E-Bow and electric guitar on 'I Wandered By A Brookside.'

Cropredy live parts on 'The Crowd':

annA: vocals and accordion

Kate Luxmoore: bass clarinet and clarinet

Chris Knibbs: trombone

Chas McDevitt: trumpet

The Cropredy Crowd: whoos, clapping etc

Recorded Summer 2001 at Woodworm Studios, Barford St Michael, Oxfordshire

Engineered, recorded and mixed by Mark Tucker

Produced by Dave Pegg and Mark Tucker

Record label: Woodworm

Released: 12 February 2002

Highest chart position: Uncharted

Length: 64:57

Current edition: 2007 Eagle Rock Records CD

Fairport Convention celebrated their 35th birthday in 2002, so it is fitting that their anniversary album should carry the very accurate and no-nonsense title of *XXXV* – that's 35 in Latin numerals, of course. Unlike *The Wood & The Wire*, which was dominated by Chris Leslie's songs and lead vocals, *XXXV* displays a greater spread of material from a number of different sources, as well as offering new takes on some old favourites. So Ric's beautiful 'Portmeirion' makes a comeback, with added flute from Peggy's Jethro Tull pal Ian Anderson, while 'The Banks of Sweet Primroses' and Dave Swarbrick and Richard Thompson's 'Now Be Thankful' are dusted off and served up in new relaxed, stately versions.

Out of the new compositions on offer, Chris shines with 'My Love Is In America' and the band get all self-referential (as they will do increasingly as they get older) with Anna Ryder's (sorry, annA rydeR's) 'The Crowd', featuring the Cropredy audience on 'clapping'. Indeed, *XXXV* features more special guests than any previous albums with the possible exceptions of *Rosie* and *Gottle O' Geer* – and that's not counting the 20,000-strong festival throng.

Apart from the aforementioned Mr Anderson, there's Julie Matthews and Chris While from The Albion Band and even engineer Mark Tucker gets in on the act with a bit of E-Bow and electric guitar.

The result is an album with a hint of a celebratory feel, although this is a band that has clearly slowed down since its folk-rocking heyday. Having said that, Ric's collection of traditional tunes is as fast and furious as any of the jigs and reels that are Fairport's stock in trade. It's probably fair to say that *XXXV* is not the best of the comeback albums either, although I feel it has more variety in style and tone than its predecessor. The cover by Mick Toole resembles the logo of a brand of intoxicating beverage – one can imagine it being printed on beermats. Indeed, the back cover shows just such an invention, with a pint of ale sitting on top. Quite appropriate for a band that's said to have done for real ale what the Grateful Dead did for LSD.

'Madeleine' (Lawrence Bristow Smith, Kenny Craddock)

Is there such a thing as folk-rockabilly? Fairport give more than a nod to Eddie Cochran's 'Somethin' Else' and 'Summertime Blues' by inserting their famous riffs into a simple-minded, uptempo song about meeting a girl called Madeleine at a country fair and deciding she would make an excellent bride. What Madeleine thinks about this arrangement goes unrecorded. The song was written by former Lindisfarne keyboard player Kenny Craddock, who sadly died in a car crash in Portugal just a few months after *XXXV* came out. Lyrics were by LAURENCE (spelling alert!) Bristow Smith, who also wrote songs for Craddock's only solo album. The Lindisfarne link is strengthened by the fact that Chris Leslie's co-writer Nigel Stonier also penned lyrics for that band's bassist Rod Clements.

'My Love Is In America' (Chris Leslie)

In the liner notes Chris says he was inspired by the book *The Living Note* by Christy McNamara and Peter Woods, which he bought in Dublin. The book travels through several generations of a fictional family to show how Irish traditional music has been preserved, passed on and spread out. Chris's song dwells on the Irish diaspora as poverty and starvation forced millions of people to emigrate. In the song, the narrator has gone to London but his love Mary has been taken by her father to America. He keeps her picture on his wall and sends her letters, but there's just silence from across the Atlantic Sea. It's a story that was probably played out thousands of times as sweethearts were parted and made new lives for themselves. The song is a stirring ballad in waltz-time with a soaring chorus that pretty much repeats the same four chords before going up a tone for a short violin instrumental. Pennywhistle, accordion and piano help build everything into a rousing climax.

'The Happy Man' (Trad arr Chris Leslie)

A morris stick and dance song from Adderbury in Oxfordshire, frequently sung while taking a rest from the jumping about. Chris Leslie no doubt knew this song very well indeed – he was a musician and dancer for the village's morris side from 1975. Fairport give it a respectful treatment, in a lurching three-quarter-time that would be very danceable with a few beers inside you, interspersed with two other Adderbury Morris tunes, 'Black Joke' and 'Constant Billy'. The former was originally a popular vulgar street song before losing its lyrics and becoming a dance tune, the second has its own dance steps involving short sticks.

'Portmeirion' (Ric Sanders)

Ric's beautiful and elegant instrumental from *Expletive Delighted!* is very similar to the original except for heavier percussion from Gerry, Chris's slightly bluesy mandolin solo and some very disciplined and tasteful flute from Ian Anderson of Jethro Tull.

'The Crowd' (annA rydeR)

Lump in the throat time. By 2002 the annual reunion festival at Cropredy had been running for approximately 23 years (depending on whether you counted the gigs held in the garden of the widow of local Labour MP Richard Crossman from 1976). It had become a fixture on the British festival calendar but was still unique, not least in the way it encouraged both artists and fans to mix with each other. So performers would stroll the field to watch other acts on stage – indeed, some would turn up even if they weren't performing. That's how Ralph McTell was inspired to write 'Red And Gold' while watching the sinking sun over the Cropredy stage, and why annA rydeR penned 'The Crowd' when Fairport asked her if she had anything for their new album.

In a loose, jaunty 6/8 the song describes the field of green, the sound of people singing and cheering, the sense of togetherness that makes the festival so special. Fairport recorded two versions – one in the studio and another live at the 2001 festival, backed by a brass ensemble, that encouraged the entire crowd to join in, singing and cheering. The two were then expertly knitted together to create one track (and a reprise later on). Peggy told the audience it would be on the next album, adding 'but don't all put in claims for royalties…I couldn't handle the maths'.

annA provides the French horn ensemble that opens the studio section of the song and almost inaudible pennywhistle, while both Ric and Chris perform some violin pyrotechnics on the extended outro. The result is a warm, emotional and triumphant song that perfectly encapsulates the experience and meaning of Cropredy.

'The Banks Of The Sweet Primroses' (Trad arr Simon Nicol, Dave Pegg, Ric Sanders, Chris Leslie, Gerry Conway)

Fairport first recorded this for the *Angel Delight* album – it was one of the least interesting cuts on that release and suffers the same fate here. Chris takes most of the vocal duties on a plodding, repetitive tune that Fairport do little with except play and then stop. As stated before, the story is of a deceiving young man who propositions a young maid, only for her to remind him he had already taken what he wanted and discarded her.

'The Deserter' (John Richards)
Another re-recording, this originally turned up on Simon's 1987 solo album *Before Your Time* then appeared on the live half of *Old New Borrowed Blue*. This version contains string support from Ric, military drum flourishes from Gerry and more vocal backing from the band, including a brief acapella section. All in all, this is a slight improvement on the original, and the extra instrumentation does not detract from the song's anti-war message.

'The Light Of Day' (Chris Leslie)
The story of a cunning fiddler who plays a trick on his pals to win a bet, this mild rocker from Chris takes a while in the telling at more than six minutes long. It opens immediately with his vocals over chopping acoustic guitar chords before Gerry enters with busy, pounding drums. There's also electric guitar in there and baritone violin from Ric. The song gallops along, apart from two gentle middle-eight sections, and Simon also takes a verse towards the end. Strangely, the song doesn't really have a chorus – it relies on its story and varied instrumentation to keep the listener's attention, playing out with a dramatic fiddle solo over almost reggae electric guitar. Yes, it does sound like an odd mix of styles, but overall it achieves its effect. The story? Blind George and his pals gather in the Chequers Inn in Hertfordshire and, as the night draws in and the shadows lengthen, they talk about a particular cave into which, according to legend, many have entered but none emerged. George is dared to enter by those with more money and sense, and he scares them all witless by making blood-curdling cries from within before emerging to play his fiddle.

'I Wandered By A Brookside' (Barbara Berry, Alfred Williams Collection, Swindon Library, arr Fairport)
The words are traditional, collected by Alfred Williams and believed to have originated in North Oxfordshire. Sometimes they are attributed to Richard Monckton Milnes, 1st Baron Houghton, who died in 1885. The tune is relatively recent, composed by Barbara Berry who was one half of The Portway Pedlars with husband Len, and released on their 1984 album *In Greenwood Shades*. Chris knew it well because he sang it with Whippersnapper on their 1987 album *Tsubo*. It has been covered many times by many people, including Eva Cassidy. Fairport give it an untypical MOR big ballad treatment, with Ric playing electric piano as well as baritone violin over Gerry's steady drumbeat. There's even some lead electric guitar there wailing away deep in the mix. The song fades out on Chris repeating the lines 'the only sound I heard' as Gerry's drumming

diminishes to just a few taps on his dhumbeks while Ric plays long, ghostly notes on his fiddle. It's a very modern and commercial take on the song – knowing Fairport's sense of humour, you wonder if it is all gently pulling the listener's leg.

'Neil Gow's Apprentice' (Michael Marra)

Michael Marra was a Dundee-born singer/songwriter who sadly died of cancer in 2012 aged 60. An accomplished musician, he worked with Van Morrison, The Proclaimers, Barbara Dickson and Deacon Blue. His work was often humorous, but he also tackled political and social issues. 'Neil Gow's Apprentice' appeared on his 1991 solo album *On Stolen Stationery* and is inspired by the famous Scottish 18th-century fiddler and composer of the same name. He was said to have composed and played many of his reels and strathspeys – a slower version of a reel – under an oak tree that still stands near the town of Dunkeld in Perth and Kinross.

Michael's song tells of two brothers, one in Scotland and the other in Australia, who both wish they could trade places. The brother in Scotland envies his sibling enjoying the summer sun in Oz, while the other yearns to be sitting under Neil Gow's Tree playing his fiddle. The song is a simple, repetitive ditty in A major that Fairport perform as a slow reel, opening with Simon on the chorus and Ric playing a traditional-sounding tune beneath him along with strummed acoustic guitar and gentle banjo picking. The chorus includes the line 'I'll sit beneath the fiddle tree with the ghost of Neil Gow next to me' – words that were engraved on a bench sited under Neil Gow's Tree and unveiled by Michael Marra's widow Peggy in 2013.

'Everything But The Skirl' (Ric Sanders)

The only new tune from Ric on the album is a Scottish-sounding jig that he originally called 'Lethal Bagpipes 3', inspired by the Mel Gibson movie *Braveheart*. The eventual title is a reference to Everything But The Girl, a pop duo formed in Hull in 1982, and a 'skirl', which is a shrill wailing sound, especially from a set of bagpipes. The tune opens with the twin fiddles of Ric and Chris imitating the 'skirl' of bagpipes before the band launch into two fast reels, one with the bow-scorching tempo of 159 beats per minute. Simon on electric guitar provides some unusual, Shadows-influenced backing riffs while Gerry gets to perform some brief drum solos before the big ending. It fits very well with the preceding track, and it's a shame Fairport could not find a way to knit the two together. Live, 'Everything But The Skirl' would segue into 'Let There Be Drums', a Gerry Conway solo that would turn into something similar to a Shadows tune but played on mandolin and fiddle. You had to be there really.

'Talking About My Love' (Chris Leslie, Nigel Stonier)

Fairport do pop! Acapella harmonies introduce a catchy chorus in this mid-tempo rocker – unfortunately, the mundane verses with their jumble of metaphors referencing nautical and ironmongering (!) themes don't do the song justice. Fairport work hard to make it interesting, with Gerry Conway using practically every percussion instrument in his armoury. But this will never be more than another pleasant but not very memorable Chris Leslie song.

'Now Be Thankful' (Richard Thompson/Dave Swarbrick)

We've already heard the current Fairport line-up perform the 1970 single in a live version included as a bonus track on *The Wood & The Wire*, and this is basically an identical studio rendition. It's sung by Chris Leslie and successfully removes any darkness or mystery that was there in the original, so it's difficult to see what the remake achieves. That said, it's still a grand song.

'The Crowd Revisited' (annA rydeR)

A reprise of track 4 comprising some of the instrumentation and Simon and annA's vocals – mandolin, penny whistle and the French horns are much more to the fore, drums, bass and guitar completely missing. In fact, it ends on a single penny whistle and then fades out on the horn ensemble. It's very pretty, but I'm not sure it makes a better ending to the album than the full song would have done, with the cheers and applause of the Cropredy crowd.

Over The Next Hill (2004)

Personnel:

Simon Nicol: vocals, acoustic & electric guitars

Ric Sanders, violin, mandolin

Dave Pegg: electric & acoustic bass guitars, mandolin, vocals, double bass on 'Auld Lang Syne'

Chris Leslie: vocals, bouzouki, mandolin, violin, Native American flute, ukulele on 'Auld Lang Syne'

Gerry Conway: drums, percussion

Additional personnel:

annA rydeR: accordion

Martin Lamble: percussion on 'Si Tu Dois Partir'

Chris While: vocals on 'Si Tu Dois Partir';

Simon & Hilary Mayo: vocals on 'Auld Lang Syne'

Recorded at Woodworm Studios, Barford St. Michael, Oxfordshire in March/April 2004

Engineered & Mixed by Mark Tucker

Produced by Dave Pegg and Mark Tucker

Record label: Matty Grooves

Released: June 2004

Highest chart position: Uncharted

Length: 51:42

Current edition: Original issue

For the next few years, Fairport Convention entered a period of uncertainty during which the future of the Cropredy festival – indeed, the future of the band itself – came under question. The cause was the marriage split of Dave Pegg and his wife Christine after 37 years. Now, we are all used to celebrities' break-ups being plastered all over the tabloids, but Fairport wouldn't normally have a high enough profile to justify much attention on their relationship woes. But Peggy's divorce was more than domestic – it forced him to sell his Oxfordshire home, Woodworms Hilton, and the adjoining studio. He also had to auction many of his vintage instruments and fold the record label that had issued all but three of Fairport's comeback albums – eagle-eyed fans noticed that *Over The Next Hill* was issued on a new label called Matty Grooves, a name inspired by a misprint on a recently-released live album.

It was also announced that 2004's Cropredy Festival would probably be the last – Christine had played a major role in its development and organisation, and Peggy admitted: 'The way Chris feels at the moment, I have to say that she is not sure she wants to continue with it. I am the guilty party in all this, and it is a very difficult time for us both.' Chris said at the time:

> I have been running Cropredy for 23 years. We do not have a big organisation behind it, and it is a huge task. I think Dave will be going to live abroad with

his new partner and I do not think I can continue. It may well be the end of an era. However, we are doing all we can to make this year's Cropredy the best ever.

In the meantime, work started on recording the latest Fairport album – and, once again, it was a solid effort following the pattern of its well-received predecessor. Indeed, *Mojo* magazine called it 'simply Fairport's best album in 25 years' which may be over-egging it a bit – most fans would probably put it somewhere in the middle if truth be told. There were plenty of tried and trusted names in the credits for the eleven tracks – three songs from Chris, two tunes from Ric, two compositions from Steve Tilston and one each from Ben Bennion, Julie Matthews and good old Trad.

Fairport also continued their recent practice of pulling out and buffing up an old classic, this time their unlikely hit single 'Si Tu Dois Partir'. In a very touching gesture, they included some percussion from the original 1968 recording, played by Martin Lamble shortly before his death in the group's van crash.

Simon Nicol was going to call the album 'Senior Moments'. The eventual title not only references the band's growing, er, maturity but also the many challenges they have faced in their long and eventful career. There would be more challenges to come.

'Over The Next Hill' (Steve Tilston)

A sprightly opener, written for the band – the demo has Peggy on the bass – and containing many lyrical and musical references to Fairport and other artists. It's 'Rising For The Moon' again but a bit less optimistic – a song about being a band on the road, the endless travel and grubby dressing rooms, and the hope that there may be, as Richard Thompson once said, a rainbow over the hill. Simon strums acoustic guitar and opens with the lines 'Forever, forever, the road goes on forever' – a reference perhaps to the 1969 song by The Highwaymen, or maybe to the record company of the same name that has in its catalogue a compilation by The Dylan Project, a Bob Dylan covers band featuring Peggy, Gerry and Simon. There's another Dylan nod in this song when Simon sings about taking 'the tambourine man's shilling'.

Then there's a reference to 'dingo days down under', about the band's enduring popularity in Australia because of the Trevor Lucas connection. Our next reference, in the middle eight, mixes Dylan's 'Like A Rolling Stone' with The Rolling Stones as the band suddenly break into the famous riff from the 1965 single '(I Can't Get No) Satisfaction'. In a reprise of the middle eight after a brief instrumental section, they play the riff from 'The Last Time', another Stones single from the same year.

Finally, there are two more song references mixed together as the track comes to a close – 'oh rainbows, rainbows, somewhere over rainbows/Over the next hill, who knows where the time goes'. Have you spotted them yet?

'I'm Already There' (Chris Leslie)

In 1845 Royal Navy officer and seasoned explorer Sir John Franklin left England with two ships, the Erebus and the Terror, to explore the last un-navigated section of the Northwest Passage. The ships became icebound in the Canadian Arctic, and the entire expedition of 129 men perished. Franklin's wife Jane persuaded the British government to launch a search, and the graves of some of the crewmen were eventually discovered on nearby islands. The evidence suggested they took a while to die and cut marks on their bones were seen as signs of cannibalism.

Nevertheless, Lord Franklin was hailed as a hero and songs began circulating about him just a few years later, including a broadsheet ballad also known as 'Lady Franklin's Lament' and 'The Sailor's Dream', and usually performed to the tune of the traditional Irish air 'Cailin Og a Stor'. It has been performed by a long list of artists including Martin Carthy on *Second Album* (1966), Pentangle on *Cruel Sister* (1970) and Nic Jones on *In Search Of Nic Jones* (1981).

Chris Leslie seems to have developed something of an obsession with the story as this is the first of three of his songs Fairport have recorded to date about the voyage. 'I'm Already There' was inspired by a stained-glass window in a church in Banbury showing a ship trapped in ice, surrounded by snow and a large polar bear, installed in the 1860s by the then vicar whose brother had died on Lord Franklin's expedition. The song tells the story of the doomed voyage but also switches about between the viewpoints of the two brothers and their completely different lives.

Chris opens by singing unaccompanied the first few lines of the original ballad in G major before a chiming acoustic backing from finger-picked guitar and strummed bouzouki in G minor leads him into the first verse of his song proper. It moves into D major for a second section and then back into G major for the chorus, with Peggy providing lovely bass runs. The result of all this chord-hopping is an interesting song packed with little melodic hooks that shift between a minor key for the serious storytelling and a major key for the imagined interaction between the two brothers. If you're a guitarist you'll find it easy to pick up and quite delightful to play.

There's a fairly fast reel planted in the middle and repeated at the end, picking up pace and volume with Gerry providing powerful drum rhythms. All in all, a very effective Chris Leslie song.

'Wait For The Tide To Come In' (Ben Bennion)

The second song Fairport have recorded by Peggy's pal Ben is a surprisingly political number that, spiritually at least, is the kin of Richard Thompson's 'Genesis Hall'. It's about eviction and homelessness and living on the back roads of life, being pushed around by the very same people in power who conspired against you in the first place. 'Do you believe the politicians?' Bennion asks, 'Do you really think they'll listen?' (Hint: The answer is no.) You would think from the subject matter that this would be a minor key lament but you would be wrong. In fact, it's a country-style rocker in D major with an added A flat, which makes it sound a bit discordant and dangerous. But any anger in the song is dissipated by Chris's vocals – he's just too nice.

Simon gets to play a bit of tasty lead electric guitar as well as providing American-sounding harmony vocals along with Peggy. In fact, if you didn't know this was Fairport, you might think it was some sort of alt-country band with a very English-sounding lead singer. This could have ended up as a somewhat nondescript rocker rather like some of the Dave Whetsone songs the band have recorded, but a certain joie de vivre and a hint of self-mockery result in an entertaining four and a half minutes.

'Canny Capers' (Ric Sanders)
Ric never disappoints with his instrumentals, whether they are O'Carolan-inspired ballads or something like this, four self-penned dance tunes that get steadily more manic as the track goes on. So we start with a jolly jig featuring Simon on acoustic guitar and the twin mandolins of Chris Leslie and Dave Pegg – which is why it's called 'Step Away From The Bass'. That leaps into 'Sir Norm De Norm', with Peggy back on the bass, Ric playing a fast reel and Simon giving us electric guitar power chords. 'My Gypsy Pal' is another, even faster, reel as Ric plays blindingly fast notes on his fiddle and, finally, 'Conway's Cognac' – dedicated to the drummer's favourite gig tipple – ends with a cacophony of fiddle, drums, bass and electric guitar. Fabulous stuff.

'Over The Falls' (Chris Leslie)
A song about Charles Blondin, the first man to walk on a tightrope across Niagara Falls in 1859. Later he did it blindfold, in a sack, standing on a chair, pushing a wheelbarrow, carrying his manager on his back and while cooking and eating an omelette. So, not a show-off then. Chris's song is an upbeat number that opens with strong harmonies on the chorus before going into a verse about standing on the edge, feeling the tension of the wire in his toes. As usual, Chris finds the personal in the history and the line 'you are the balance on the wire' seems to be addressed to one of Blondin's three wives. Gerry provides some clattering drum sounds and Ric a pleasant but unremarkable violin solo.

'The Wassail Song' (Trad arr Fairport Convention)
A mixture of two songs, actually, beginning with a brief mention of the tune to 'Here We Come A-Wassailing', a Christmas carol composed around 1850. The main song is the 'Gloucestershire Wassail', which dates back to the Middle Ages. The word comes from the Anglo-Saxon for 'be hale and hearty' and wassailing originated when peasants would go to their lords' homes at Christmas and request food and drink, banking on a certain amount of festive generosity.

Plenty of artists in the folk and folk-rock fraternity have performed at least one of the songs. Fairport's version unusually decides to resurrect Maartin

Allcock's favourite time signature of 5/4, which gives it a jaunty feel rather reminiscent of Jethro Tull's 'Living In The Past' but occasionally introduces some awkward moments in the chorus as the band try to fit the lyrics in. Towards the end, there's an instrumental in straight 4/4 rock style. A drum roll introduces Chris with the first verse, Peggy takes the second and Simon the last. Like 'The Card Song' on *The Five Seasons* this is a jolly singalong that should be performed with copious amounts of quaffing.

'The Fossil Hunter' (Chris Leslie)

Chris usually scores a two out of three success rate with his songs, and he's had his successful two on this album. So 'The Fossil Hunter' – based on the story of 19th-century palaeontologist Mary Anning, who supported her family by selling fossils after her father died – is a little underwhelming. It is a pleasant-enough, slightly maudlin ballad, with the repeated refrain that 'she won't find love any more'. But it is perhaps a little too nice and bland compared to his other compositions and palls in comparison. However, his Native American flute solo at the end is a nice touch. By the way, Mary Anning was supposedly the inspiration for the 1908 tongue-twister 'She sells seashells by the seashore'.

'Willow Creek' (Steve Tilston, Chris Parkinson)

British folk musician Parkinson was inspired to write the tune by the town of Willow Creek in Ohio (although there are 14 other Willow Creeks in the US!). Steve Tilston supplied the words, which tell of a meeting with a strange, wild woman on a nut-brown mare who is apparently being pursued by 'five of King George's men', which suggests it is set during the American Revolutionary War of 1775-1783 in the reign of King George III. However, there is no geographical hint in the song at all and no explanation of why the five men are pursuing the girl so desperately that there is blood on their spurs.

The hero of the song sends them in the wrong direction, then sees the girl on a ridge waving her thanks. Like Tilston's 'The Naked Highwayman', 'Willow Creek' cracks along at a fair old pace and presents a bit of a challenge for the singer to squeeze all the words in. Fairport's version opens with Gerry playing all manner of percussion instruments almost in the style of Latin jazz (it would become even more South American when performed live, with shouts of 'Arriba!') with acoustic guitar, plucked violin and bouzouki accompaniment. Simon and Chris share the verses, there's a fiddle solo from Ric, and the song crashes to an end after nearly four exhilarating minutes. Steve Tilston recorded a version for his 2005 album *Of Many Hands*.

'Westward' (Julie Matthews)

A track from Julie Matthews and Chris While's 2004 album *Perfect Mistake*, 'Westward' is a simple, optimistic country song that, lyrically, appears to be inspired by the Westward Expansion of the US in the early 19th century. This was encouraged by the Homestead Act that provided 160 acres of land to anyone prepared to up sticks and move into the wilderness – it was reckoned 100 acres was the minimum required to support a family, so the acre of land mentioned in the song would not have gone very far. The lines 'They promise you silver, they promise you gold/Not one word of truth in the lies that they told' seems to reference the California Gold Rush of 1849, when for every lucky 'Forty-Niner' who found any precious metal there were probably thousands who were disappointed. Fairport perform 'Westward' at a surprisingly fast gallop – certainly quicker than Julie and Chris's version – with Simon taking most of the vocal duties, Chris on mandolin and Ric providing country 'n' western fiddle licks, while Peggy plays solid two-to-a-bar double bass. It ends on plucked strings from Ric and a descending, sliding bass note from Peggy.

'Some Special Place' (Ric Sanders)
Ric's second self-penned tune on the album is a slow fiddle duet with Chris that opens almost like a Scottish pibroch then turns into an O'Carolan-style waltz. Mostly gentle and contemplative, it picks up at the end with some slow, heavy drumming from Gerry. The ending is a bit odd – it sounds like the performance has fallen apart with some misbowing. It is no doubt deliberate but mars an otherwise enjoyable and calming tune.

'Si Tu Dois Partir/Auld Lang Syne' (Bob Dylan/Traditional)
The evolution of Dylan's 1965 song 'If You Gotta Go, Go Now' into a Cajun-style Top 30 hit sung in French is chronicled in the *Unhalfbricking* section. This is a more straight-forward version, with Gerry playing proper drums instead of the original's stacked chair backs, although there is a brief reprise of Martin Lamble's percussion in the middle. Simon takes most of the vocal duties, with Chris While helping out on backing vocals and annA rydeR on accordion. The addition of a fiddle solo section makes this about a minute longer than the 1969 version. There are 32 seconds of silence before a hidden track, a brief burst of Auld Lang Syne sung by the band and Simon and Hilary Mayor – poignant perhaps when one considers three of the musicians on the original recording of 'Si Tu Dois Partir', Sandy Denny, Martin Lamble and Trevor Lucas, had by now all passed away.

Sense Of Occasion (2007)

Personnel:
Simon Nicol: guitars, vocals
Chris Leslie: vocals, mandolin, bouzouki, violin
Ric Sanders: violin, keyboard
Dave Pegg: bass guitar, vocals
Gerry Conway: drums, percussion, Indian harmonium on 'Best Wishes'
Recorded at Woodworm Studios, Barford St. Michael, Oxfordshire in November 2006
Engineered & Mixed by Mark Tucker
Produced by Mark Tucker with Fairport Convention
Record label: Matty Grooves
Released: 12 February 2007
Highest chart position: Uncharted
Length: 60:07
Current edition: Original issue

There must have been times between 2004 and 2006 when Fairport Convention thought they might not make it to their 40th anniversary. The band had been faced with many challenges and obstacles before and come out the other side, still playing, recording and touring. But one of the constants, the rock on which the post-1969 band was built, was bass player Dave Pegg – cheerful, smiling, down-to-earth, dependable, unflappable-unless-drunk Peggy. So to see him suddenly go through an emotional crisis that threatened the future of Fairport must have been as bewildering and worrying to the band as it was to the fans.

The split from wife Christine after 37 years was professional as well as personal and could have scuppered Cropredy, of which Mrs Pegg had been such a vital part. But there was good news on that front – the band created a company called Fairport Convention Ltd and recruited 'Independent Entertainment Professional' Gareth Williams to run the festival, so it could continue. At the time of writing, it has just celebrated its own 40th anniversary. After 2004's Cropredy and the release of that year's *Over The Next Hill* the band performed virtually non-stop into 2005. But things came to a head when Fairport reached the States for an acoustic tour without Gerry Conway. In his autobiography, Peggy says:

> I was in a bit of a state: I was drinking a lot, even by my standards, and I was in the process of getting divorced from Christine. My head wasn't in a good place, and to say I'd become unpredictable would be an understatement. I gather I was a bit of a nightmare to be with ... I do remember having a lot to drink. Before the next gig they decided I wasn't in a fit state to play. Next day we had a meeting and it was decided that I should take a break and do something about getting myself together.

Peggy played just two dates on the US tour – the band fulfilled three more, then cancelled the rest and flew home, unhappy to be just a three-piece. But Peggy and his new partner Ellen remained in the States, meeting up with old friends there and just getting his head together. By the time Cropredy 2005 came around a new, refreshed and happier Peggy joined Fairport on stage and resumed his bass-playing duties. But it took another year and a half for the band to get back into the studio and craft its 40th-anniversary celebration album, *Sense Of Occasion*. The result is a collection that sits pretty much in the same territory as its two predecessors – entertaining and comfortable, beautifully played but with few surprises in its blending of contemporary folk-rock, Chris Leslie originals and a couple of old favourites.

In fact, Chris has no fewer than five songs here although they are not quite as inspired as some of his previous efforts (and he had better to come). Ric's three instrumentals seem more subdued than usual and the reworkings of the two classics, 'Polly On The Shore' and 'Tam Lin', don't outshine the originals, although they give Simon a chance to plant his vocals on songs originally sung by Trevor Lucas and Sandy Denny. The best tracks on the album come from some unexpected sources – a Beatle-y ballad from Glenn Tilbrook of Squeeze and a breezy cover of XTC's 'Love On A Farmboy's Wages'.

But it's fair to say *Sense Of Occasion* is a lesser effort from Fairport and, at 60 minutes, it could have lost of couple of the weaker tracks. Some reviewers criticised it for being too smooth and polished, and twee and sentimental. Even stalwart Fairport supporter Allmusic dismissed it as 'more a holding action than a step forward'. But after what the band had gone through we should now be thankful there was any new album at all.

'Keep On Turning The Wheel' (Chris Leslie)

A 1966 split-screen VW camper van eulogised as, er, a woman – 'So admired for your body/So bewitching are your eyes'. Chris's best track on the album is a pleasant, catchy song about the iconic mode of transport, referencing the 1960s, *Magical Mystery Tour* and The Beatles. Bouncy and melodic, it does have a certain McCartney-esque charm about it, with Peggy and Simon offering cheeky 'yeah, yeah, yeah' backing vocals. The title comes right at the end as the song plays out with indistinct 1960s radio sounds in the background.

'Love On A Farmboy's Wages' (Andy Partridge)

XTC were a punk band from the late 1970s that evolved into one of the most interesting and original groups of the '80s and '90s. Their songs, mostly written by guitarist and singer Andy, were quirky, witty, clever and musically ingenious, drawing from the likes of The Beatles and The Kinks but with added aggression and cynicism. 'Love On A Farmboy's Wages' comes from their overlooked sixth album *Mummer* (1983) which, like its successor *The Big Express*, suffers from being sandwiched between the sprawling but wonderful *English Settlement* and the polished and professional *Skylarking*. The song, as the title suggests, is about a farmboy getting married and worrying about how he can support a wife on his lousy agricultural-worker wages. Unfortunately, it's the only job he knows 'and it's breaking my back'. Fairport's version is pretty much a clone of the original, except with fiddle playing the original tricky acoustic guitar riff and Simon's sunny vocals replacing Andy Partridge's cynical snarl. If Fairport are looking for another XTC song to cover I would humbly suggest 'All The Pretty Girls' from *The Big Express*.

'The Bowman's Return' (Ric Sanders)

On *Who Knows Where the Time Goes?* (1997) the bowman retreated, quite rapidly. Here, the bowman returns but his experiences have clearly slowed him down somewhat. He's plodding a bit on this fiddle tune, frequently pausing for breath as Gerry hits a few percussion instruments. Thankfully, things speed up in the second section, a jig that subtly changes time signatures, and gets even faster in a reel, with added electric guitar chops and phrases. The twin fiddles of Ric and Chris build up and up into a dramatic, screaming finish.

'South Dakota To Manchester' (Chris Leslie)

Nicholas Black Elk was a Lakota medicine man who fought at the Battle of the Little Bighorn and the Wounded Knee Massacre in 1890. In 1887 he joined Buffalo Bill Cody's Wild West Show and travelled to England, putting on a command performance for Queen Victoria and staying for five months in Salford near Manchester. Chris's song is inspired by that period of his life, recounted in his book Black Elk Speaks, and contrasts South Dakota with the alien landscape of Manchester. Despite the melancholic subject matter, the song is quite upbeat, driven by swiftly strummed mandolin and Gerry's heavy drums (I swear they are getting louder with every album. Soon Gerry will be as loud as Dave Mattacks). But it lacks some catchy melodic hooks, especially in the rather dreary chorus, and fails to make itself very memorable.

'Spring Song' (Chris Leslie)

We're in, the liner notes suggest, the beautiful countryside around Morvah in West Penwith, Cornwall – it lies slap-bang in the Cornwall Area of Natural Beauty and the South West Coast Path passes close by. Chris's pretty song in a happy 6/8 extols the beauties of the landscape and recalls the history of those who passed this way 'from tinner to weaver, saint and believer'. He seems to be particularly happy to be in Morvah in springtime when the ale tastes so much better for being drunk in the gentle sunshine. The song ends with a minute and a half of 'Princess Royal', a morris tune from Bampton-in-the-Bush, Oxfordshire, which is about 260 miles away from Morvah via the M5.

'Polly On The Shore' (Music: Dave Pegg, Lyrics: Swarbrick, Lucas)

The late Trevor Lucas sang this on *Nine* during Simon Nicol's absence from the band so it's interesting to hear his take on the track. It's pretty much a clone of the original except for busier drums from Gerry and Chris's mandolin replacing Jerry Donahue's electric guitar. It lacks the drama of the original and, try as he might, Chris cannot match the peerless guitar licks Jerry brought to the track 34 years ago.

'Just Dandy' (Ric Sanders)

Mandolin and fiddle duet on a stately, Irish-sounding jig – this was accompanied by Irish dancers when Fairport played it at Cropredy in 2007. The composition consists of three melodies of eight bars each – for the first half of the tune mandolin plays first and fiddle repeats, then both work in unison for the second half. It's pretty but not distinctive enough to distinguish it from the many mando-fiddle tunes the band have recorded over the years.

'Tam Lin' (trad arr Dave Swarbrick)

'Tam Lin' was one of the tunes used to audition new bass players when Ashley Hutchings left the band in 1969. If they could cope with its alternating bars of 3/4 and 4/4 then they could probably play anything. Peggy passed with flying colours, but the band rarely performed this live without Sandy Denny – Swarb certainly did it in 1971 while Vikki Clayton and Chris While have filled in for Sandy at Cropredy. Here, Simon takes lead vocals and does a good job, making the song as much his own as he did with 'Matty Groves'. But in terms of energy and dark foreboding, I wouldn't say this betters the original.

'In Our Town' (Chris Leslie)

As Chris says in the liner notes: 'When children leave the nest, it's a bittersweet journey – who knows where the time goes?' Anyone who has waved their kids off to a new life (sob!) will appreciate the sentiments in Chris's gentle little song, in which an 18-year-old girl leaves home, presumably to go to university. Ah, stop your sobbing, she'll be home every weekend with her dirty laundry. A brief drum roll from Gerry introduces a pretty melody with the repeated refrain of the title. But who is Emily Lewis in the lyrics? Most likely, she is Eleanor Rigby – a sequence of syllables that fit the song.

'Edge Of The World' (Chris Leslie)

Chris leaves his comfort zone of pretty ballads with this more muscular track, based around a fast guitar and violin riff, in which he tells the tale of a pirate character condemned to sail for all eternity on legendary ghost ship The Flying Dutchman. Chris credits fan Rebecca Maxfield for recounting the story of the cursed vessel after a gig at The Town Crier in Pawling, New York. In the song, his pirate character is 'carried away through the sea over hundreds of years as the world comes and goes through the veils of eternity'. Musically, there's some slightly funky electric guitar and bass here with drums and bongos from Gerry. Chris's voice is a little too nice for the song – it would have been a better vehicle for Simon, who brought a bit more menace to Chris's previous salty seadog saga 'Spanish Main' on *Who Knows Where The Time Goes?*. But it has a bit of swing to it, a catchy refrain and Ric plays some fiddle improvisation before the track ends on the fast riff. It is, of course, the second song about the ghost ship Peggy has played on – he provides bass for Jethro Tull's track 'Flying Dutchman' from *Broadsword And The Beast* (1982).

'Hawkswood's Army' (Pete Scrowther)
Sir John Hawkwood was an English soldier who fought under King Edward II at the battles of Crecy and Poitiers in the 14th century. After a peace treaty was signed between England and France, he joined a band of mercenaries and fought for whoever paid the most, including the Pope. He died on 17 March 1394 and had a magnificent funeral in the Duomo in Florence.

Scrowther's song tells the story from the point of view of an unnamed soldier who joins Hawkwood's army after the peace treaty of Bretigny and helps him 'rob and rape' across Italy and France. Like the pirate on the Dutchman, our soldier knows he is damned because of his bloody deeds and will die alone, 'my bones upon this dusty plain so far away from home'.

Simon takes lead vocals on a composition that bears some similarities in tone and style to Ralph McTell's 'Wat Tyler' on *Gladys' Leap* – guitar, bass and drums power along a medium-paced rocker with traditional-sounding verses and a rip-roaring chorus. There is a fiddle and mandolin instrumental played as a reel but with the unusual chord sequence of A minor to G minor and back to A minor again. Simon does an excellent job putting a bit of aggression into the song, which ends rather abruptly after the final chorus.

'The Vision' (Bill Miller, John Flanagan)
A pretty ballad based on Simon's finger-picked acoustic guitar and Gerry's steady, unobtrusive drums, with lyrics about following your vision on the journey of life. You wouldn't guess from the tune or words that Bill Miller is a Native American singer/songwriter whose Mohican name is Fuah-Ya Heay Aka, which means 'bird song'. He plays guitar and Native American flute – he's on 'Colors Of The Wind' from the Disney film *Pocahontas* – and has toured with Tori Amos, Richie Havens and Arlo Guthrie. 'The Vision' comes from his 1999 album *Ghostdance* where it has a bit more of a swinging, country 'n' western vibe, with a bit of cheesy organ and female backing singers. Fairport strip it of all its idiosyncrasies and produce a more straight-laced version, although Miller and Chris Leslie have a similar, gentle vocal style.

'Your Heart And Mine' (Ric Sanders)
Another slow, contemplative violin ballad from Ric, dedicated to the love of his life, Angie. It opens with finger-picked acoustic guitar from Simon before Ric

135

plays long, sweeping fiddle notes and Chris adds gentle mandolin. It's pretty but is unlikely to unseat 'Portmeirion' as his best O'Carolan-style composition.

'Untouchable' (Glenn Tilbrook, Christopher Braid)

One of the few composers in the known universe who can write Paul McCartney songs almost as well as Paul McCartney, Tilbrook was lead singer and guitarist with British band Squeeze, who had considerable chart success from the late 1970s to the mid-1980s with most of their hits penned by him and songwriting partner Chris Difford. When Squeeze eventually broke up for good in 1999 Tilbrook released solo albums including *Transatlantic Ping Pong* (2004) which included his version of 'Untouchable', a plaintive power-pop song packed full of endearing melodic hooks.

Fairport produce almost a carbon copy of the original track, with Chris's gentle voice sounding eerily similar to Tilbrook's. Ric replaces the original's keyboards with fiddle plucking and bowing and Chris provides a mandolin solo. They even keep the atonal chords Tilbrook throws into one of the choruses (because that's the sort of thing Squeeze would do) and the dramatic, extended outro with its hints of 'I Am The Walrus'.

'Galileo's Apology' (PJ Wright)

Born in Leicester, guitarist PJ has worked extensively as a session player and in groups such as Little Johnny England and the Steve Gibbons Band. In fact, it was as a member of the latter outfit that he became involved in *The Dylan Project* (1998), a tribute album of Bob Dylan songs mixing members of the Steve Gibbons Band with Fairport Convention. That evolved into a group with the same name as the album and including PJ on lead guitar and Peggy on bass. The pair struck up a friendship and have worked together as a duo, releasing the albums *Galileo's Apology* (2006) and *Double At T'Mill* (2007).

The first album's title song is a gentle anti-religion polemic that says 'spare me the fairytale, dogma and theology' and points out that it took 300 years (actually 350) for the Roman Catholic Church to apologise for putting the 17th century Italian astronomer and physicist under house arrest over his insistence that the Earth orbits the Sun (which it does). Spoiler alert – PJ also reveals 'I don't believe on Christmas Eve Santa climbs the chimney'. All these radical sentiments are wrapped up in a loose, country chug of a song performed mainly by Simon, with Ric having fun playing slightly humorous fiddle solos and Chris on his trusty mando. There are some very nice vocal harmonies towards the end, and the song slips cheerfully by in three minutes.

'Best Wishes' (Steve Ashley)

Londoner Steve has been part of the folk-rock 'mafia' since the late 1960s when he sang on albums by Shirley Collins and joined the first incarnation of the Albion Band in 1972. His 1974 solo album *Stroll On* featured Simon, Peggy and Dave Mattacks and he has been a close friend of the Fairports for decades. So it's a surprise to realise that this is the first time they have recorded one of his songs for a studio album. 'Best Wishes' comes from *Time And Tide* (2007) and is an appropriate number for a birthday album and a cousin to Bob Dylan's 'Forever Young' – may you have good fortune, good company, good health and good music. In fact, the lyrics suggest it may well have been written with Fairport Convention in mind in the lines 'Long may the music keep you underneath its spell/And long may you keep it live and always play it well'.

It's a slow, stately song performed in three-part harmony throughout by Simon, Peggy and Chris with just acoustic guitar backing, a Ric fiddle solo and Gerry playing gentle chords on an Indian harmonium. There are 30 seconds of silence at the end before a short hidden track slowly appears – the verse melody of 'Untouchable' repeatedly played and at a faster pace on mandolin with cymbal percussion from Gerry.

Festival Bell (2011)

Personnel:
Simon Nicol: vocals, acoustic and electric guitars, bass ukulele
Chris Leslie: vocals, bouzouki, mandolin, Portuguese guitar, D whistle, low D
whistle, violin, footsteps
Rick Sanders: violins, keyboards, bass ukulele
Dave Pegg: bass guitar, tenor ukulele, backing vocals
Gerry Conway: drums, percussion, washboard
Additional personnel:
Joe Brown: ukulele, backing vocals on 'Ukulele Central'
Frank Skinner: banjolele on 'Ukulele Central'
Recorded, mixed and mastered at The Bowman's Retreat, Oxfordshire, 2010
Recorded, engineered and mixed by John Gale
Drums recorded at Sound By Design's Delta Studios
Frank Skinner recorded by Vo Fletcher
Produced by John Gale and Fairport Convention
Record label: Matty Grooves
Released: January 2011
Highest chart position: Uncharted
Length: 52:25
Current edition: Original issue

You know you've made it when they name a bell after you. Well, almost. It's
actually the Festival Bell, freshly cast and hanging in St Mary's Church in
Cropredy, Oxfordshire, and the Fairport Cropredy Convention doesn't start
until the bell has been rung at 4pm on the first day. You can't become more
Establishment than being embraced by the Church of England – and it's only
taken Fairport 45 years!

It was inevitable, then, that their 26th album (including *Live 1987* – see
previous chapters for justification) would be called *Festival Bell* and Chris
Leslie would pen a merry ditty to celebrate its existence. In fact, there's a
celebratory feel to a lot of the album – it's optimistic, upbeat, tuneful and
positive. It is, without a doubt, better than *Sense Of Occasion* – magazine
Record Collector said it was 'a work of maturity and depth, yet delivered with a
lightness of touch that will delight fans old and new'.

At first sight, the mix of compositions suggests it's business as usual in the
song-spotting department – five Chris Leslies, five from Ric (including one
written with Chris and one with Dave Pegg), some Ralph McTell, a few new
names and, finally, a reworked classic in 'Rising For The Moon'. What the
album lacks is any Trad, which you may consider to be odd for a FOLK-rock
band. But Fairport had long ago taken their hand from behind their ear and
embraced a more contemporary repertoire – and plenty of these songs are in
a traditional style, telling stories from the past and using the structures and
repetitive melodies of folk music.

As usual, Gerry Conway's inventive and distinctive percussion lifts up many of these songs, the instrumentals are a lot of fun and there's even a ukulele sextet, which you will either embrace or run away from while screaming. On a few occasions, Chris takes a lead vocal that would really work better for Simon, and there's a couple of songs that come and go without making a huge impression. But overall, this is the work of a band that has put its most recent troubles behind it.

'Mercy Bay' (Chris Leslie)

Another song inspired by the doomed expedition of Sir John Franklin to find the Northwest Passage. In the years after his ships disappeared somewhere in the ice off Greenland more than a dozen expeditions were launched to find Franklin and his gallant crew, including HMS Investigator in 1850. That, too, was stuck in ice in Mercy Bay for three terrible winters until the surviving sailors were rescued by HMS Resolute. In 2010, in the year *Festival Bell* was recorded, the wreckage of Investigator was found buried in silt and water, its masts torn off by the ice flows, and this is no doubt what inspired Chris to take up pen, paper and mandolin to write the song. It opens with a repetitive, ringing three-note motif in G minor with simple bass drum accompaniment. Simon sings in his baritone growl, with Chris and Peggy joining in on the words 'go down', which appear in every verse. The simplicity of the verse melody creates tension, accentuated by Peggy's brooding basslines, which is released as Simon's vocals hit higher notes in the chorus. The final rendition of the chorus is given slightly atonal backing vocals to create a sense of unease. There are acoustic and electric guitars, Chris on bouzouki and mandolin while Ric plays both violin and keyboards. It's an effective opener, although the listener keeps expecting the arrangement to burst into more life at the end. Instead, the song broods all the way to the finish.

'Rui's Guitar' (Chris Leslie)

Chris composed this on a Portuguese guitar given to the band by Fairport friend Rui Vasco Godinho Mendes, from Lisbon. The instrument looks more like a bouzouki than a guitar, with six sets of two strings, and is associated with a style of music known as fado – mournful, melancholy songs of longing and melancholy. Chris's composition is probably a little too upbeat for fado, with its fast opening melody line played almost in baroque style over a descending bass, and the words are definitely much too positive and uplifting as Chris sings about a 'lazy, hazy day' with sunshine, flowers and ripening fields of maize. The nod to the fado comes in the third verse, which references the danger and loneliness in being a sailor, a frequent preoccupation of the genre. It's a pleasant number with warm harmony vocals on the refrain of 'So I'll sing this song for you on Rui's guitar' – no doubt Rui himself is very touched.

'Danny Jack's Chase' (Ric Sanders)

By his own admission, Ric found himself at this time writing a lot of 'piratey' tunes, influenced no doubt by the film series *Pirates Of The Caribbean* – part three, *At World's End,* had been released in 2007. In live performance, he would explain that, instead of a violin, he wrote the song using a ukulele and a bottle of Jack Daniels (referred to by vegetarian Ric as 'a meat substitute'). Perhaps that explains the unusual, thrashing chord sequence at the start of G, G7, C, B flat and A major, the almost flamenco guitar rhythm and the unpredictable fiddle and mandolin melody that reels all over the tune like a drunken sailor on a heaving deck. There's moments of jazzy improvisation then a final flourish of notes over the intro chords before we crash to a finish. It's mad but it works, partly because Gerry's drumming is so versatile and creative. It's also a bit of a return to form for Ric, whose instrumentals had began to sound a bit tired on the previous album.

'Reunion Hill' (Richard Shindell)

Shindell is an American folk-singer who now lives in Buenos Aires. He frequently writes historical songs from the first-person perspective – 'Reunion Hill' is penned from the viewpoint of a Civil War widow, somewhere in Confederate country in the south-east of the US, who waves her husband off to battle then tends to a stream of injured soldiers returning from defeat while mourning her fallen man. It's a surprisingly breezy tune repeating the chords G, D, A minor and C major – perilously close to the overworked G, D, E minor and C major sequence that seems to adorn most country-rock songs these days. Originally penned for Joan Baez, who released it on her 1997 album *Gone From Danger,* Shindell also recorded it as the title track of a solo album the same year. His version is gentle and wistful, with a simple acoustic guitar accompaniment, while Joan's is upbeat and rhythmic, and it's her rendition that seems to have provided the inspiration for Fairport. Strummed acoustic guitar and mandolin open proceedings before Simon sings the first verse, then drums, bass and organ come in, with fiddle and mandolin playing the refrain. At the end, Chris adds wistful whistle. It's a pleasant tune but, bearing in mind the downbeat subject matter, some listeners may think Shindell's original version has the edge in style and tone.

'Wouldn't Say No' (Chris Leslie)

The idea of the tough, no-nonsense US cop secretly fighting his inner demons has become a bit of a cliché these days in endless crime novels and TV shows but rarely does such a character appear in a song performed by a British folk-rock band. So we have Chris to thank for this, a medium-paced piece of, well, country-pop I guess. Apparently the image of the lovelorn law enforcement officer driving a big convertible car through a wood, looking for a jailbreaker, came to his mind as he played a mandolin riff one sunny morning in his garden. The riff doesn't sound particularly cop-like or lovelorn – instead, it's a twisty, country-style tune that's more *Dukes of Hazzard* than *Dirty Harry*, especially when Ric doubles up on fiddle. Electric guitar chords and Gerry's pounding drums drive the song along with a bit of a Sixties vibe – in fact, there's more than a hint of Squeeze in there for me in the density of chords in the chorus and the bright harmony refrain of the title. It ends a little abruptly, but it's a catchy, bright and arresting (pun intended) track.

'Around The Wild Cape Horn' (Ralph McTell)

There's seems to be an American theme to this album – it's the third song in a row to have its roots in the Land of the Free. The inspiration this time is Massachusetts adventurer Irving McClure Johnson, who sailed around Cape Horn while a merchant seaman on the barque Peking. An amateur film-maker, he took footage of the voyage which was later released as a movie in 1929. With his wife Exy, he circumnavigated the world seven times, documenting the voyages in books and films before dying in 1991.

Ralph's song is a bright, cheerful narrative full of his particular songwriting tricks – the first-person narrative, the descending E minor, D and C sequence (although with a capo on the second fret to put the song itself in A), the doubling up of lines at the end of the verses to put in an extra bar of music, the fairly predictable way the melody swings up then comes down as the song returns to its home chord. There's a similarity in style and tone to 'Travelling By Steam' on *Jewel In The Crown*, except that song is a jig, and this is in 4/4 time. The band clearly enjoy playing this – it's catchy, easy to listen to and is performed with pace and enthusiasm.

'Celtic Moon' (Mark Evans, Carolyn Evans)

Mark and Carolyn are a duo from Birmingham known as Red Shoes who have, to date, released three albums with the help of Peggy and Ric. 'Celtic Moon' comes from their Peggy-produced debut album *Ring Around The Land* (2010) and is a simple folk tune about a woman who loved and lost but finds strength from the Celtic moon (which is, of course, the same moon as the rest of us just viewed from a very slightly different angle).

Strangely, this is performed without Simon – Peggy plays very accomplished acoustic guitar and mandolin and takes lead vocals in his gentle, deliberate Brummie voice. Chris plays violin and supplies backing vocals while Ric is on bass ukulele! How did that happen? Peggy really loves this song and plays it faster than Red Shoes do – personally, I think it has little to offer apart from some nice mando and violin action from Peggy and Chris.

'Ukulele Central' (Chris Leslie, Ric Sanders)

A potted history of the ukulele, performed not only by Simon, Peggy, Chris and Ric on the four-stringed little instrument but with the help of comedian Frank Skinner and musician Joe Brown. Ric was inspired by seeing Joe play the instrument at the concert for George Harrison recorded at the Royal Albert Hall in 2002 – he freeze-framed the DVD to see where Joe's fingers went. Words come from Chris and tell how the little uke arrived in Honolulu, Hawaii, from

Spain in 1879 and started a craze among the locals. The song is predictably silly and fun, with the band's three singers and Joe Brown harmonising the letters U-K-U-L-E-L-E before a medium-paced strum allows Chris to sing the verses. There's a minor key chorus during which there's a short-lived attempt to have a bit of fun with the similar-sounding 'uke' and 'you can'.

'Albert And Ted' (Dave Pegg/Ric Sanders)

Peggy's dad Albert and Ric's dad Ted worked together at Hartfield Crescent School in Hall Green, Birmingham, as respectively caretaker and English teacher, later headmaster. In his biography, Peggy tells how his father knew Mr Sanders was into music and played him a recording of his son's first band, Dave And The Emeralds. Mr Sanders' response was positive; he also mentioned that his son Ric was learning violin. A couple of decades later… Peggy wrote a bass instrumental on his new Ibanez 505 and Ric had a tune that he thought would fit over the top of it. The result is this short but enjoyable little instrumental that opens with Gerry hitting woodblocks and bongos before the band launch into a jig-like tune led by Ric on fiddle. Then there's a sudden change as Peggy plays a fiendishly-difficult bass run, joined by Chris on mandolin and finally Ric on violin. It's fun while it lasts.

'Darkside Wood' (Chris While)

Lancashire lass Chris While is a singer/songwriter who toured with her husband Joe before joining the Albion Band in 1993, working with Simon on the albums *Acousticity*, *Albion Heart* and *Demi Paradise*. Later she formed a duo with another former Albion Band member, Julie Matthews. 'Darkside Wood' comes from their 2010 album *Hitting The Ground Running* and is set in the forests of Australia. A couple go walking together but are trapped by a ferocious bushfire. They try to escape by plunging into 'the Wilson dam', but the water is too hot, and the song suggests the girl expires in the mud. Eventually, the man gets home safely with the body of his young lady in his arms.

While Chris performs the song with medium-paced acoustic guitar picking accompaniment, Fairport's version is more busy and muscular, with Simon strumming acoustic guitar in G major, bubbling bass from Peggy and steady drumming from Gerry with the occasional offbeat percussion. Chris sings and Ric provides a fiddle solo full of foreboding in a G minor instrumental section before the song goes back to G major for the remaining verses. The song ends in G minor again with Chris, Peggy and Simon harmonising on the lines 'we were running'.

'London Apprentice/Johnny Ginears (Ralph McTell/Ric Sanders)

Another McTell number, like 'Around The Wild Cape Horn' but slower with a more plodding rhythm. Being an apprentice requires no explanation – the song suggests that no matter how long you live in London and walk the city's streets you will never really get to know it. To drive the point home the track starts with Chris Leslie's footsteps – according to the liner notes 'using the most modern recording techniques, he put down his right foot first and then overdubbed his left foot just moments later, a trick he developed while on manoeuvres with the Adderbury Morris Men'. The lyrics reference Sir Christopher Wren, designer of the replacement St Paul's Cathedral after the medieval original was burned down in the Great Fire of London in 1666, and English writer Dr Samuel Johnson, who famously said 'when a man is tired of London, he is tired of life'. Simon sings – his first lead vocal since the previous McTell track – and plays acoustic guitar, with violin, mandolin, bass and drums accompaniment.

It is followed by a Ric tune, 'Johnny Ginears'. The title comes from recording engineer John Gale, who mixed the album while drinking gin and tonic. After a while, he would announce it was time to stop work because he had his 'gin ears' on. The tune, played on fiddle and mandolin in a minor key, continues the same plodding rhythm, ending with versatile Chris's footsteps.

'Rising For The Moon' (Sandy Denny)
A remake of Sandy's song that provided the title for Fairport's attempted 'breakthrough' album in 1975. It follows the same template with fiddle arpeggios to start and Chris replacing Sandy on vocals. Even the instrumental is identical to the original, just substituting Jerry Donahue's lead guitar with fiddle and mandolin duet. The band do a solid job with it but I would suggest we all go back and listen to the original.

'Danny Jack's Reward' (Ric Sanders)
The ubiquitous DJ returns (he will appear again on a later album) in this instrumental that opens with five thumping chords and then settles into a minor key 'straight jig' in 2/2 time. Parts alternate between eight bars of C minor played on fiddle and then eight bars of E minor on mandolin. In concert, Ric will claim it grew out of his classical training, and there's a certain baroque feel to the melody lines. Indeed, he will suggest Handel as an inspiration, going on to claim that Handel joined with Hinge And Bracket (briefly popular late 70s, early 80s female impersonators) to form The Doors. Thank you Ric. There's a drum 'n' bass solo in the middle, with reggae guitar from Simon, followed by a fast, thrashing section. So, a slightly Jamaican, Handel-inspired, piratey folk tune.

In 2014 this would be performed on the Cropredy stage with an additional 45 string players dubbed the Conservatoire Folk Ensemble.

'The Festival Bell' (Chris Leslie)
Chris's song about the bells in Cropredy parish church is, as you would expect, a bright, celebratory end to the album. The track moves along at a fair old clip, with the first verse telling the story of the original six bells cast for the church by William Bagley of Chacombe in 1690. The second verse is a brief instruction

on bell-ringing, while the third suggests that all the music played at Cropredy –
along with peace, love and copious amounts of Wadsworth ale – have somehow
been condensed into the new Festival Bell. It's a short but catchy little tune
that successfully encapsulates everything the festival stands for – and ends,
rightly so, with the bells of St Mary's fading into the distance.

By Popular Request (2012)

Personnel:
Simon Nicol: vocals, acoustic and electric guitars
Chris Leslie: vocals, mandolin, bouzouki, violin, banjo, whistles
Ric Sanders: violins, keyboards
Dave Pegg: vocals, bass guitar
Gerry Conway: drums, percussion
Additional personnel:
Edmund Whitcombe: cornet on 'Red And Gold' and 'Meet On The Ledge'
Recorded, engineered and mixed by John Gale
Produced by John Gale and Fairport Convention
Record label: Matty Grooves
Released: January 2012
Highest chart position: Uncharted
Length: 54:42
Current edition: Unavailable except as a digital stream or download

In 2011 fans were asked to vote for the Top 20 Fairport Convention songs they would like rearranged and recorded for the band's 45th anniversary. Fairport then whittled those down to thirteen for an album that was initially expected to be available before Christmas but didn't arrive until the New Year. Of the baker's dozen all but three came from the classic Fairport period of 1969 to 1973 and one of them, 'The Hiring Fair', had already been recorded twice since the band's 1985 comeback. Many were staples of the current band's stage act and can be found on various live albums – Chris's version of 'Rosie', for example, is on recordings of a 2003 gig in Canterbury, released as *And The Band Played On* (2012) and *The Journeyman's Grace* (2003). And, of course, there are so many renditions of 'Matty Groves' you could spend the rest of your life listening to them.

So who needed yet another studio version of these songs, especially since they were unlikely to top the originals? Well, there are a few renditions here that we haven't heard before – Chris performing 'The Hexhamshire Lass' Simon doing justice to 'Fotheringay' and the band tackling 'Farewell, Farewell' and 'Sir Patrick Spens'. If you regard this collection not as an attempt to rewrite the past but as an affectionate nod to the songs that made Fairport, and the place they occupy in the hearts of the fans, then this is a very enjoyable selection of classics, played with the band's usual enthusiasm and musical dexterity.

The harmony vocals are particularly impressive – age has not wearied them – and the cover is striking, designed by Mick Toole in the style of a 45rpm single (remember those, grandad?) in a picture sleeve showing the current line-up.

'Walk Awhile' (Dave Swarbrick, Richard Thompson)

The opener on *Full House* is played here with same joyous gusto and at about the same speed as the original, with Simon providing confident electric guitar parts, Ric outdoing Swarb on violin and the vocal harmonies absolutely spot-on. The only real difference is, of course, Chris Leslie on mandolin and his gentle, melodic un-Swarb-like voice on the second verse. What it loses is a bit of dark humour – what it gains is energy and a clear affection, as well as the greater audio clarity provided by more modern recording techniques. Is it me or does the original sound a bit woolly? Ric, in particular, excels, playing those fiddle solos like a Tasmanian devil on speed. Oh, and this version throws in the sudden lurch from G to F and back to G in the final repeat of the chorus, which Fairport started doing with live versions of the song back in the late 1970s. The song came fifth in the Top 20 list with 466 votes.

'Crazy Man Michael' (Dave Swarbrick, Richard Thompson)

It's impossible to expect this to outshine the classic *Liege And Lief* recording – Sandy's voice always contained a hint of something slightly off-kilter in it, as if she could easily identify with poor, tortured Michael, which Simon's more straight-forward baritone fails to convey. Unlike both previous studio versions, there's no electric guitar here – Chris blends in acoustically on his bouzouki (I think!). And I would question the wisdom of replacing the original electric guitar solo with Chris on low D whistle – for me, it's too much like he's picked up his old school recorder, and it jars. Others disagree – I've seen reviews praising this aspect of the recording. But for me, this doesn't quite capture the dark, haunted quality of the original. Fourth in the list with 516 votes.

'The Hiring Fair' (Dave Mattacks, Ralph McTell)

Look up this song on Discogs, and you will find no fewer than 74 entries, including all the live versions. It's a great song and a 'Fairport Reconvention' classic but...did we really need another one? This version loses the short keyboard intro that Dave Mattacks provided for the 1987 recording, instead opening with Simon's acoustic guitar and Chris's mandolin. After a minute and a half Gerry adds percussion – a monotonous thump of bass drum and a bit of shaker. No, it doesn't work, damaging the steamy, sensual atmosphere. Chris's mandolin licks between verses lack any real focus and certainly don't compare to what Maart could do in the song. It also fades out, instead of coming to a satisfying, er, climax. On the plus side, Simon sings it well, and Ric's violin is tasteful and appropriate. 463 votes put this in at No 6.

'The Hexhamshire Lass' (Trad arr Fairport Convention)

When this was originally recorded for *Nine* it was during Simon's break from the band – in fact, only the loyal and stalwart Peggy was there from the current line-up. The new version takes a few liberties with the original arrangement – it opens in a similar manner, with rhythmic percussion and vocals from Chris, then suddenly goes up a key with a driving rock beat from Gerry and Peggy. Simon's on electric guitar and, so far as I can tell, Chris doesn't contribute instrumentally at all. I like the result, though – it has the same manic energy and the twin electric guitar and violin attack in the instrumental works well. So a yes from me. At No 18 in the list with 259 votes.

'Red And Gold' (Ralph McTell)
A very nice rendition of the title track from *Red & Gold*, with Chris's mandolin picking under Simon's voice and martial cornet flourishes from guest Edmund Whitcombe replacing the original's keyboards. It's a little less portentous and self-important than before, a little less over-egged in the instrumental backing. Simon sings it beautifully, and that cornet gives it a yearning, melancholy feel, like reveille sounding in the misty early morning. At 6:42 it's almost exactly as long as the original but sounds shorter, which is a tribute to the remake's ability to keep the listener interested all the way through. No 8, 455 votes.

'Sir Patrick Spens' (Trad arr Fairport Convention)
Another song with three studio versions floating around. Surprisingly, this goes at virtually the same speed as the *Full House* version – I say 'surprisingly' because, despite being just four seconds longer, it feels too slow. Instrumentally, there are no issues here – Simon does a creditable job replacing Richard's original electric guitar licks. It's just that you want the whole thing to pick up its britches and gallop along a bit more. I could also do with a bit more attack in the drum department, which feels too laid back. I've certainly heard this line-up perform the song with considerably more pace and energy. No 13, 312 votes.

'Genesis Hall' (Richard Thompson)
Thompson's blast at uncaring landlords and the 'sheriffs' who do their dirty work was originally sung by Sandy on *Unhalfbricking*. However, this is one of the rare occasions where Simon's vocal actually trumps her. Why? Because the song is angry and needs a bit of bite in the vocal – Sandy's rendition is a little too resigned and weary. Simon gives it a bit of grit – so do Gerry's busier drums – while the harmony vocals on the chorus are absolutely superb. No 14, 290 votes.

'Farewell, Farewell' (Richard Thompson)
On *Liege And Lief* this is a fragile song of longing and regret, sung solo by Sandy with subdued instrumental backing. Here, it's been turned into a choral singalong as the combined voices of Simon, Peggy and Chris burst out of the speakers in all their harmonic glory. Then the band thumps in with an uptempo instrumental rendition led by Chris's whistle before Simon alternates lines with Peggy and Chris as a kind of call and response. There's another instrumental section before the song winds down, but by then it is too late – what was a tender ballad about loss has become almost a late-night drinking song. No 19 with 257 votes.

'Rosie' (Dave Swarbrick)

Some songs are so indelibly linked with their creators or original singers that it's difficult to imagine – or even accept – someone else giving it a go. 'Rosie' is not just one of Swarb's finest songs, his performance on the 1973 album of the same name is restrained, subdued and touching, with a sense of real agonised longing. Chris Leslie, on the other hand, doesn't do agonised longing. Sure, he has a lovely voice, but he's not got any inner demons lurking beneath the surface. What you see (or hear) with Chris is what you, apparently, get. So he does a fine job with the song – certainly performing it with more sensitivity and grace than he does on the 2003 live recording in Canterbury – but it's not quite the same. Having said that, the musical backing is warm and supportive, with Ric's violin playing long flowing lines beneath Chris's voice (although he gets a bit wild in the instrumental). No 9, 355 votes.

'Matty Groves' (Trad arr Fairport Convention)

So here we go with possibly Fairport's most performed track (not 'Meet On The Ledge,' which didn't become a regular part of the band's repertoire until the late 1970s), the mammoth murder ballad that, in some incarnations, could stretch to almost 13 minutes, depending on what other tunes would bookend the song. So what do Fairport do with this version? Well, it has a pretty powerful opening, heavier than on the original, with driving drums from Gerry and a bit of a bluegrass feel from Chris playing banjo (with a capo quite high up on the strings). Simon must be able to sing this in his sleep but he still manages to invest it with the right amount of drama and menace (in a live setting he would leaven the drama with humour, throwing in lines such as 'How do you like my feather bed, how do you like my sheets/And how do you like my curtains that I bought from Ikea last week'). Let us not overlook Simon's electric guitar – he's playing a lot of interesting phrases here, so it's not just a D minor thrash. Ric's violin screams and swoops and the whole things end with a satisfying flourish. Yes, this is another worthy addition to the long list of Mattys. No 3, 532 votes.

'Fotheringay' (Sandy Denny)

See what I said about 'Rosie' above? You could say the same about Sandy's beautiful and moving ballad on the pending execution of Mary, Queen of Scots. Can you imagine anyone else singing it? I can find no evidence that, without Sandy in the band, Fairport ever played it except at the Cropredy festival with guest female singers. Until now, that is. Simon takes lead vocals and, you know, I think he does okay. It's actually quite a difficult song to sing, with lots of different stresses, pauses and note-lengths and the like, but he performs it with an easy flow, and his voice carries just the right amount of pathos. Unlike the original, this remake opens with keyboards playing some slightly cheesy 'aahs' and 'oohs' before the acoustic guitar figure comes in. Gerry's bass drum is a bit obtrusive – in the original, it was Ashley Hutchings' bass that provided rhythm

– but the combined strings of Ric and Chris are gorgeously done. All in all, it's a fine, respectful version. No 7, 456 votes.

'Jewel In The Crown' (Julie Matthews)

A surprise entry, just creeping into the list at No 20, is the title track from the band's 1995 album. Wot, no 'Angel Delight' or 'The Journeyman's Grace'? No 'Polly On The Shore' or 'John Gaudie'? No 'White Dress', 'Reynard the Fox', 'The Widow of Westmoreland's Daughter', 'Poor Will And The Jolly Hangman'? Nothing at all from *'Babbacombe' Lee*? Ah well, perhaps it should have been a Top 30. Anyway, I can't hear much that's different between this remake and the original – there's more treble on the 1995 version while the new one has a bit more fret squeak! Gerry's drums aren't quite as interesting as DM's were and there's a distinct lack of abrasive electric guitar. But Simon's voice sounds warmer and fuller, the harmonies are perfect, and the whole thing comes in at just one second shorter than the original. So not the most vital remake on the album but a solid effort nonetheless. No 20, 241 votes.

'Meet On The Ledge' (Richard Thompson)

In 1987 Ric joked: 'We're going to release this every twenty years until it's a hit!' In fact, it's been 25 years since the last remake – and the song has been played at every gig and every Cropredy since. It still packs an emotional wallop, which is why it was voted the fans' No1 favourite Fairport song of all time, so there. What differences do the band bring to this, the third studio version of the song? There's some mandolin notes from Chris and unobtrusive cornet from Edmund Whitcombe, while Gerry's drums sound a little 1980s as if they've been digitally generated. Otherwise, this is a reprise of the 1987 version with the added instrumental section. It still works, still gives you that lump in the throat. And that ends the album because, in the words of John 'Jonah' Jones when the song was first played as the band's encore number: 'That's it. That's the last song. You cannot follow that. We simply cannot follow that.'

Myths & Heroes (2015)

Personnel:
Simon Nicol: vocals, acoustic and electric guitars
Chris Leslie: vocals, mandolin, bouzouki, Celtic harp, banjo, whistles, tenor guitar, harmonica, violin
Ric Sanders: violins, keyboards, bass ukulele
Dave Pegg: vocals, bass guitar, bass ukulele, bouzouki, banjo, mandolin, double bass,
Gerry Conway: drums, percussion
Additional personnel:
Matt Pegg: bass on 'Myths And Heroes', 'Theodore's Song', 'Grace And Favour', 'Home'
Joe Broughton, Paloma Trigas & Aria Trigas: violins on 'The Gallivant'
Jake Thornton & Benjamin Hill: alto saxophone on 'The Gallivant'
Emma Jones: tenor saxophone on 'The Gallivant'
Recorded by John Gale at Woodworm Studios
Mixed by John Gale at Galeforce Sound, Dublin
Produced by John Gale and Fairport Convention
Record label: Matty Grooves
Released: January 2015
Highest chart position: Uncharted
Length: 51:19
Current edition: Original release

Another album, another drama. Dave Pegg cut a tendon on the first finger of his left hand, rendering him unable to play on some of Fairport's 2014 winter tour – he was deputised by his son Matt (who stood in for dad with Jethro Tull, too, in 1991 and 1994). It hadn't healed by the time the band went into Woodworm Studios to record their 28th album. In fact, Peggy feared his playing days were over – so Matt is credited with bass on the four first tracks to be recorded, as listed above.

Of course, Peggy's fears were unfounded, and soon he was back plucking his Ibanez and plinking his mandolin on what the band and fans consider to be the best Fairport album since *Jewel In The Crown*. It's built around Chris Leslie's song 'Myths And Heroes', which the band had been playing at gigs for a few years before finally recording a definitive version. Simon and Peggy came up with the wheeze of recreating the *Full House* cover, with its five rectangular segments and the title in the middle, but this time disguising Fairport as their own favourite heroes, real and fictitious. This led to an online competition to identify the slightly-dodgily Photoshopped characters and win tickets to Cropredy plus a signed copy of the album.

So we have Simon Nicol as Renaissance artist and scientist Leonardo da Vinci; Ric Sanders as Kwai Chang Caine, the character portrayed by actor David Carradine in the 1970s TV series *Kung Fu*; Gerry Conway as comedian Spike Milligan; Chris Leslie as 1920s violin-maker Lloyd Loar (and I bet few fans got that one); and, finally, Dave Pegg as bass player Rick Danko of The Band.

While not a concept album, there are a few tracks on the myths and heroes theme: a song about John Condon, the (allegedly) youngest soldier to be killed in World War I; one about an itinerant Oxfordshire watch and clock repairer; one about Grace Darling, who rescued nine people from the sea in 1838; and a tune dedicated to all the Fairport members and friends who have gone to meet on the ledge.

In the liner notes Peggy says 'In my humble, we have come up with one of our best Fairport albums' and it is true that there is a confidence and an energy to *Myths & Heroes* that may have been missing in some of the previous albums. There are six Chris Leslie compositions, which usually means we're in for a nice but bland experience, but on this occasion his personal quality-control is working well and he has come up with four catchy songs with quite a bit of oomph in them, plus a sedate minor key reel tacked on the end of 'Weightless' and half a mandolin instrumental with Dave Pegg.

Ric offers two compositions, the touching and Carolan-ish 'Jonah's Oak' and a sprightly minor-key tune in the style of 'Danny Jack's Reward', with added strings and horns. Fairport favourites Ralph McTell, annA rydeR, PJ Wright and Rob Beattie contribute some enjoyable songs, plus there's a number inspired by the 2013 movie *Gravity*.

The album was released on CD and limited edition vinyl, at first available only online and from the band during their 2015 winter tour.

'Myths And Heroes' (Chris Leslie)

With a blast of Eddie Cochran-style rockabilly, Chris's title track fairly rips along as a warning to humanity not to put its 'faith and hope in things that aren't always what they appear to be'. It's almost as if he was predicting Brexit. This is one of the four songs here featuring Matt Pegg on bass, and he appears to have learned all his dad's old licks, while Peggy himself makes his presence felt on backing vocals. Simon helps to power things along on electric guitar and Gerry is steady and strong in the engine room, but this is Chris's show as he tells of Romulus and Remus (mythical founders of Rome), references the astrological 'influence' of the stars and the 'yearly hope for peace on earth'. Starting in F major the chords slide down to D major for the verse, moving into D minor for the bridge (a frequent Chris Leslie device) before ending quite suddenly after one more verse and chorus. As usual, there are a few musical larks in the song – a reference to a 'million dollar mandolin that played a bluegrass tune' gives Chris an opportunity to play a quick run on his mando. It's a strong, upbeat opener and a song that works well in a live setting, too.

'Clear Water' (Ralph McTell)

A song about Fairport from Ralph, although it could apply to any of us wishing for a quieter, calmer twilight. As Mr McTell says in the liner notes: 'The well-worn metaphor of the good ship sailing on to represent the crew pulling together is a heartfelt wish for continuation of their voyage which began so long ago. Only now the hope is for a safer journey on calmer water.' Simon takes lead vocals on this surprisingly sprightly number, which opens with unaccompanied three-part harmonies on the chorus before launching into a fairly brisk trot on the verse. Like a lot of McTell songs, the chords and melody lines are fairly safe and predictable, but there are some touching lyrics with oblique references to the band itself – 'the rising of the moon proved to be a fickle guide'. The whistle and fiddle instrumental is endearing, while Simon's voice here is so rich it could almost be coming from Mr McTell himself. Simon's on acoustic guitar with Peggy playing bass ukulele.

'The Fylde Mountain Time / Roger Bucknall's Polka' (Chris Leslie / Dave Pegg)

In the liner notes, Peggy says: 'The Fylde Guitar Company built a beautiful bouzouki for Chris Leslie with a wonderfully thin neck. I was very jealous. On hearing of my interest Roger (Fylde's supremo) built one for me.' If that's all it takes to get a bespoke instrument from Fylde then I, too, am very jealous. Both Peggy and Chris resolved to write a tune on their new bouzoukis – with Peggy still recovering from his finger injury – and found to their delight that they could fit them both together even though they are, erm, completely different. Chris's is a stately, swaying 4/4 tune in G major while Peggy's is a bouncing 2/4 polka in D taken at what seems like twice the speed. But Fairport have always been adept at fitting different tunes together into one cohesive track and both these compositions share the same spirit of joyous celebration. Both Peggy and Chris multi-task on bouzouki, mandolin and banjo while Ric plays that bass ukulele.

'Theodore's Song' (Chris Leslie)

An appealing ballad about Theodore Lamb, 'an itinerant Oxfordshire watch and clock repairer and musician who travelled the lanes and byways of the county pre-1950', says Chris. He was apparently well-known in the village of Sibford, where he lived like a hermit in a shack, with long matted hair and beard. He died of pneumonia in 1950 aged 70. Chris's song is an affectionate tribute to a recluse with hidden talents and a hidden story – others may see him as a raggle-taggle gypsy-oh, but it seems his heart was broken on his wedding day, which is not a nice thing to happen. It's packed full of lovely melodic lines, with quite an unusual chorus in C but with a G flat in there as well. The song slides beautifully from G major to D flat minor for a short ukulele instrumental from Ric before heading back into G major again. This is the second song with Matt on bass and Peggy providing backing vocals.

'Love At First Sight' (Chris Leslie)

There's an old rock 'n' roller in Chris Leslie, judging by the openings to 'Myths And Heroes' and this 1950s-style rocker. A folk-ish bouzouki and fiddle riff is backed with some Cochrane-style chords before settling down into a steady chug led by Simon's electric guitar. Chris adapts a traditional theme of a woman dressing as a man to enter a forbidden masculine world, only on this occasion, it's to join a morris dancing team, as you do. While there she falls in love with the Fool and they live happily ever after, producing enough children to make their own morris side. It's true that during the 1950s and 1960s there was much debate over whether women should be allowed to participate in what was until then seen as the strictly male pursuit of dancing about with bells on your ankles. These days there are probably as many female as male morris dancers, although it took a threat of a legal challenge under the Equalities Act to force national organisation the Morris Ring to allow women to join.

'John Condon' (Richard Laird, Sam Starrett, Tracey McRory)

More than 200,000 young Irishmen volunteered to fight for the British in the First World War. They included John Condon from Waterford who, the stories say, lied about his age when he signed up and was just 14 when he died shortly after arriving in Flanders, Belgium, in 1915. His headstone in Poelkapelle Cemetery lists him as having been born in late 1900 and is one of the most visited graves in the European war cemeteries. More recent research suggests he was probably 18 or 19 – but it's still no age to die. This song was penned by three Northern Ireland artists – pianist Laird had the initial idea and co-wrote it with All-Ireland champion fiddler McRory and playwright Starrett, who was working on a production about the 1917 Battle of Messines. The song formed part of an album called *Boys Of The Island* and was originally performed by Mary Black. Fairport heard it sung by Co Armagh singer Janet Dowd and, said Peggy, 'we jumped at the chance to perform it'.

The first slow ballad on the album, it opens with finger-picked acoustic guitar and Chris playing plaintive harmonica before Simon sings about finding John Condon's grave beneath a Belgian sun. There's a moving chorus of 'Wee lad who'll not grow old – heroes that don't come home' and an instrumental section of fiddle and harmonica – it's a little corny but very moving. Peggy on double bass adds to the old-fashioned feel, while Simon's honest and open voice adds a sense of yearning and loss. It's a lovely song performed with style and sensitivity.

'The Gallivant' (Ric Sanders)

Peggy had the idea of bringing in Joe Broughton's Conservatoire Folk Ensemble – a 50-piece funky string and brass orchestra – to help play Ric's tune 'Danny Jack's Reward' at Cropredy in 2014 and the result was one of the highlights of Fairport's performance. He also suggested they play on this tune, which is in a similar vein, but space restrictions in the studio meant only Joe and six other musicians could squeeze in. However, they still manage to pack plenty of drama and menace into another pirate-y composition. Descending chords in quick succession lead into a G minor mandolin tune with swiftly-strummed acoustic guitar chords. Then bass and drums crank in, along with stabs of brass with strings and keyboard backing. Halfway through Peggy gets into a funky bass groove in B minor with Chris improvising on mandolin over the top, before the tune lurches back into its original G minor, ending with a bit of a rock 'n' roll riff in D. Yes, this tune goes all over the place like a lost caravan driver. Chris's playing is particularly impressive here, with nimble fingers flying over the mando fretboard, producing some astonishingly fast and intricate little runs and flourishes. All in all, this is a fine instrumental from Ric and one of the highlights of the album.

'The Man In The Water' (Rob Beattie)
When you approach Rob Beattie for a song, you know you're not going to get something with a lot of laughs. He penned the depressing 'Red Tide' on *Jewel In The Crown,* and this is equally miserable. It's about the mystery of a drowned man in a river and asks if he got there through accident or suicide. There's a wife 'cursing at the cameras' and something about a diary with missing pages – and, at the end of the song, a suggestion that the depressed narrator could join him in the watery depths. However, one would hope Mr Beattie would know better because, as well as being a songwriter, he wrote *The Boating Handbook: All You Need To Know About Life On The Water*.

Fairport manage to counteract the misery in the song by turning in a performance that doesn't sound anything like them. Taken at a steady pace, with Gerry playing restrained rimshots, Chris sings in quite a high key with Simon copying his vocal lines an octave lower. There's a Celtic harp being plucked and strummed, gentle string backing and unobtrusive bouzouki chords – no guitars, acoustic or electric. Peggy's restrained bass rarely strays away from providing steady rhythmic support. The result is an unusual but attractive track that illustrates why the Fairports have long been sought after as session musicians because of their ability to adapt to many different musical styles.

'Bring Me Back My Feathers' (annA rydeR)
The third song recorded by Fairport from the peculiarly capitalised annA, this was composed on a four-string banjo while producing a show about a parrot at the Fox Hollies Summer Scheme for special needs children in Birmingham. She says: 'I meant to replace the words which turned out to be the title of the song, but this line stuck, and I'm glad it did as it's slightly peculiar.' The result is something that sounds a little like a bluegrass children's song, with repetitive verses that ask to 'bring back' various things, including feathers, my sweetheart, my tears and my footsteps. There is, however, a line about taking a young lady to bed, which renders it wholly unsuitable for tender young ears.

Chris opens on banjo and lead vocals for the first two verses and the chorus, which pretty much repeats part of the verse before the rest of the band join in with steady, rock-solid bass from Peggy and electric guitar chords from Simon. There's a bluegrassy instrumental melody in the middle from Ric and Chris that also plays out the end of the song, rather like the reels that finished off 'John Gaudie' on *Who Knows Where The Time Goes?*. Simple but appealing, it was a popular part of the band's set at this time.

'Grace And Favour' (Chris Leslie)
Written by Chris after he visited the Grace Darling Museum at Bamburgh, Northumberland. Grace was the daughter of a lighthouse keeper and, on 7 September 1838, she and her father rowed out in tempestuous seas and gale-force winds to rescue nine survivors of a stricken steamship that had crashed into Big Harcar Rock. Grace became a Victorian hero and received several awards, including £50 from the Queen. Chris's song tells the straightforward story of the ship setting out from Hull, developing a boiler leak and then being broken into pieces against the rock. 'Darling daughter launched the boat' sings Chris, and she rows towards the wreck, 'keeping it steady now...now that she knows death is a breath away'.

Performed in a slightly uncomfortable 7/8 rhythm, the song chugs along more like a wounded steam train than a ship, with Chris and Simon repeating five-note riffs on bouzouki and electric guitar, occasionally slowing things down for emphasis during some of the more dramatic verses. The last verse borrows the opening lines from 'A Sailor's Life', recorded by Fairport on *Unhalfbricking*, and the song ends with Ric's violin over triumphant chords.

'Weightless / The Gravity Reel (James Wood / Chris Leslie)
Sheffield-born musician James Wood wrote the first of these two compositions – inspired by the 2013 film *Gravity* – after his daughter Helena was killed in a car crash in 2004. Most of us know the film as Sandra Bullock spinning around in space after cosmic debris smashes into her space shuttle – James, however, identified with the fact that her character is fighting to rebuild her life after the death of her daughter. He says: 'It's about being in freefall but at the same time being tied to the ground, unable to move. It's about feeling powerless and unable to breathe. It's about loss. But it's about striving to overcome that loss.'

James recorded it with Peggy, Chris and Gerry for his first solo album *The Last Journey* (2016) after meeting the Fairports during recordings for Alan Simon's Excalibur project – both men lived in Nantes, France, at the time. Fairport immediately grabbed the song for themselves and produced a stately version that captures some of the ponderous movement from the less frantic scenes in the film, adding a minor key reel written by Chris. It's not the most interesting of songs, being mostly based around alternating chords of A minor and G but Chris sings it well and it moves just about fast enough to keep the listener interested.

'Home' (PJ Wright)
Peggy's pal PJ wrote this while on walks with his dog – it's an unashamedly corny tribute to the simple joys of home life, with a gentle warning about the condition of our planet. Sung by Simon with a slow, gentle acoustic guitar

strum, it is pleasant and unremarkable, with fairly basic instrumentation from the rest of the band. They do it well, of course, with occasional harmony vocals, Ric's languid violin and gentle mandolin plucking from Chris, but it is a little plodding and surprisingly downbeat considering its subject matter.

'Jonah's Oak' (Ric Sanders)

Here's Ric: 'In the corner of the Cropredy field there's a big old oak which has become a tree of remembrance for Johnny Jones, Rob Braviner, Geoff Hughes and all those we have lost but still love.' John B Jones was Fairport's (and Ralph McTell's) manager who became synonymous with the Cropredy Festival – he was, said Simon, the only MC that could make every act sound like a stripper. He died in December 2003. Rob Braviner was Fairport's long-running tour manager, who died in 2009. Actor Geoffrey Hughes, who played Eddie Yeats in Coronation Street and Onslow in Keeping Up Appearances, was a big Fairport fan and regular festival compère. He died in 2012 after suffering from prostate cancer. Also by this time, Fairport had lost the following former band members: Martin Lamble, Sandy Denny, Trevor Lucas, Roger Hill and Bruce Rowland. Oh, and Dave Swarbrick had been accidentally killed off by the Daily Telegraph.

So this bitter-sweet waltz from Ric carries a certain poignancy – similar in style to 'The Rose Hip' from *Red & Gold*, it is by no means depressing but, thanks to Ric's long violin melodies it allows the listener to sit and contemplate with everlasting affection all those who have gone on to meet on the ledge.

50:50@50 (2017)

Personnel:
Simon Nicol: vocals, guitars
Chris Leslie: vocals, mandolin, bouzouki, banjo, ukuleles, D whistle, harmonica
Ric Sanders: electric violins, keyboards
Dave Pegg: 5-string bass, mandolin, double bass, backing vocals
Gerry Conway: drums, percussion
Additional personnel:
Robert Plant: vocals and harmonica on 'Jesus on the Mainline'
Jacqui McShee: vocals on 'Lady of Carlisle'
Joe Broughton, Paloma Trigas & Aria Trigas: violins on 'Danny Jack's Reward'
Natasha Davies & Arjun Jethwa: flutes on 'Danny Jack's Reward'
Rose Rutherford: clarinet on 'Danny Jack's Reward'
Rob Spalton: trumpet on 'Danny Jack's Reward'
Jake Thornton: alto and tenor saxophone on 'Danny Jack's Reward'
John Gale: engineer
Record label: Matty Grooves
Release dates: January, 2017
Highest chart positions: Uncharted
Running Time: 64:17
Current Edition

A golden wedding anniversary always calls for a lavish celebration, and being in a band is almost like a marriage. Both call for the ability to communicate well and work as a team, with a high degree of tolerance (especially after living on a tour bus for months). In 2017 Fairport Convention hit this milestone. Although not all of them have been there for the full 50-year slog, Simon has been in and out since the beginning and Peggy started his journey with Fairport three years later, so a celebration is still deserved.

The album is entitled 50:50@50, which at first glance looks a little horrifyingly like a maths equation, but it is simply descriptive. Half the album is brand-spanking, hot-off-the-press new studio material and the other half is a collection of live recordings (hence 50:50 at 50 years old). The majority of the live material comes from the Cropredy warm-up gigs at The Mill in Banbury between 2014 and 2016, with the exception of 'Portmeirion' which was recorded on tour in Holland and 'John Condon' recorded on the same tour in, appropriately, Belgium.

The track-list is a real eclectic mix that acts as a showcase of what Fairport have done best over the last half-century. 'Jesus on the Mainline' is a nod to their 'British Jefferson Airplane' beginnings, and the live classics remind us of their commercial heyday in the early 1970s. A song dedicated to the Fairport Cropredy Convention is included to remind us of the band's contribution to one of Britain's best music festivals.

Absent on this anniversary album is 'Meet On The Ledge', which has gained so much weight and gravitas over the years as a way to collectively wave at all members, past and present. It's been replaced by 'Our Bus Rolls On', a cheerful Chris Leslie song – perhaps the group want to stop dwelling in a maudlin manner and prefer a happy remembrance. It also reflects the stability the band has enjoyed since 1998 compared to the turmoil of the early years.

Guest songwriters and performers including Robert Plant, Jacqui McShee and Joe Broughton's Conservatoire Folk Ensemble help Fairport celebrate and the album is full of references to time passing by – and why shouldn't it be after 50 years? In the opening track, 'Eleanor's Dream', Chris Leslie sings 'this world won't see their like again' and, in Fairport Convention's case, truer words have never been spoken.

'Eleanor's Dream' (Chris Leslie)

We're back to the ill-fated expedition by Sir John Franklin to discover the North-West passage – this is the third song written about the doomed voyage (the others being 'I'm Already There' and 'Mercy Bay', the latter of which is included as a live version on this album). It's written from the perspective of Franklin's wife, Eleanor, upon receiving the news that her love and all his men have been lost to the deep. The first verse starts out with gentle mandolin, but it isn't long until we get the full folk-rock treatment, for this song appears not to be a lament. It isn't slow; it isn't pretty; it has a driving tempo and, although it's in a minor key, the overwhelming emotion is anger. The run-time is a comparatively short three minutes, which leave you wanting more.

'Ye Mariners All (Live)' (Trad arr Fairport Convention)

Continuing with a maritime theme this is a rollicking rendition of the *Tipplers Tales* opener, complete with the sprightly, instrumental introductions played on mandolin and fiddle. Chris Leslie takes the vocal duties with Simon on slightly tinny electric guitar.

'Step by Step' (Chris Leslie)

Another new composition by Chris paints a picture of beautiful scenery and sweet love. We take a walk by cliffs and countryside, our steps accompanied by guitars continually tinkling, soft taps on the hi-hat and warm vocal harmonies. The mellow level is maintained throughout the track, with occasional instrumental interludes of soaring violin.

'The Naked Highwayman (Live)' (Steve Tilston)

Crime, deception, sex, nudity and cross-dressing – they are all here in Tilston's challenging tongue-twister originally recorded for *Jewel In The Crown*. Fairport play it at a slightly slower speed so Simon can get all the words in, with Gerry adding interesting percussion noise.

'Danny Jack's Reward – Expensive Version!' (Ric Sanders)

Originally on 2011's *Festival Bell*, Ric's tricksy composition was turned into something epic for 2014's Cropredy with the addition of Joe Broughton's 35-strong Conservatoire Folk Ensemble. Later Ric squeezed as many of them as he could into the studio to produce this orchestral version of the tune, bulked out with extra string, brass and woodwind sections. This is certainly the 'expensive version' as it is rich in sound (not to mention how much it cost to hire all the extra musicians!).

'Jesus on the Mainline (Live)' (Trad arr Fairport Convention)

Robert Plant of Led Zeppelin fame has made frequent Cropredy appearances – his connection to the band goes back to at least to 1970 when they shared the Troubadour stage in Los Angeles, and Peggy knew him before that. This live recording from a warm-up gig in Banbury shows him having a lot of fun with a simple blues spiritual that dates back to the 1920s, although the most influential recording is probably Ry Cooder's on his 1974 album *Paradise And Lunch*. The premise is fairly simple (as is the tune) – Jesus can now be communicated with through the modern invention of the telephone, so call him up and tell him what you want. It's clear that everyone is having fun on this, from the wild harmonica flailing to the fiddle sliding. Plant, in particular, is enjoying himself immensely, cheekily adding a reference to Led Zep's 'Whole Lotta Love'.

'Devil's Work' (Chris Leslie)

As if to make a point that you can extract a good folk song out of any kind of material, 'Devil's Work'concerns the joys and, indeed, the trials of DIY. The melody trips happily along on the mandolin, and the bass line walks and slides around the scales. A little tongue in cheek, it isn't without its slightly darker metaphor in the chorus where he's 'shoring up this house of cards while life it slips away'. A violin instrumental section confirms the darker notions we've been fed by switching entirely to a minor key accompanied by ominous thumps (possible hammering maybe?) from the bass drum. Very soon we go right back to bobbing along in the major key until the big finish.

'Mercy Bay (Live)' (Chris Leslie)

A perfect example of how Fairport turn an established studio track into something quite unique and different at a gig. When this song was performed on stage, the lighting was blue and flickering, placing you right in the middle of that ice-bound Arctic sea. The microphones are set to echo, and the violin interjections feel organic, less like music and more like the faint whistle of the wind or the calling of a whale. The instrumentals are extended and Ric Sanders has room to explore the arrangement fully, which is not always feasible in the studio but sounds beautiful in a big performance space.

'Our Bus Rolls On' (Chris Leslie)

Another autobiographical song about how Fairport Convention are still rolling on, despite everything. Think 'Three Wheels On My Wagon' as inspiration. The tune is unerringly steady, bright and upbeat, while the lyrics run through a roll-call for the current line-up, with a mini-verse for each member. The final verse raises a glass to 'the band called family and those blown off that mountain' – a reference, of course, to 'Meet On The Ledge'.

'Portmeirion (Live)' (Ric Sanders)

Ric's much-loved instrumental returns again in a live version similar to the arrangement on the *On The Ledge 35th Anniversary Concert* album.

'The Lady of Carlisle' (Trad arr Fairport Convention)

Jacqui McShee sings on Fairport's version of a traditional song recorded by her band Pentangle in 1972. The tale concerns a beautiful young lady who is in the enviable position of being sought after by two high-ranking soldiers. She can only choose and marry one, so she devises a test and throws her fan into a lion's den – one soldier chickens out, but the other bravely dives in and retrieves the fan and claims his bride. The song has existed under various other names, including the 'The Lion's Den', 'The Fan', 'The Bold Lieutenant' and various different nationalities of Lady. It has been performed freestyle time, five-four time, in major and in minor keys. This particular Lady is performed as an upbeat, major key, four-four time with a real foot-tapping feel. Minimalist banjo opens proceedings while the melody plays on whistle and harmonica. Restrained accompaniment places Jacqui's vocals centre stage, creating a clear focal point for the story being told.

'Lord Marlborough (Live)' (Trad arr Fairport Convention)

This live version of another Fairport classic, the opener to *Angel Delight*, shows the musical agility of the group on stage. The fluctuating time signatures demand careful counting and the fact that the performance is so tight rhythmically is a testament to the teamwork and musical talent within the band. With the change of line-up since 1971, this live version features Simon on lead vocals instead of Dave Swarbrick, giving the song a more stately air.

'Summer by the Cherwell' (PJ Wright)

Another celebration of the Cropredy festival, the River Cherwell passes four miles north of the village, and the verses capture the atmosphere of being on the hill with 20,000 other folk-lovers. Bright, positive, festival vibes are channelled in this tune, helped by all three vocalists singing in rich harmony, and the walking bass-line.

'John Condon (Live)' (Richard Laird, Sam Starrett , Tracey McRory)
The album ends on one of the saddest songs Fairport have performed – the
moving tale of the (possibly) youngest soldier to die in the First World War.
Appropriately, it is performed in Belgium, the country where the young
soldier boy is buried, which brings the tragic reality a little closer to home.
Accompanied by a slow, finger-picked guitar, a plaintive harmonica and simple
fiddle line, Simon's vocals have a slight catch to them, as if he was struggling to
control his emotions while singing it. Quite frankly, if this does not bring a tear
to your eye then you are made of the most solid granite. It brings the album to
a sad but beautiful ending.

Shuffle And Go (2020)

Personnel:
Simon Nicol: lead vocals, electric guitars, acoustic guitars
Dave Pegg: backing vocals (lead vocal on 'Linseed Memories'), electric bass, acoustic bass, ukulele, bass ukulele
Ric Sanders: violin, keyboards, resonator ukulele, electric ukulele
Chris Leslie: lead vocals, acoustic guitar, mandolin, Celtic harp, violin, harmonica, kalimba, whistles, ukulele, bouzouki
Gerry Conway: drums, percussion, handclaps
John Gales and Stuart Jones: handclaps on 'Good Time For A Fiddle And Bow/The Christmas Eve Reel'
Recorded and engineered by John Gale at Woodworm Studios, Barford St Michael, Oxfordshire in October 2019
Assistant engineer: Stuart Jones
Fiddles recorded by Ric Sanders at The Bowman's Retreat, Bloxham, Oxfordshire
Additional recording: Mark Lee at Blue Moon Studios, Oxfordshire, on 'Linseed Memories'
Record label: Matty Grooves
Release dates: February 28, 2020
Running time: 52:32
Current edition: Original release

In the 50th anniversary year of *Full House*, Fairport released an album that bore little resemblance to that folk-rock classic of 1970. In place of energy, excitement and boundary-busting experimentation, came relaxed contemplation and a comfortable predictability.

But what do you expect from a band that has been around for an astonishing 53 years, and whose oldest member Gerry Conway (he beats Dave Pegg by a month) is 72? All five of them should be sitting at home drinking cocoa and contemplating an early night, not touring around the country in a van strumming and bowing and banging things for our entertainment. But the bus rolls on – it may rattle a bit now, and there are probably a few surprise leaks, but the engine is still well-tuned and the timing spot on. Piston broke? Not quite yet...

So, on to the 30th studio album. Is there a hint in the title that Fairport themselves were about to shuffle off the stage and go? *50:50@50* was a perfect ending album, as it seemed to knit together most of the threads of their long career, but clearly the band thought otherwise. Apart from the title, there's no clue on the cover or in the music that the bus is about to be parked, with the possible exception of the final track, 'Precious Time'. A slow, sad waltz, it speaks of endings – after all, as we get older time does indeed become more precious. But it's dedicated to 'Angie', not to the band, so I am probably reading too much into it.

The songs follow the pattern of most of Fairport's 21st-century releases

– five Chris Leslie numbers that range from the very good to the somewhat forgettable, two excellent-as-always Ric Sanders instrumentals and sturdy compositions from some tried and trusted Fairport friends. There's a slice of social comment about Kenya (including a brief rendition of a Kenyan pop song) and the second cover on a Fairport album of a James Taylor song.

Everything is tastefully played with skill and precision, and the vocal harmonies are, as usual, absolutely impeccable. Some of the songs are catchy and memorable, and hold their own among the best Fairport have recorded over the last twenty years or so. A few are less than impressive and slip by without making a mark and, sadly, the James Taylor track is one of them.

Some fans may long for the band to step out of its comfort zone and attempt something a bit more challenging, but I guess Fairport have long ago decided to do what they want, and play the songs they like, rather than dance to the tune of fickle public opinion. Look back at the times they've tried to create a 'hit' album and remember how well that went…

The CD cover sports a painting by Mick Toole, Fairport's go-to man for artwork, and it references some of the songs inside. There's the rocker from the song 'Shuffle And Go', sinking a pint in one of 'A Thousand Bars' and gazing mournfully at a pram, a green Gretsch guitar propped up against a table. Standing on an incongruous pedestal is something that looks a bit like the Apollo 11 command module, set against a black moon. Slipping round on to the back cover are some morris men ordering a pint – or they could be cricketers in their whites sharing some 'Linseed Memories'. And are those discarded cricket stumps behind a 1950s suitcase tube guitar amplifier?

This is Fairport Convention in 2020 – 53 and not out.

'Don't Reveal My Name' (Chris Leslie)

The album opens with Chris's best song here, a slow, brooding, minor-key blues that could have come from the pen of Richard Thompson, and wouldn't be out of place on a rootsy Robert Plant album. It's inspired by a book he read about Dai Vernon, a magician who learned the tricks of card sharps and cheats to put into his act. Dai – born David Frederick Wingfield Verner in Ottawa, Canada, in 1894 – was known as The Professor because of his sleight of hand skills and once baffled Harry Houdini, who watched the same card trick seven times but couldn't work it out. After that, Dai billed himself as The Man Who Fooled Houdini.

Chris's song is not about Dai but invents a card sharp who's on the run after cheating one too many suckers and jilting too many women. We seem to be in 19th century America – there are a bar and a gunfight and a hangman's noose waiting for him if he's captured, and a hint of Christian revivalism in the references to the waters that 'call the faithful' and the 'pride of old Elijah'. There's even a nod – deliberate or otherwise – to a Richard Thompson song in the opening line 'When you get to the border'.

Musically, this is an atmospheric ballad in D minor, opening with Gerry's funereal percussion with considerable echo on the bass drum. Chris strums acoustic guitar, while Simon's electric guitars carry plenty of reverb, giving the song a haunting quality. In true folk style, there's no chorus or middle eight, just five verses sung to the same repetitive melody. In the hands of Thompson, these would be separated at some point by a blistering, spiky guitar solo but Fairport opt for a low-key instrumental doubled up on mandolin and fiddle.

If this all sounds somewhat dull and unadventurous, well, think again. The result is quite hypnotic and the track's four minutes pass quickly. In fact, I think Fairport could have put an additional instrumental section on the end and easily taken this to six minutes without trying the listener's patience. It's an example of how, sometimes, less is more and a simple, minimalist approach can be more effective than flinging around chord changes like confetti.

'Cider Rain' (James Wood, Luc Boisseau, Philippe Richalley)

We've met James Wood before, back on the *Myths & Heroes* album. Luc and Philippe are fellow members of the band Rosemary and the Brainless Idols, based in Nantes – not far from where Peggy now lives in Brittany, France. To date, they have self-released one album, *Tales From The Bottom Of Our Garden* which, as the title suggests, was recorded in Studio Woodland at the, er, bottom of their garden.

'Cider Rain' opens as an upbeat acoustic guitar strum in E major with a simple, five-note riff and, to be honest, my initial reaction was not terribly enthusiastic. It appeared we were in for a fairly bland, predictable, three or four-chord experience that would slip into one ear and immediately exit through the other. But wait! A surprise C major takes the melody into interesting directions; then it moves into G major for the chorus before transitioning beautifully back into E major again. Simon's baritone is strong and joyful, the harmonies (especially in the transition) are warm and uplifting and the whole thing bounces happily along thanks to Gerry's understated pop-rock beat.

There are a couple of other tricks to keep the listeners on their toes. Simon sings the first verse with simple acoustic guitar backing, and you expect the rest of the band to come in at the start of the second verse. But wait (again)! They leave it until the second line of the second verse, confounding your expectations and creating a nice bit of musical tension. There's a brief but lovely slice of soaring violin from Ric, and the whole thing ends not on the chorus but on a repeat of the first line. These are simple things, but they help to raise the song to a different level.

Subject matter matches the melody and treatment – it's about wandering along the waterside getting out of your skull on cider (and they make some very nice fermented apple juice in Northern France). If there was any musical taste in the world – apart from yours and mine, of course – this would be *BBC Radio 2's* song of the week. It's certainly one of my songs of the album and, in the words of the Electric Light Orchestra, I can't get it out of my head.

'Good Time For A Fiddle And Bow / The Christmas Eve Reel'
(Chris Leslie / Tommy Coen)

In the liner notes, Chris says the song was 'inspired by the life of Donegal fiddler John Doherty, who was also a tinsmith and storyteller. He was even known to make tin fiddles!' In fact, he came from my favourite place in Co Donegal, the west coast town of Ardara where I have played many times in The Corner House, and there's a sculpture of him standing virtually opposite. As iconic Irish fiddlers go he's actually fairly recent – he died in 1980 – so there are recordings and some movie footage of him playing in his distinctive, flowery style. He's also honoured with an annual festival in the town at the end of September, and there's a very nice bar named after him known locally as Doc's (the Irish 'h' can sound a bit harder than in English).

Doherty was in demand as a player all over Ireland and his travels are reflected in Chris Leslie's lyrics – 'Boots on the ground / Fiddle in hand / Old rock road / Stone of sand' – although the fiddler famously didn't take his instrument with him, knowing he would have one thrust into his hands wherever he went.

The song is a bright, cheerful number in a brisk 4/4 time, based on 'The Christmas Eve Reel' by Tommy Coen, another 20th-century fiddler but this time from East Galway. Ric opens with the tune before Chris sings about Donegal in winter, and how nice it is to be snug and warm somewhere listening to music. 'Every fiddle in Donegal / Plays such magic when you call' he sings, and I can confirm from personal experience that he is absolutely spot on. There's a chorus of 'Frost it lies on the top of the hill', and this is repeated as the song comes to an end. The melody is not terrifically distinctive, and Fairport have recorded many similar songs, but the track gives Ric a chance to play a good, old-fashioned Irish reel and the whole thing bounces along merrily for nearly four and a half minutes. And it's about Ardara, which is always a bonus.

'A Thousand Bars' (Rob Beattie)

This is another song that starts off sounding like many ballads Fairport have recorded over the years but, like 'Cider Rain', the arrangement, harmonies and a few little musical tricks give it a bit more personality. We know Rob Beattie – this must be his fourth composition to be covered by the band – so we are well aware that he is not the most cheerful of songwriters. This is a little more upbeat – no-one is dead or depressed – but is still unlikely to have you dancing on the tables, singing along. It's about how important the pub is to society and how all manner of human life is to be found there, singing, fighting, reminiscing, drowning sorrows and getting bladdered.

The chorus is a list of evocative pub names, including The Horse and Groom, The Pig and Poke, The Sun and Moon, The Piston Broke (yes, there is one, in Shoreham-by-Sea near Brighton). It also mentions my favourite bar, The Corner House. But I take issue with the suggestion that there is or has ever been a pub called The Fox and Flagon – my extensive researches have established no such hostelry. There is, however, a Flour and Flagon in Manchester and, if we're prepared to go international, a Fool and Flagon in Ontario, Canada. But I suppose Rob had to find something to rhyme with George and Dragon.

The liner notes remind us that the pub is an institution that is in danger of dying out. In Britain, they are closing at the rate of fourteen a week, while Ireland has 1500 fewer pubs than in 2006, victims of higher prices, stricter drinking laws and the availability of cheap supermarket booze. Times change, of course, but where will folk groups play if there are no pubs left?

The song opens with the whole band playing a steady two-chord intro drawn from the chorus, with Simon finger-picking acoustic guitar, Chris on harmonica and Gerry playing laidback 'tocks'. Simon takes lead vocal for a verse with a fairly predictable melody over D, G and A chords with the odd B minor thrown in. Everyone comes in for the litany of pub names in the chorus, which is no more than a slight variation on the verse melody. But it's lifted by a repeat of the last two lines moving from what sounds like Em7 with an added sixth to A, with some lovely harmonies from Chris and Peggy repeating Simon's lines, and it's just enough to produce a little sentimental lump in the throat. In fact, Simon seems to have a catch in his voice as he sings the middle eight 'And here's the Sussex Yeoman / Her door is open wide / A stone's throw from the station / And all my friends inside'.

We end, appropriately, on the sound of bar chatter and the ringing of the bell for last orders. Mine's a pint of Old Peculier, thank you.

'Shuffle And Go' (Chris Leslie)

The title song is, for me, one of the weakest on the album, and I say this with love and respect to Mr Leslie, who has in the past written some of my favourite Fairport songs. The problem, I think, is that it's a bit of a rehash of Madeleine, the opening track on the *XXXV* album, with the same Eddie Cochran intro from 'Summertime Blues'. Adding to the 'ho-hum' feeling are some simplistic melody lines and a chorus that fails to take off.

I also feel some of the lyrics really don't stand up – 'more love than you could fit into an old cocked hat'? A 1950s-influenced song quoting headwear not seen after the early 19th century? And the phrase is 'knocked into a cocked hat', which means 'to out-do or to defeat someone'.

Look, it has its good points. It powers along breathlessly at a fair old crack and there's a nice, brief acapella section towards the end. And it's only three minutes and 14 seconds long. The subject matter is a young rocker who sweeps a girl off her feet and gets her in the family way thanks to his 'shuffle and go', whatever that is. But it has a bit too much of a novelty feel about it and, despite repeated listens, it's not growing on me.

'Moses Waits / Jambo Bwana' (Rob Beattle / Teddy Kalanda Harrison, Peter Bischoff-Fallenstein)

Fairport cover a Kenyan pop song? I am not sure how that would go down with the PC brigade. In fact, they may have something to say about Rob Beattie's song and the way it seems to depict African people as passive victims waiting for someone to bring them aid and a stable economy – apparently, wherever you go in Kenya as a crass Western tourist you will see 'Moses' standing there waiting for something. Having said that, Simon insists that it is accurate. According to his liner notes he 'toured there in 1993. Vivid memories of Nairobi and Mount Kenya, and I remember the 'Moses' he brings to life in this song. He was most places we went'.

It's true that Kenya is one of the most corrupt countries in the world – it ranks 139th out of 176, with the least corrupt at the top – and recent elections have been accompanied by violence and allegations of vote-tampering. It's also true that the country has become a popular holiday destination, worth £644 million to the Kenyan economy, so it must be galling for the ordinary people if they fail to see any of that tourism money trickling down to them. As the middle-eight remarks: 'The country needs a hard man / The country needs a saint / And Moses waits for someone in between / Someone not on someone else's payroll / To make the country that he clings to great again.'

Political correctness aside, this is a gentle, finger-picked ballad that opens with Simon's acoustic guitar notes doubled by Chris on Celtic harp, with Gerry on some unobtrusive ethnic percussion. The verse melody, in the key of F major, is not very distinctive and the 'hook' of the song lies in the repeat of the title and an up-and-down five-note motif. Then things pick up as we go into the short Jambo Bwana section, with Chris on whistle and Ric playing some 'township'-style violin.

Now, you may raise an eyebrow at the idea of five old white guys in Oxfordshire playing a 1982 Kenyan pop song (first released by Them Mushrooms and later covered by German group Boney M) but Fairport could be making a subtle point here. It's become what is known as a 'hotel pop song', aimed squarely at the tourist population, so could be another example of how the country has become a white Westerners' playground. Jambo Bwana is Swahili for 'Hello, sir!' and contains the line 'hakuna matata', used as the title of a song in the Disney film *The Lion King*.

I realise both Fairport and I may have strayed into controversial territory here, so I apologise in advance for anything we've done that's insensitive, tone-deaf or just plain wrong. It is, after all, only a song.

'Steampunkery' (Ric Sanders)
Ric rarely disappoints with his instrumentals and they are frequently among the high points of a Fairport album. 'Steampunkery' is no exception, highlighting the band's musical dexterity and sense of fun, and, for me, its DNA contains traces of every instrumental Fairport have performed, right back to 'Dirty Linen' and 'Flatpack Capers' on *Full House*.

It opens with a steady, 4/4 beat, Peggy's meaty, dirty bass powering things along like an old rock 'n' roll number. Ric plays a cheerful tune over E and B majors and is doubled up by Chris on mandolin, while Peggy throws in some cheeky, funky bass slaps and Gerry bashes away powerfully. It very quickly goes into a spirited dance tune in D major that bears some stylistic similarities to 'Sack The Juggler'/The Rutland Reel' but slightly less frantic. Then we're back into the original tune in E major before ending with a cheerful, noisy flourish.

According to the liner notes, the title is inspired by the *Steam, Smoke & Mirrors* novels of Colin Edmonds, author, screenwriter and, for more than 30 years, head gag writer for comedian Bob Monkhouse. His books sit firmly in the 'steampunk' genre, a form of science fiction writing that mixes Victorian settings with futuristic technology powered by burning fossil fuels, and Ric's tune certainly suggests something weird and fantastic chugging along merrily, spewing sparks and smoke.

'Linseed Memories' (James Wood)

I would not have been surprised to see Dave Pegg's name on this song because it reminds me of a gentler version of his 'Hungarian Rhapsody' from 1973's *Rosie* album. It's an upbeat, swinging, ukulele-led ditty, sung by Peggy, celebrating the joys of village cricket. But it has a bittersweet tinge to it because the narrator is a cricket bat that is no longer used by its owner. It 'hangs in the shed in the yard' and has to make do with memories of past glories between the stumps. For those unschooled in the arcane mysteries of the sport, linseed is an oil extracted from dried, ripened flax seeds and used as a protective coating for willow wood cricket bats.

Peggy first recorded the song with PJ Wright for their 2006 album *Galileo's Apology* and it seems his original bass, ukulele and vocal tracks were extracted and the rest of Fairport, minus Simon, played their parts over it. So Chris provides more uke and gentle harmonica, Ric adds two more ukes in case there aren't enough and Gerry backs them up with restrained percussion.

There may be another level to this song because, according to Peggy, the unused bat's name is Willy, and he doesn't score any more. I'll leave you to make the humorous connection. Suffice to say, this is a pleasant, undemanding but somewhat corny little tune.

'The Year Of Fifty Nine' (Chris Leslie)

It seems extra-terrestrial life, if it really exists, is remarkably fond of folk music, and should aliens actually attempt to make contact with the human race they are likely to say 'Take me to your morris team leader.' That's the only conclusion that can be drawn from the little-known fact that Banbury and the surrounding area has seen quite a bit of UFO activity over the past 70 years. Chris's song tells of one such sighting back in 1959, when he was just three. 'It flew up in the sky like a spinning wheel', he sings, 'never seen before'. Apparently, 'people ran indoors, others hit the floors' and the local paper suggested it may have been a Russian Sputnik satellite.

Chris wonders if Dan Dare – a British science-fiction hero whose adventures were serialised in *The Eagle* comic from 1950 to 1967 – could fly in to save the show and then, in a massive anti-climax, the mysterious vessel just disappears. Was it real, or had the inhabitants of Banbury imbibed just a little too much of the Hook Norton brewery's products at the Coach & Horses?

Despite the other-worldly subject matter, this is a bright, uptempo rocker with a catchy chorus of 'doo doo doo-doo doo doo', suggesting the occupants of the UFO may have travelled light years to Earth to enter the *Eurovision Song Contest*. It opens with alternating A and E chords on Simon's electric guitar with Ric playing a little fiddle phrase over the top before Chris comes in, strumming acoustic guitar and singing the verses, ending each one with a repeat of the title.

It moves along at a fair old pace, if not at warp speed, and the silly chorus is a bit of an earworm that will lurk in your head for some considerable time. I'm not sure if the style of the song really fits the subject matter – it's a bit too much of a singalong compared to 'Calling Occupants Of Interplanetary Craft', say – but it's an entertaining three and a half minutes.

'The Byfield Steeplechase' (PJ Wright)

Another composition by Peggy's pal, this one masquerading quite successfully as a traditional folk song about a horse race. Think of 'Skewball', the ballad of a champion 18th-century galloper who starts off as the underdog (or underhorse) but goes on to triumph on the plains of Kildare. PJ Wright's hero here is not a horse but 'Martin Chad, a local lad, on a lively chestnut mare' who sets out to win a race from Culworth churchyard in Northamptonshire to the steeple of Byfield church, galloping through and over anything that happens to stand in between (which is why it's called a steeplechase).

The favourite to win is Lord Wilkin of Marston Hall, but a dense mist and the misleading ringing of a bell send him and the rest of the runners and riders in the wrong direction, leaving wily Martin, who knows the terrain, to take the right road to Holy Cross church in Byfield.

Fairport's arrangement of the song shares many similarities with their version of 'Claudy Banks' on 1990's *The Five Seasons*. It has the same brisk pace and several key changes to keep the listener interested, opening in A for the intro but shifting up into C for the first verse. Simon takes lead vocals, Chris supports vocally and plays mandolin and harmonica and Ric takes a short instrumental that copies the melody line.

The song then goes into an unidentified instrumental reel that, again, goes up a key to build excitement until the triumphant finish. It's a cracking number driven by Gerry's powerful drums and sung with gusto by Simon, and it's one of the highlights of the album.

'Moondust And Solitude' (Chris Leslie)

From UFOs to Apollo 11. 'Moondust And Solitude' is an affecting ballad about

Michael Collins, the astronaut left on his tod in the Command Module while Neil Armstrong and Buzz Aldrin bounced about on the lunar surface, taking giant 'Leaps for Mankind'. Told from Collins' point of view, it imagines his thoughts as he floated 60 miles above the surface of the Moon, encapsulated in the chorus of 'In my mind / Here confined / Ever primed / In solitude'.

Chris is not the first to consider the plight of the astronaut who got so far but no further – Peggy's other band, Jethro Tull, did it on their 1970 album *Benefit* in the song 'For Michael Collins, Jeffrey And Me' – but the upbeat nature of his song suggests someone at peace with his role in the ultimate adventure. In reality, Collins was haunted by the possibility that he might have to leave his fellow explorers on the Moon and return without them if something should go terribly wrong, writing at the time: 'If they fail to rise to the surface, or crash back into it, I am not going to commit suicide; I am coming home, forthwith, but I will be a marked man for life and I know it.'

It opens with Simon's strummed acoustic guitar and Chris on bouzouki, with Ric playing a wistful violin melody and Gerry giving us a swoosh of cymbals. Bass and drums enter properly for the second verse as the song gently swings along, then Chris slips into a different key for a 'call and response' middle eight that allows Simon and Peggy to croon along distantly as if from the dark side of the moon. The song ends on a strummed G major, with a brief snatch of conversation between Collins and Ground Control.

It's a lovely little song with thoughtful lyrics, some sweet melodic moments and sensitive playing from all concerned. Sometimes Chris can slip into blandness, especially when writing songs with well-worn chord sequences, but he and the band manage to make something special out of this.

'Jolly Springtime' (James Taylor)

James Taylor has written many great songs – Fairport covered one of them, 'Frozen Man', on 1996's *Old New Borrowed Blue*. But this time they have gone for something relatively obscure, a mock traditional ditty originally tacked on the end of the title track to Taylor's 2015 release *Before This World*. It is a repetitive chant, utilising such cliche-ridden lines such as 'in the merry month of May', and it works for Taylor because its simple, upbeat nature counterpoints the rather depressing sentiments that come before it. But taken out of context and made to stand alone, it comes across as, well, a bit naff.

It doesn't help that it seems to be in too low a key for two of the Fairport singers. Peggy handles it okay, but Chris sounds a bit uncomfortable and Simon appears to be channelling Paul Robeson on Ol' Man River. Meanwhile, the percussion track was pieced together by sound engineer John Gale because Gerry Conway was too ill to make the last recording session.

According to the liner notes, the song gave Peggy the chance to play his 1918 Gibson F4 mando and Ric the opportunity to pluck Kala bass ukulele, but I'm not sure if those are good enough excuses. Anyway, the whole thing lasts just two minutes so we can forgive them their indulgences.

'Precious Time' (Ric Sanders)

Who knows where it goes? Blink, and decades have passed. Sorry for ending this chapter on such a depressing note but it's the tune that's doing it to me. It's sombre, emotional and lyrical, even slightly dark and mysterious. Simon opens with a gently-plucked acoustic guitar in G minor before Ric plays long, mournful notes over a slow three-quarter time beat, with occasional little jumps in the tune that remind me of O'Carolan's 'Sigh Beg Sigh Mor'.

Peggy provides 'woody' bass ukulele, Chris plucks tasteful mandolin, Ric adds unobtrusive keyboards and Gerry gently taps ethnic instruments. There's a middle section concentrating on Simon's guitar-picking that has a certain Tudor feel to it – imagine courtly ladies and gentlemen walking through those stately dances they used to do, but in a mournful minor key as if they're all going to be beheaded by King Henry VIII afterwards.

Towards the end, mando and violin harmonise beautifully with each other before ending the song with a final, rising phrase. It's sad and lovely, and not what you would expect from an album that has generally been quite upbeat and positive. But it shows, once again, what a fine composer Mr Sanders is and how he has the ability to move both your heart and your feet.

Fairport Collections

It would take another book at least three times this size to detail all the compilations and live recordings under the Fairport Convention name that have poured down like silver over the last 50 years. Some are essential listening for every Fairport fan, others are cheap, nasty cash-ins for which we should not be thankful. If you are reading this book, then I shall assume you are keen to dig deeper into the catalogue and prise out those hidden gems, the audio treasures that have unaccountably lain dormant in musical vaults for decades on end, and the live recordings that capture the band at its best.

Let's begin, then, with *Heyday – The BBC Sessions 1968-1969* (Island remasters IMCD 290, Island Records 586 542-2), which contains 20 tracks recorded mostly by the second line-up of the band after Judy Dyble's departure and Sandy Denny's arrival. What you have here is a selection of the West Coast sounds that filled Fairport's live sets in those early days but didn't make it on to the original albums – Eric Anderson's 'Close The Door Lightly When You Go', Richard Farina's 'Reno Nevada', Leonard Cohen's 'Suzanne' and 'Bird On A Wire', Johnny Cash's 'I Still Miss Someone', the Everly Brothers' 'Gone, Gone, Gone' and Gene Clark's 'Tried So Hard'. There are a few tracks from *Liege And Lief* – if you want more BBC versions of the folk-rock stuff then hunt down the four-disc set *Live At The BBC* (Universal Music Catalogue) that goes up to 1974.

For a live document of the *Full House* line-up go for *House Full: Live At The LA Troubadour* (Island Records, 2007), which contains the non-album tracks 'Staines Morris', 'The Mason's Apron', 'Battle Of The Somme' and 'Yellow Bird', alongside powerful renditions of Fairport favourites.

Fairport Live Convention (Commercial Marketing, 2005) captures the return of Sandy Denny, although you may do better finding the deluxe version of *Rising For The Moon* with a second live CD from the LA Troubadour in 1974 or, failing that, *Before The Moon* (Burning Airlines, 2002) recorded live in Detroit, although the sound quality is sometimes a bit dodgy.

The late 1970s four-piece with the return of Simon Nicol is chronicled on *Encore, Encore* (Brilliant, 2006). Originally released as *Farewell, Farewell* on the band's Woodworm label, this version has extra tracks plus a rare live rendition of 'John Lee' and Fairport's 1979 dying-breath single 'Rubber Band'. A more complete record of the band's setlist is available as *4Play* (Shirty Records, 2012), a double CD constructed out of tapes Dave Swarbrick carried around with him for years. The sound quality is as you would expect under the circumstances.

The band managed to release three live albums while officially disbanded, all chronicles of the reunion concerts in Cropredy that kicked off in 1979. *Moat On The Ledge: Live At Broughton Castle* (Talking Elephant, 2003) is of interest because it marks the first time Judy Dyble appeared with the band since 1967. She sings a charming, if slightly unsteady, version of Joni Mitchell's 'Both Sides Now' alongside a frantic rendition of Bob Dylan's

'Country Pie', Richard Thompson's 'Woman Or A Man' and rock 'n' roll standard 'High School Confidential', all by the *Full House* line-up.

AT2 (1983), *The Boot* (1984), *The Other Boot* (1987) and *The Third Leg* (1988) were cassette tape souvenirs of Cropredy recorded and released by Dave Pegg on Woodworm Records. They are very hard to get hold of these days but some of the recordings have turned up on other compilations. To get most of *The Other Boot* and *The Third Leg* try *More Things We Did On Our Holidays* (Secret Records, 2011), which includes a stonking version of 'Serenade To A Cuckoo' by the 1987 line-up with Ian Anderson and Martin Barre of Jethro Tull. *AT2* and *The Boot* were released as a 4CD set in 2000 but you're more likely to find Lord Lucan riding Shergar.

Proper CD mementoes of the Cropredy festival began with the 25th anniversary concert in 1993 – currently available as *The Anniversary Concert* (Talking Elephant Records, 2008) – which features Chris Leslie playing with the band for the first time after Ric Sanders put his hand through a plate-glass window. If you feel you only need one Cropredy collection in your life, then make it *The Cropredy Box* (Talking Elephant, 2017) – three CDs featuring all the members of the band who were alive in 1997 apart from Iain Matthews. It contains two bonus tracks: 'Seventeen Come Sunday', recorded for Ken Russell's TV documentary *In Search Of The English Folk Song*, and 'April Fool', a prank phone call to Dave Swarbrick that turns the air blue. For some later live Fairport try *Off The Desk* (Matty Grooves, 2008), a collection of recordings from 2004 and 2005 with Chris Leslie on fiddle and Gerry Conway in the engine room.

Between 1998 and 2008, Fairport were among the many musicians who worked with Breton composer Alan Simon on his Excalibur concept albums. *Fame And Glory* (2009) compiles 15 tracks from Simon's five albums, featuring the current line-up along with appearances from Martin Barre, John Wetton, Pentangle's Jacqui McShee and Supertramp's John Heliwell. The result is an intriguing mix of Celtic and British folk-rock. Simon's flute dominates, giving the album a definite Jethro Tull vibe.

Did I say you only need one Cropredy recording? Well, I was wrong – you need this one too. *What We Did On Our Saturday* (Matty Grooves, 2018) is the band celebrating its 50th anniversary with a career-spanning set across two CDs. Iain Matthews is there this time.

On Track series

Queen – Andrew Wild 978-1-78952-003-3

Emerson Lake and Palmer – Mike Goode 978-1-78952-000-2

Deep Purple and Rainbow 1968-79 – Steve Pilkington 978-1-78952-002-6

Yes – Stephen Lambe 978-1-78952-001-9

Blue Oyster Cult – Jacob Holm-Lupo 978-1-78952-007-1

The Beatles – Andrew Wild 978-1-78952-009-5

Roy Wood and the Move – James R Turner 978-1-78952-008-8

Genesis – Stuart MacFarlane 978-1-78952-005-7

Jethro Tull – Jordan Blum 978-1-78952-016-3

The Rolling Stones 1963-80 – Steve Pilkington 978-1-78952-017-0

Judas Priest – John Tucker 978-1-78952-018-7

Toto – Jacob Holm-Lupo 978-1-78952-019-4

Van Der Graaf Generator – Dan Coffey 978-1-78952-031-6

Frank Zappa 1966 to 1979 – Eric Benac 978-1-78952-033-0

Elton John in the 1970s – Peter Kearns 978-1-78952-034-7

The Moody Blues – Geoffrey Feakes 978-1-78952-042-2

The Beatles Solo 1969-1980 – Andrew Wild 978-1-78952-030-9

Steely Dan – Jez Rowden 978-1-78952-043-9

Hawkwind – Duncan Harris 978-1-78952-052-1

Fairport Convention – Kevan Furbank 978-1-78952-051-4

Iron Maiden – Steve Pilkington 978-1-78952-061-3

Dream Theater – Jordan Blum 978-1-78952-050-7

10CC – Peter Kearns 978-1-78952-054-5

Gentle Giant – Gary Steel 978-1-78952-058-3

Kansas – Kevin Cummings 978-1-78952-057-6

Mike Oldfield – Ryan Yard 978-1-78952-060-6

The Who – Geoffrey Feakes 978-1-78952-076-7

Camel – Hamish Kuzminski 978-1-78952-040-8

Thin Lizzy – Graeme Stroud 978-1-78952-064-4

The Clash – Nick Assirati 978-1-78952-077-4

On Screen series

Carry On... – Stephen Lambe 978-1-78952-004-0

Powell and Pressburger – Sam Proctor 978-1-78952-013-2

Seinfeld Seasons 1 to 5 – Stephen Lambe 978-1-78952-012-5

Francis Ford Coppola – Cam Cobb and Stephen Lambe 978-1-78952-022-4

Monty Python – Steve Pilkington 978-1-78952-047-7

Doctor Who: The David Tennant Years – Jamie Hailstone 978-1-78952-066-8

James Bond – Andrew Wild 978-1-78952-010-1

Decades Series

Pink Floyd in the 1970s – Georg Purvis 978-1-78952-072-9

Marillion in the 1980s – Nathaniel Webb 978-1-78952-065-1

Curved Air in the 1970s – Laura Shenton 978-1-78952-069-9

Other Books

Not As Good As The Book – Andy Tillison 978-1-78952-021-7

The Voice. Frank Sinatra in the 1940s – Stephen Lambe 978-1-78952-032-3

Maximum Darkness – Deke Leonard 978-1-78952-048-4

The Twang Dynasty – Deke Leonard 978-1-78952-049-1

Maybe I Should've Stayed In Bed – Deke Leonard 978-1-78952-053-8

Tommy Bolin: In and Out of Deep Purple – Laura Shenton 978-1-78952-070-5

Jon Anderson and the Warriors - the road to Yes – David Watkinson 978-1-78952-059-0

Derek Taylor: For Your Radioactive Children – Andrew Darlington 978-1-78952-038-5

and many more to come!

Would you like to write for Sonicbond Publishing?

At Sonicbond Publishing we are always on the look-out for authors, particularly for our two main series:

On Track. Mixing fact with in depth analysis, the On Track series examines the work of a particular musical artist or group. All genres are considered from easy listening and jazz to 60s soul to 90s pop, via rock and metal.

On Screen. This series looks at the world of film and television. Subjects considered include directors, actors and writers, as well as entire television and film series. As with the On Track series, we balance fact with analysis.

While professional writing experience would, of course, be an advantage the most important qualification is to have real enthusiasm and knowledge of your subject. First-time authors are welcomed, but the ability to write well in English is essential.

Sonicbond Publishing has distribution throughout Europe and North America, and all books are also published in E-book form. Authors will be paid a royalty based on sales of their book.

Further details are available from www.sonicbondpublishing.co.uk. To contact us, complete the contact form there or email info@sonicbondpublishing.co.uk